Multinational Corporations and European Regional Systems of Innovation

In globalising economies, particularly those going through a process of economic integration, such as economies within the EU, regions forge an increasing number of technological linkages with other locations both *within* and *across* national borders. This is largely carried out by the technological efforts of multinational corporations (MNCs).

This book explores localised technological advantages and the location of innovative activities by MNCs in Europe. Using an empirical analysis, John Cantwell and Simona Iammarino cover such important themes as:

- the geographical distribution of MNC technological activities and economic wealth,
- MNCs and the regional systems of innovation in Italy, the UK, Germany and France,
- the geographical hierarchy within and across European national borders.

This comprehensive, readable book will be of interest to students and academics involved in such areas as the economics of innovation, economic geography, and corporate strategy. The book also has important policy implications and will be required reading for corporate managers and policymakers.

John Cantwell is Professor of International Business at the Rutgers Business School, New Jersey, USA, and is Professor of International Economics at the University of Reading, UK.

Simona Iammarino is Lecturer in International Economics at the University of Rome 'La Sapienza' and is affiliated researcher at the Department of Economics, University of Reading, UK.

Studies in Global Competition

A series of books edited by John Cantwell, The University of Reading, UK and David Mowery, University of California, Berkeley, USA

Japanese Firms in Europe
Edited by Frédérique Sachwald

Technological Innovation, Multinational Corporations and New International Competitiveness
The case of intermediate countries
Edited by José Molero

Global Competition and the Labour Market
Nigel Driffield

The Source of Capital Goods Innovation
The role of user firms in Japan and Korea
Kong-Rae Lee

Climates of Global Competition
Maria Bengtsson

Multinational Enterprises and Technological Spillovers
Tommaso Perez

Governance of International Strategic Alliances
Technology and transaction costs
Joanne E. Oxley

Strategy in Emerging Markets
Telecommunications establishments in Europe
Anders Pehrsson

Going Multinational
The Korean experience of direct investment
Edited by Frédérique Sachwald

Multinational Firms and Impacts on Employment, Trade and Technology
New perspectives for a new century
Edited by Robert E. Lipsey and Jean-Louis Mucchielli

Multinational Firms
The global–local dilemma
Edited by John H. Dunning and Jean-Louis Mucchielli

MIT and the Rise of Entrepreneurial Science
Henry Etzkowitz

Technological Resources and the Logic of Corporate Diversification
Brian Silverman

The Economics of Innovation, New Technologies and Structural Change
Cristiano Antonelli

European Union Direct Investment in China
Characteristics, challenges and perspectives
Daniel Van Den Bulcke, Haiyan Zhang and Maria do Céu Esteves

Biotechnology in Comparative Perspective
Edited by Gerhard Fuchs

Technological Change and Economic Performance
Albert L. Link and Donald S. Siegel

Multinational Corporations and European Regional Systems of Innovation
John Cantwell and Simona Iammarino

Multinational Corporations and European Regional Systems of Innovation

John Cantwell and
Simona Iammarino

Routledge
Taylor & Francis Group

LONDON AND NEW YORK

First published 2003 by Routledge
11 New Fetter Lane, London EC4P 4EE

Simultaneously published in the USA and Canada
by Routledge
29 West 35th Street, New York, NY 10001

Routledge is an imprint of the Taylor & Francis Group

Typeset in Bembo by Wearset Ltd, Boldon, Tyne and Wear
Printed and bound by Gutenberg Press Ltd, Malta

British Library Cataloguing in Publication Data
A catalogue record for this book is available from the British Library

Library of Congress Cataloging in Publication Data
Cantwell, John.
  Multinational corporations and European regional systems of
  innovation / John Cantwell & Simona Iammarino.
    p. cm. — (Studies in global competition ; v. 18)
  Includes bibliographical references and index.
  1. International business enterprises–European Union countries.
  2. Technological innovations–Economic aspects–European Union
  countries. 3. Technology transfer–Economic aspects–European
  Union countries. 4. Industrial districts–European Union countries.
  5. Regional planning–European Union countries. I. Iammarino,
  Simona. II. Title. III. Series.

  HD2844 .C36 2003
  338.8'884–dc21

                                                              2002036921

ISBN 0-415-27140-1

Contents

List of figures   x
List of tables   xi
Acknowledgements   xiv
List of abbreviations and acronyms   xv

1 Introduction   **1**

**2 Regional systems of innovation in Europe and the
    globalisation of technology**   **7**
Introduction 7
*The location of innovative activities and regional systems of
    innovation 8*
The globalisation of technology 14
*'Local' versus 'global': cumulative causation and regional
    hierarchies 17*
Conclusions 21

**3 MNC technological activities and economic wealth: an
    analysis of spatial distribution in the European Union**   **22**
Introduction 22
Technological growth and regional convergence 23
Patent data at the regional level 26
The spatial distribution of MNC technological activity and GDP 28
MNC technological activity, regional cores and attractiveness 33
*Technological growth patterns in EU regional systems of
    innovation 41*
Conclusions 43

**4 Geographical hierarchies of research locations in the
    European Union**   **46**
Introduction 46

The internationalisation of MNC technological activities: an
*   overview 47*
The European Union: some national features 50
Technological specialisation profiles: methodological issues 56
Geographical agglomeration within EU national borders 56
Conclusions 60

5   **Multinational corporations and the Italian regional**
    systems of innovation   **61**
    Introduction 61
    The location of MNC technological activities in the Italian regions 62
    Technological specialisation and the regional hierarchy in Italy 68
    Conclusions 73 ·

6   **Multinational corporations and the UK regional systems**
    of innovation   **76**
    Introduction 76
    The location of MNC technological activities in the UK regions 77
    Technological specialisation and the regional hierarchy in the UK 85
    Conclusions 91

7   **Multinational corporations and the German regional**
    systems of innovation   **93**
    Introduction 93
    The location of MNC technological activities in the German
    *   regions 93*
    Technological specialisation and the regional hierarchy in Germany 100
    Conclusions 106

8   **Multinational corporations and the French regional**
    systems of innovation   **108**
    Introduction 108
    The location of MNC technological activities in the French
    *   regions 109*
    Technological specialisation and the regional hierarchy in France 117
    Conclusions 125

9   **The geographical hierarchy across European national**
    borders   **128**
    Introduction 128
    Cumulativeness, change and differentiation of regional technological
    *   innovation: concepts 128*

Cumulativeness, change and differentiation of regional technological innovation: methodology 131

Cumulativeness, change and differentiation of regional technological innovation: results 137

MNC technological strategies: EU versus non-EU MNCs 146

Conclusions 155

10 Conclusions: the global–local nexus in technological innovation: what implications are there for the future?   **157**

Some issues for public policies 157

Some open questions for future research 162

Appendices   165

Notes   172

Bibliography   181

Index   196

Figures

3.1 MNC technological activity and GDP in the EU regions   30

3.2 (a) MNC technological growth and GDP growth in the EU regions, 1978–95   32

3.2 (b) MNC technological growth and GDP growth in the EU regions, 1985–95   32

3.3 PCA and cluster analysis – plane of the selected EU regions   37

4.1 Patenting activity attributable to European-owned (EU15, Norway and Switzerland) research outside the home country by host area, 1969–95 (%)   49

5.1 Foreign shares (foreign-owned companies' percentage of total patents granted to large firms for local research in Italy), by year and region, 1969–95 (%)   67

6.1 Population (000s) and R&D personnel (absolute numbers) by UK region, 1995   77

6.2 R&D expenditure by UK region, business sector, 1995   78

6.3 EPO requests and USPTO patents by UK region, 1995   79

6.4 Government research grants to higher education institutions by region, 1994–7 (percentage of UK total)   81

6.5 Patents by year, UK total, 1969–95   84

6.6 Foreign shares (% of total patents) by year and UK region, 1969–95   85

7.1 Inter-regional, intra-sectoral technology flows through time   105

8.1 French regions, GDP per inhabitant, 1996 (EU15 = 100)   111

8.2 French regions, R&D expenditure (% of GDP) and R&D personnel (% of active population), 1995   112

8.3 Patents by year: France total, 1969–95   116

8.4 Foreign shares (% of total patents) by year and region, 1969–95   117

9.1 Technological higher order regions in Europe – shares of total country's patents, 1969–95   132

9.2 Shares of regional patents by the home country of large firms, 1969–95   149

Tables

2.1 MNC networks for innovation 16
3.1 Regional dispersion of MNC technological activity (1991–5) and per capita GDP (1995) 29
3.2 US patents granted to large firms and ranks of patent counts in 1969–77 and 1987–95 for 30 EU regions 34
3.3 (a,b) Principal component analysis: results 35–6
3.4 (a,b) One-way ANOVA: results 39–40
3.5 World US patents granted to large industrial firms 41
4.1 Share of US patents of the world's largest firms attributable to research in foreign locations, organised by the nationality of the parent firm, 1969–95 (%) 48
4.2 Patenting activity attributable to research outside the home country by nationality of the parent firm and host area/country, 1969–95 (%) 51
4.3 Distribution (D) and penetration (P) (%) of foreign-owned patenting activity by host country, 1969–95 52
4.4 Patenting activity attributable to European-located foreign-owned research by host EU country and nationality of the parent firm, 1969–95 (%) 53
4.5 Geographical composition of foreign-owned research by host EU country and nationality of the parent firm, 1969–95 (%) 55
4.6 Regional breakdown of US patent grants to large firms, 1969–95 (% of each group's patent grants on national totals); population and output by region (1995) 58
4.7 Sectoral dispersion (standard deviation) of technological specialisation, 1969–95 59
5.1 Shares of US patents of the largest Italian firms attributable to research in Italian regions relative to Italy as a whole, and the equivalent regional shares for the Italian-located research of foreign-owned firms, by technological sector, 1969–95 (%) 64
5.2 Foreign shares (foreign-owned companies' percentage of total patents granted to large firms for local research in Italy), by sector and region, 1969–95 65

5.3   RTA (Italian and foreign firms) relative to the world by sector
and region, 1969–95   69
5.4   RTA correlation matrix   71
5.5   Results of the regressions for Piemonte   73
5.6   Results of the regressions for Lombardia   74
5.7   Results of the regressions for Italy   75
6.1   Shares of US patents of both the largest UK firms and the
UK-located foreign-owned firms, attributable to research in
UK regions relative to the UK as a whole, 1969–95 (%)   79
6.2   Foreign shares (foreign-owned firms' percentage of total
patents granted to large firms for local research in the UK) by
sector and region, 1969–95   82
6.3   RTA index (UK and foreign firms) relative to the world, by
sector and region, 1969–95   86
6.4   RSA index relative to the UK, by scientific field and region,
1994–7   87
6.5   Results of the cross-sectoral regressions of foreign-owned
RTA on indigenous RTA in the UK as a whole, and in the
three UK regions   90
7.1   USPTO patent grants to large firms located in Germany by
region, 1969–82 (t_1) and 1983–95 (t_2)   95
7.2   Shares of US patents of the largest German firms attributable
to research in German regions relative to Germany as a whole,
and the equivalent regional shares for the German-located
research of foreign-owned firms, by technological sector,
1969–95 (%)   96–7
7.3   Foreign firm share by technological sector and region,
1969–95 (%)   99
7.4   RTA index (German and foreign firms) relative to the world,
by sector and region, 1969–95   102–3
8.1   Shares of US patents of both the largest French firms and the
French-located foreign-owned firms, attributable to research
in French regions relative to France as a whole, 1969–95 (%)   113
8.2   Foreign shares (foreign-owned firms' percentage of total
patents granted to large firms for local research in France) by
sector and region, 1969–95   115
8.3   RTA index (French and foreign firms) relative to the world by
sector and region, 1969–95   119
8.4   RTA correlation matrix   121
8.5   (a,b) Results of the regional regressions   123–4
9.1   RTA index for the eight European regions relative to the
world, by technological category, 1969–95   133
9.2   Results of the regression analysis of regional RTA in 1987–95
on RTA in 1969–77: $\mathrm{RTA}_{ij1987–95} = \alpha + \beta \, \mathrm{RTA}_{ij1969–77} +$
$\varepsilon_{ij1987–95}$ 137

9.3 Technological specialisation indicators derived from the
    regression analysis of regional RTA in 1987–95 on RTA in
    1967–77 for the eight European regions   139
9.4 The dynamics of regional technological profiles (1987–95
    versus 1969–77)   144–5
9.5 Regional bi-lateral technological specialisation index
    (correlation coefficients), 1969–77, 1978–86, 1987–95   147
9.6 RTA index for eight European regions (nationally-owned
    firms, EU-owned firms and non-EU-owned firms) relative to
    the world by technological category, 1969–95   152–3

Acknowledgements

The authors gratefully acknowledge financial support from the project on 'Assessing the impact of technological innovation and globalisation: the effects on growth and employment (AITEG)', funded under the EC's Targeted Socio-Economic Research (TSER) programme (contract number: CT-1999-00043).

John Cantwell is also grateful for financial support from the project on 'Dynamic capabilities, growth and long-term competitiveness of European firms (Dynacom)', funded under the EC's Targeted Socio-Economic Research (TSER) programme (contract number SOE1-CT97-1078).

Simona Iammarino wishes to acknowledge the support of the EU Commission under the TMR Marie Curie Research Training Programme (category 30, contract No. ERBFMBICT961062), which provided her with a two-years postdoctorate grant for working at the University of Reading.

The authors wish to thank the participants of a number of international conferences, in particular those participants in the Conference on 'Technology Policy and Less Developed Research and Development Systems in Europe', Seville, Spain, October 1997; the 45th North American Regional Science Association International, Santa Fe, USA, November 1998; the International Economics Study Group meeting at the London School of Economics, London, UK, March 1999; the 39th ERSA Conference, Dublin, Ireland, August 1999; the DRUID Conference, Aalborg, Denmark, June 2000; the ICTPI Kansai Conference, Kyoto, Japan, August 2002.

John Cantwell's former PhD students – Camilla Noonan and Grazia Santangelo – provided us with valuable help in the tedious regionalisation of the University of Reading database. At various times we have received useful comments and helpful suggestions or ideas from Daniele Archibugi, Stefano Breschi, John Dunning, Maryann Feldman, Peter Hart, Phil McCann, Rajneesh Narula, Andrés Rodriguez-Pose, Stefano Usai and anonymous referees. We are grateful for the interest they have shown, subject to the usual qualifying remarks that none of them is to be held responsible for the final contents of the book, or for any errors that remain. We must also thank those who have assisted us through the final stages of publication at Routledge: Robert Langham (Economics editor) and Terry Clague (desk editor). Finally, we are particularly grateful to John, Daphney, Guido and Leli for their invaluable practical and psychological support.

Abbreviations and acronyms

ANOVA	Analysis of variance
CA	Cluster analysis
CIS	Community innovation survey
CV	Coefficient of variation
EC	European Community
EPO	European Patent Office
EU	European Union
EU15	15 EU Countries
FDI	Foreign direct investment
GDP	Gross domestic profit
GPT	General purpose technologies
HEI	Higher education institution
HSD	Honestly significant difference
ICT	Information and communications technologies
MNC	Multinational corporation
NSI	National system of innovation
NUTS	Eurostat nomenclature of territorial units for statistics
OLI	Ownership–Location–Internationalisation
OST	Office of Science and Technology
PCA	Principle component analysis
PPS	Purchasing Perity Standards
R&D	Research and development
RSA	Revealed scientific advantage
RSI	Regional system of innovation
RTA	Revealed technological advantage
SMEs	Small and medium enterprises
USPTO	United States Patent and Trademark Office

1 Introduction

According to Paul Krugman 'the most striking feature of the geography of economic activity is surely concentration . . . production is remarkably concentrated in space' (Krugman, 1991a: p. 5). However, usually we refer to 'economic activity' and 'production', having especially in mind the creation of goods and services, and this attitude has tended somehow to obscure another crucial feature of the geography of economic activity: innovation is *even more* concentrated in space. The evidence suggests that technological and innovative activities not only generate externalities (spillovers), but these are often geographically bounded within the region or local context where the new knowledge was initially created.

Especially over the last decade, a substantial body of research has sought to establish the importance of the spatial dimension in the study of technological innovation, firm competitive advantage and overall economic growth (among others Cantwell and Janne, 1999; Enright, 1998; Martin and Ottaviano, 1998; Porter, 1990, 1994). Although the physical agglomeration of industrial and technological activity is readily visible, the precise origins and dynamics of these agglomerations vary across locations and there is therefore no single explanation for their existence. For instance, as noted by Cooke and Morgan (1994), in some European Union (EU) regions it is clear that localised buyer–supplier networks, together with robust institutional support mechanisms at the local level, have played a major role in promoting localised patterns of innovative activity.

Yet, until recently, comparatively little research has empirically investigated the sub-national concentration of technological activities in Europe, mainly because of the lack of data on innovation at detailed geographical level. Several studies exist for the US (among others, Feldman and Audretsch, 1999; Audretsch and Feldman, 1996; Feldman, 1994; Jaffe et al., 1993), which observe the concentration of innovative and economic variables both across regions and sectors. Using European Patent Office data, Breschi (2000) finds evidence of considerable differences in the spatial concentration of innovation across sectors in Europe; Caniëls (2000) shows that the top 12 EU regions account for 70 per cent of the total number of patents in the period 1986–90; Paci and Usai (2000a, 2001) demonstrate that the degree of geographical concentration of innovative activities in the Union is much higher than that of production.

However, for the most part, both theory and empirical analysis have paid only scant attention to the nationality of ownership of innovative activity, or, in other words, to the particular characteristics of foreign-owned, as opposed to domestically-owned, technological activities. Indeed, while traditional analyses of multinational activity emphasise the centralised nature of research and development efforts of multinational corporations (MNCs), contemporary contributions highlight the potential redundancy of this thesis. The trend toward globalisation of research and innovative activity has resulted in a questioning of the rather narrow role conferred upon the subsidiary by Vernon (1966), and attempts to redefine the role of the subsidiary as a key creator of innovation and technological knowledge – a role originally suggested by Dunning (1958) and later developed by Chesnais (1988), Cantwell (1994) and Fors (1998).

The increasing appreciation of the role of MNCs in the generation of technology (and not just in its international transfer) has been facilitated by the recent trend for MNCs to establish internal and external networks for innovation. Internationally integrated networks within the firm may lead, through a greater focus on the specialisation of technological efforts in affiliates, to an improvement of innovation capacity, both of the MNC and of the host location. Inter-firm networks established between MNC affiliates and local firms may, in addition, amplify the advantages of geographical agglomeration in some particular lines of technological development. In other terms, in order to consolidate existing competencies, it is generally necessary for a firm to extend those capabilities into new related fields of production and technology, and across a variety of locations. The firm is thereby able to benefit from the dynamic economies of scope that derive from the technological complementarities between related paths of innovation or corporate learning in spatially distinct institutional settings or environments. In this perspective, MNCs spread the competence base of the firm and acquire new technological assets, or sources of technological advantage. For their part, indigenous firms benefit from localised knowledge spillovers from MNCs, given the access of the latter to complementary streams of knowledge being developed in other regional locations. The precise form that such knowledge networks take depends upon the nature of the extant agglomeration forces that shape the spatial organisation of activity.

The ongoing reorganisation of multinational operations further confirms the fact that technological know-how is undoubtedly the *key* factor of production operating through these dispersed but interdependent global networks. Indeed, as highlighted by Dunning and Wymbs (1999), the decision of firms to extend their innovative activity to a number of foreign locations is closely linked to the perception that such strategies can greatly enhance the firm's international technological advantage by extracting local knowledge for its global network. Knowledge is therefore transferred in a two-way direction

– from the parent to the subsidiary (as was traditionally believed to be the case) and also, by tapping into the host's knowledge base, from the subsidiaries to the parent.

Although these trends have long been apparent, their persistence and evolution within the current climate of declining transportation and communication costs (and amongst high-tech firms for whom the 'friction of distance' was perceived to be largely irrelevant) seem to warrant investigation. The resolution of the paradox 'does the *local* continue to matter in a world increasingly relying upon apparently space-less globalisation and virtual communications and exchanges?' lies in the crucial distinction between knowledge and information. 'While the costs of transmitting information may be invariant to distance . . . the cost of transmitting knowledge, especially what von Hippel (1994) refers to as *sticky knowledge*, rises with distance' (Feldman and Audretsch, 1999, p. 411). As firms cluster, therefore, knowledge can be more easily transferred between them and the resulting interfirm interaction (be it coordinated or uncoordinated) serves to consolidate and promote the future attractiveness of the location.

In emphasising the *public good* characteristics of research output (or potential for technological spillovers), traditional research in this area focused upon the inadequacies of the market if left to provide such goods. The non-rivalrous and non-excludable nature of knowledge renders it very difficult for the producers of that knowledge fully to appropriate social returns on their investments, which means that other actors in the economy can enjoy positive externalities (or research spillovers). As a result of this so-called market failure and implied divergence between private/social costs and benefits, a sub-optimal level of R&D would be undertaken at firm level (Cantwell and Noonan, 2001).

Since knowledge was considered to be the 'quintessential public good' (Geroski, 1995, p. 91), one of the central concerns of the literature is how to define the property rights associated with the creation of new knowledge, i.e. how to correct the *market failure*. Although such contributions have greatly enhanced our understanding of research spillovers, they fail to acknowledge the tacit component implicit in the innovative process. This, in turn, has led to an overestimation of the importance of the appropriability argument – a hypothesis confirmed by recent work in the field (Hall and Ham, 1999; Cohen *et al.*, 2000).

While knowledge is free in principle, the absorptive capacity of the firm determines the degree to which knowledge created outside the firm infiltrates its activities. Building and sustaining this capacity is, in turn, costly and dependent, *inter alia*, upon the amount of technological innovation undertaken by the receiving firm (Rosenberg, 1976, 1982; Cantwell, 1989a, b), which has become increasingly costly in recent years. Following on from this point, Nelson and Winter (1982) highlight the importance of location for the firm that wishes to take full advantage of inter- and, indeed, intra-industry innovations. Because the innovative process is believed to be path-dependent and firm-specific in nature, the technological advances that result are partially embodied, not just in the final output, but also in the organisational structures of companies engaged in such activities. The costs associated with the articulation of such newly created knowledge thus determine the degree to which this knowledge remains tacit over time. Such costs may be reduced via the physical reduction of distance; that is, the geographical clustering or agglomeration of research activity. Such clustering of firm activity serves to highlight the fact that knowledge spillovers are essentially geographically bounded (Jaffe *et al.*, 1993; Almeida and Kogut, 1997). Dispersion of multinational R&D activity across many locations is therefore believed to facilitate the accumulation of knowledge, which feeds directly into the company's competitive position internationally. While there is evidence that much of the technology developed abroad by large firms lies in their core areas of strength – suggesting that adaptation and technical support to foreign manufacturing plants continues to be major explanatory factors – MNC research in foreign locations is also increasingly associated with a higher probability of entry into new and more distantly related fields of technology. Such knowledge-seeking activity is undertaken to help define the future directions in the evolution of the corporations' sources of competitiveness (Pearce, 1999). Furthermore, since knowledge creation is a cumulative process, and certain locations boast certain technological expertise, the knowledge-seeking activity of MNCs is believed to be self-reinforcing, leading in turn to further geographical agglomeration over time.

There is a strong interdependence between geographical, technological and sectoral 'systems of innovation', particularly when looking at sectoral boundaries as multidimensional, integrated and dynamic, rather than static and delimited in terms of technological opportunities. As argued by Malerba (2002), the notion of a sectoral system of innovation (and production) actually complements both that of a geographical system of innovation and that of a technological system, where the latter focuses mainly on the networks for the generation, diffusion and use of new technologies (Carlsson and Stankiewitz, 1991). Following Malerba's definition of sectoral systems – in which the agents are individuals and organisations with different degrees of aggregation and specific learning processes, competencies, institutional and organisational structures and objectives – it may be maintained that, as a sectoral system undergoes the processes of change through the coevolution of its various elements, so does a local or regional system, underlying the transformation of certain socio-economic environments and the factors at the base of the different performances of firms across locations. In fact, according to the evolutionary theory, environments and contextual conditions in which firms and agents operate may substantially differ. Firms embedded in the same institutional context are likely to share some common behavioural and organisational traits and develop some common learning and absorptive modes. Exactly as interdependence and complementarily mark the real boundaries of a sectoral system, they define the actual borders of a regional system, rendering boundaries and borders quite dynamic and subject to evolutionary change.

On the other hand, cumulativeness is indeed observed at various levels – technological, sectoral and local. Technological change is a path-dependent process in the sense that the probabilities of adopting a certain kind of technology are influenced by past decisions, which in turn constrain the range of existing choices. Therefore, the industrial composition of innovative activities in a given location reflects past technological accumulation (Cantwell, 1991). From the systemic view of technological change, it turns out that a system is a collective emergent outcome of the interaction and coevolution of its various constituting elements, and the appropriate level of analysis depends on the specific research goals.

The aim of this book is to examine one crucial aspect of the nexus between global and local processes: that is, how the particular corporate technological trajectories of multinational corporations have interacted with spatially-specific resources for the creation of new competencies in some of the leading (sub-national) regions in the European Union. Particularly within the latter, the reorganisation of operations of MNC affiliates has been spurred to a much greater extent than in the case of affiliates based outside the area (Cantwell, 1987, 1992b; Dicken, 1994), as a consequence of the completion of the Single European Market and the pursuit of economic and monetary union.

The theoretical and analytical approach from which this work draws comes from the evolutionary theory and the system approach. It is within such a framework that key concepts such as knowledge, learning, competence, interdependence and dynamics, have particularly been developed. And, as a consequence, that relationships and networks have become the main elements of innovative and production processes.

The focus on 'systems of innovation' has led to a different contribution of the geographical dimension to the study of innovative phenomena. Yet, along with the importance of context-specific factors, the presence of systemic interactions in the process of generation and diffusion of innovation has also been recognised as a key determinant of the technological and economic performance of countries and regions. However, proper regional systems of innovation are found only in a few well-defined areas: in most regions, systemic interactions and knowledge flows between the relevant actors are simply too sparse and too weak to reveal the presence of systems of innovation at work. By contrast, regions that have developed high endogenous scientific and technical capabilities over time are likely to be net providers of technological knowledge to the rest of the country, as well as to appear very 'attractive' for the localisation of innovation activities and facilities by global actors. Indeed, the development of cross-border corporate integration and intra-border inter-company sectoral integration, as new forms of governance, makes it increasingly important to examine where and how innovative activity by MNCs is internationally dispersed and regionally concentrated.

This book addresses some of the most relevant questions in this field of research, such as: what are the main features of the nature of interactions between local and corporate knowledge? Is there a positive correlation between MNC technological profiles and regional technological specialisation? Can a hierarchy of regional centres of technological excellence be established within and across national boundaries? What are the dynamics of regional patterns of technological specialisation? Which implications can be drawn from the evidence on the EU regions?

The conceptual framework on MNC strategies for innovation and the crucial link between the global and the local dimensions of technology creation is summarised in Chapter 2. Actually, each chapter contains some background that clarifies the most crucial themes related to the subsequent discussion. This is also because the literature has been particularly prolific in the last few years and, without claiming to be exhaustive, we have tried to take into account at least the main lines of evolution of the current debate. Chapter 3 provides an overview of the spatial distribution of technological operations of MNCs across European regions, illustrating some basic links between technological growth and systemic characters and giving account of the data used in this book as a proxy for both MNC and regional technological profiles. Chapter 4 introduces, in comparative terms, the national case-studies reported in the following four chapters, which address, respectively, Italy (Chapter 5), the UK (Chapter 6), Germany (Chapter 7) and France (Chapter 8). Our hypothesis that MNC networks for technological innovation conform to a hierarchy of regional centres *within* national systems is tested for each of the four major EU economies. Chapter 9 explores the dynamics of both technological capacity and specialisation of the leading European regional cores for innovation, supporting our second hypothesis that a geographical hierarchy can also be established *across* European national boundaries. Finally, Chapter 10 concludes, by drawing some implications of our work and highlighting the main directions of our future research efforts.

2 Regional systems of innovation in Europe and the globalisation of technology

Introduction

In this chapter, we will summarise the conceptual framework and the current debate on the evolution of regional systems of innovation in the European Union, adopting a globalisation–localisation perspective. Spillovers, particularly those associated with new technological knowledge, tend to be highly concentrated at the geographical level. The convergence/divergence tendencies of regional development in the EU seem to depend increasingly on regional innovative capabilities and on localised learning, which in turn shape the attractiveness of the region towards outside resources. The regional dimension of the cumulative nature of the innovation process, which also includes social, cultural and institutional factors, is thus becoming central in explaining the locational choices of multinational corporations, especially with regard to their innovative activity.

We argue that these choices depend upon the number and the characteristics of regional centres and their relative position in a geographical hierarchy, and upon the different strategies for technological upgrading and diversification developed by MNCs. The ultimate implication is that public policies on a far wider range than those currently practiced are required in order to reap the benefits associated with the globalisation of innovation and to offset the risk of increasing regional inequalities.

The 'local' dimension of innovation phenomena is the subject of the following section, in which we give an overview of the increasing function of regional innovation systems. The 'global' dimension of technological innovation is discussed in the third section of this chapter. In it we explore the change of MNC innovatory strategies, according to the recent trend for large industrial firms to establish internal and external networks for innovation. The 'local' versus the 'global' is considered in the fourth section, addressing the cumulative causation mechanisms that may arise from the interaction between the two dimensions of innovative processes.

The location of innovative activities and regional systems of innovation

There are two clear observations pointing towards the link between geographical location and industrial performance. The first is that economic and technological activities show a strong tendency to agglomerate in certain locations, giving rise to patterns of national and regional specialisation. The second is that the performance and the growth of firms depend, to a large extent, on the conditions of the environment in which they operate, and particularly on those in the immediate proximity (Malmberg *et al.*, 1996).

The phenomenon of the concentration of economic activities in space, and its persistence over time, was first observed by Marshall (1891), who listed three fundamental advantages (or externalities) that cause firms to agglomerate:

- a pooled market for skilled workers with industry-specific competencies;
- the availability of non-tradable and intermediate inputs provided by local suppliers;
- the easy transmission of new ideas, which increases productivity through technical, organisational and production improvements.

Both static and dynamic economies were thus identified by Marshall as possible causes of spatial agglomeration, enhancing the efficiency and the growth of firms in the same location.

The foundation of traditional location theory can be traced in part to Weber (1929) – who first used the term *economies of agglomeration* for those kinds of external economies of scale previously described by Marshall – and to Lösch (1954), both of whom identified the proximity to either the market for products or the source of inputs as the key explanation of agglomeration. However, the focus on distance and on the non-linearity of transport costs – which nowadays have actually diminished in importance to the point of irrelevance for many firms' location decisions (Malecki, 1997; McCann, 1995, 2001) – does not give a full account of the determinants of spatial concentration, particularly when looking at innovative activities.

Already, François Perroux (1950), in his distinction between different types of economic space, defined the firm as a 'field of forces': economic space consists of centres (*pôles de croissance*) that emit centrifugal impulses and attract centripetal forces, thus exerting influence over areas larger than the centre itself. Economic activities would therefore be better defined in terms of space and networks of forces, which escape the national dimension insofar as they 'can never be made precise by their outline or by their container' (Perroux, 1950: 102).[1]

As well as production, innovative activity turns out to be spatially concentrated and this can mainly be attributed to the benefits that stem from a specific case of agglomeration economies, i.e. knowledge externalities or spillovers. Reference may once more be made to Marshall's pioneering work, suggesting that accumulation of skills, know-how and knowledge takes place within spatially bounded contexts, promoting a kind of 'industrial atmosphere' capable of enhancing economic growth. Following this line, Kaldor highlighted that the advantages of dynamic economies of scale originate mainly from 'the development of skill and know-how; the opportunities for easy communication of ideas and experience; the opportunity of ever-increasing differentiation of processes and of specialisation in human activities' (Kaldor, 1970, p. 340). It should be noted, however, that such kinds of externalities go beyond the concept of spatial agglomeration, insofar as they affect managerial and organisational practices, market structures, growth processes and a wide range of activities not necessarily confined to specific spatial configurations. On the other hand, a common location offers cultural similarities that improve the ease and the speed of knowledge diffusion, providing the right environment for the development of a common language, shared codes of communication and interaction, collective values and institutions (Sölvell and Bengtsson, 1997). Therefore, more recent approaches to the analysis of the benefits of agglomeration have shifted attention away from traditional purely economic factors towards the characteristics of social and institutional localised systems, supposing that they can provide a better understanding of the geographical concentration of economic and innovative activity, as well as of the dynamics of technological specialisation patterns. Hence, the broad literature on the advantages of the geographical agglomeration of technology and innovation has developed along a twofold perspective. The first, and antecedent to the other, kind of approach has followed the Marshallian tradition in trying to identify such advantages and their implications for the overall economic growth (see, for instance, Perroux, 1955; Pred, 1967, 1977; Malecki, 1980, 1983). Within this approach, the spatial dimension represents a factor characterising economic development, in relation to which the local innovation potential is assumed to be only one variable among others. The second and more recent line of research has instead addressed the localised structural factors that shape the innovation capacity of specific geographical contexts. This has given rise to heterogeneous subnational typologies of innovative activity – all returning to a broadly defined form of spatial organisation, i.e. the innovative cluster.[2]

The significance of the 'regional dimension' of an innovative system has emerged as the logical consequence of an interactive model (Kline and Rosenberg, 1986) – which led to the substitution of the linear model with the chain-linked model based on feedbacks, interactions and networks – putting the emphasis on the relationships with information sources external to the firm. Such relationships – between firms and the science infrastructure, between producers and users at the inter-firm level, between firms and the institutional environment – are strongly influenced by spatial proximity mechanisms that favour processes of polarisation and cumulativeness (De Bresson, 1987; Lundvall, 1988; von Hippel, 1989). Furthermore, the employment of informal channels for knowledge diffusion (so-called *tacit* or uncodified knowledge) provides another argument for the tendency of innovation to be geographically confined (Hägerstrand, 1967; Lundvall, 1992). Although a break has thus occurred with the conventional economic approach – in which spatial factors shaping innovation were usually considered secondary (if not thoroughly negligible) – the regional scope is still rather indeterminate with respect to the geographical location of innovatory capacity in the global economy.

A useful distinction is usually made between two different types of agglomeration forces that shape spatial organisations, pushing related firms and industries to cluster and possibly leading to patterns of uneven regional development – i.e. the emergence of cores and peripheries at the global and national level (Malmberg *et al.*, 1996). On the one hand, there are general external economies and spillover effects – so-called urbanisation economies – that attract all kinds of economic activities in certain areas. This provokes the emergence of regional cores with broad sectoral specialisations varying across different locations. On the other hand, localisation economies are fostered in spatial clusters of firms undertaking similar or related activities. These kinds of forces are likely to be industry-specific and to produce cumulative mechanisms that enable host locations to increase their production, technological and organisational competence over time (Richardson, 1969; Dicken and Lloyd, 1990).[3] Agglomeration forces tend to be deeply conservative and self-reinforcing, thus leading to a strong path-dependency of regional agglomeration patterns. In Krugman's words: 'If there is one single area of economics in which path dependence is unmistakable, it is in economic geography – the location of production [*and innovation*] in space' (Krugman 1991b, p. 80). However, both agglomeration in general and industry- or sector-specific agglomeration have usually been considered in static terms, driven by efficiency considerations such as economies of scale – both in production and/or in R&D – transaction and transport costs, input–output linkages, etc. As pointed out by Kaldor (1970), dynamic agglomeration economies refer rather to the occurrence of technological learning and knowledge accumulation, which are more likely to affect growth processes than simple unit costs of production (Harrison *et al.*, 1991).

The characteristics of innovation processes can therefore provide further support to the actual importance of the local dimension in an era of increased globalisation. To summarise, the rising function of local and regional innovative contexts can be explained by: (a) the relations with the sources of information external to the firm, which are strongly influenced by spatial proximity; (b) the use of informal channels for knowledge diffusion (tacit knowledge), which spur the tendency of innovation to be geographically polarised; (c) the nature of innovative capabilities, which is highly cumulative and path-dependent.

The importance of contextual factors and systemic interactions in the generation and diffusion of innovation has been recognised as a key determinant of the technological and economic performance of countries and regions. In particular, the notion of regional system of innovation (RSI) has emerged as a different perspective of analysis from the broader concept of a national innovation system, which was introduced by the evolutionary theorists in the late 1980s (Freeman, 1987; Lundvall, 1992; Nelson, 1993; Nelson and Rosenberg, 1993). Following this stream of literature, a RSI may thus be defined as 'the localised network of actors and institutions in the public and private sectors whose activities and interactions generate, import, modify and diffuse new technologies'. Referring to Howells (1999) for a comprehensive discussion on the extent of applicability of such a definition to a smaller geographical scale than the national one, the highly uneven pattern and spread of innovation in space suggest that such a phenomenon could be better depicted by assuming subnational units of analysis, which can avoid the distortions and the loss of information of hypothesising national systems as homogeneous entities. Indeed, as Carlsson and Stankiewicz accurately remarked, 'high technological density and diversity are properties of regions rather than countries' (Carlsson and Stankiewicz, 1991, p. 115).

Moreover, it has been stressed that learning dynamics and exchanges of tacit knowledge are usually embedded in distinct environments of interactions among different subjects, sharing common attitudes towards particular types of learning (Lundvall, 1988). Therefore, 'social capabilities' (Abramovitz, 1986), along with 'technological congruence' (Fagerberg *et al.*, 1994), have emerged as crucial localised factors that also determine the degree of attractiveness and the amount of spillovers that a region is able to draw. While the first – i.e. social capabilities – refers to the overall ability of the region to engage in innovative and organisational processes, the technological congruence points to the distance of the region from the technological frontier, or, in other words, the region's capacity to adapt and implement the technical properties connected to the new knowledge.

Within this systemic approach to the geographical dimension of technological innovation, the distinction between the aspects related to the geographical agglomeration of innovative activity (i.e. the Marshallian type of agglomeration forces) and the issues connected with the geographical diffusion of innovation – i.e. the impact of space on technology dissemination and transfer through networks, both informal and formal – has become increasingly blurred. The implication of putting together the two sides is that the 'top/down' perspective – that is, based on the transferability of the features characterising the national innovation system to the subnational scale – may reflect only the *necessary* conditions to distinguish RSIs. The *sufficient* conditions, instead, are represented by elements that are eminently contextualised; therefore, there is the need to integrate the top/down view with a 'bottom/up' perspective, which also tackles the internal dynamics of the regionally embedded socio-cultural and socio-economic structures (Asheim, 1995). In other words, it should be highlighted that the local competitive advantages are mainly dependent on attributes such as 'untraded interdependencies' and informal flows of knowledge (Storper, 1995), which in fact generate the bulk of territorialised externalities. These are crucial elements, insofar as regions with a similar response to the general comprehensive RSI criteria may show different capacities to accommodate innovation and adjust in ways that enhance innovative capability (Evangelista *et al.*, 2002).

Yet, the integration of the two approaches – top/down and bottom/up – helps define what can be labelled the 'hypothetical' RSI, insofar as the above features, in practice, combine in different ways, and have different intensity, quantity and quality. Indeed, the presence of strong geographical asymmetries in both economic and innovative variables poses the question of to what extent the criteria for defining the RSI can be applied, or, in other terms, if the identification of 'systems' as such is always feasible. Thus, can the observation of the criteria justify in all cases the applicability of the concept of regional system of innovation (even accounting for strong and weak RSIs)? Are all administratively and economically well-recognizable regions 'innovation systems'? The answer is clearly negative, as any 'system' – particularly with reference to innovation and technology – needs, in order to be distinguished as such, to have an internal coherence, a collective identity and 'rules of the game', which result in a regional 'whole' or model (Cooke *et al.*, 1997). It is not only the lack of a critical mass to generate, import, modify and diffuse new technologies that prevents the attribution of the distinctive status of 'innovation system' to the local context, but, even more, the lack of coherence among the structures that make up the regional governance. Weak and vulnerable regions are in fact bound to be highly dependent upon actual innovation systems; their need for new technologies is satisfied mainly by the mere adoption of imported knowledge and innovation; the intensity of relationships for innovation is higher with the outside world, due to the scarcity of endogenous capabilities; in addition, the strong dependency from external providers couples with a low degree of openness and attractiveness towards external resources (weak regions are usually dependent on the outside, simultaneously showing rather high levels of closeness in terms of participation in networks and activation of inflows/outflows of innovation). Moreover, there are also 'midway' regional cases, i.e. either those regions whose industrial base is open to innovation, showing at the same time a feeble scientific system; or regions where, in spite of the relative strength of the localised scientific and research system, this is not sufficient to ensure spillover effects.

All these are elements that may question the coherence of the system as a 'whole', posing further problems to the description of the potential of the region to be actively identified in the global knowledge-based or learning economy. However, it has been shown that the capacity of regions to hold within the process of technological and economic globalisation is determined by the comparative advantage on which they can rely, and that the nature of the region's internal organisation changes over time (as learning processes are not stable by definition), possibly leading to the strengthening or the breaking up of the consistency of the regional structure, even where a system can be neatly identified (Maillat and Grosjean, 1999).[4]

The importance of the above considerations confirms the complexity of locational choices for innovation, especially in the ongoing process of globalisation. Indeed, while traditional factors of production are becoming increasingly mobile across countries, other location-specific factors remain highly concentrated in space, boosting differentiation between regions. Furthermore, the attraction of external sources of innovation and technology depends both on the strength of the regional innovative capacity and on the regional pattern of sectoral specialisation, and it is a crucial aspect of regional change in the increasingly globalised economy.

The local interaction between economic, socio-cultural and institutional actors follows patterns of both collaboration and competition, which can produce stable mechanisms of collective knowledge accumulation. On the one hand, as also suggested by Porter's 'diamond approach' (Porter, 1990), competitive pressures and the associated push to innovation provide the dynamics of the advantage which firms derive in this virtuous circle. The competitive advantage of a regional system is thus created and sustained through highly localised processes, which in turn are reinforced by their own capacity to attract resources from outside. On the other hand, spatial concentration boosts the intensity of interactions within the regional system, thus increasing the extent of collaboration and the attitude towards innovation (a localised system helps reduce the elements of dynamic uncertainty).

On the other side, weak and backward regions are those that have an inadequate innovative base in order to compete with other locations and to be attractive for external flows of knowledge and technology. According to the traditional theory, the interaction of dynamic agglomeration forces might, in principle, be offset by supply considerations – such as high wage differentials, rising prices of land, increasing costs due to congestion, etc. – pushing towards the geographical dispersion of economic activity (what Weber called *deglomerative tendencies*) and causing relocation to backward regions. In practice, however, negative externalities of this kind do not always succeed in offsetting the centripetal forces of agglomeration, as the (re)location of economic and innovative activities strictly depends on the type and the sectoral characteristics of the regional cluster. As shown by Baptista and Swann (1998), agglomeration spillovers may operate for intra-industry clustering, while instead congestion effects may dominate, offsetting positive spillovers, in the inter-industry case. The price mechanism plays a role in spreading the location of industrial activity, but it is certainly not the only cause of the reversal of virtuous and vicious cycles in the patterns of regional growth.

As a consequence, a growing differentiation in economic and technological performance between successful and unsuccessful regional systems is likely to emerge, thus showing the local innovative potential of strategic importance in determining regional futures.

The globalisation of technology

The increasing interest of economists in the globalisation of production and technology reached its peak with the arrival of the current millennium. The term 'globalisation' refers to a wider dimension than the one evoked by prefixes to the word 'national', such as inter-, multi- or trans- (see, among many others, Howells and Wood, 1993; Perraton *et al.*, 1997; OECD, 1999). More specifically, in the present context, by 'globalisation' we refer to a high degree of interdependence among units that constitute the MNC. In principle, therefore, we could have a higher interrelatedness among geographically dispersed units, even with the same level of internationalisation of innovative activities of the MNC. However, the difficulty in assessing the actual stage and the implications of globalisation, especially as far as innovative phenomena are concerned, has led to rather dissimilar views, still inadequately supported – at least in most cases – by significant empirical evidence.[5]

The expression 'globalisation of innovation' is used to describe the recent increase in the intra-firm coordination of innovative activities of MNCs. On the one hand, the strength that allows a firm to invest and govern its operations across national boundaries is its ability to innovate and to take advantage of such innovation in different locations through its own organisation. The authentic global generation of innovations requires, on the other hand, a wide range of skills and capabilities that only firms with specific infrastructure, organisation and management can attain (Archibugi and Iammarino, 1999). This explains why there has been a shift in attention away from the MNC as a mere vehicle of technology transfer towards the crucial role it plays as a creator of innovation and technological knowledge (Chesnais, 1988; Cantwell, 1994).

The 'state of the art' on the international generation of innovation – leaving aside the current academic debate[6] – may be depicted as a trend towards increasing shares of innovation generated outside the home country and integrated within the MNC. The share of US patents of the largest industrial firms attributable to research undertaken in foreign locations rose from 12.2 per cent in the period 1969–72 to 18.6 per cent in the years 1987–90 (Cantwell, 1995: tables 1–2). Moreover, in the latter period, European parent firms showed, on average, a share of patents granted for research located outside their home country of higher than 30 per cent, indicating a greater propensity to internationalise their innovatory capacity than firms of US or Japanese origin.[7]

The traditional advantages of the centralisation of research and innovative activities – basically connected to economies of scale and scope in R&D, control on innovation and linkages with national business and non-business sectors – thus seem to be increasingly counterbalanced by those associated with decentralisation (see Pearce and Singh, 1992; Howells and Wood, 1993; Miller, 1994). From the perspective of the investor, the advantages of decentralisation can be summarised in terms of the linkages between innovatory activity and foreign production, local markets, suppliers and clients, and the exploitation of technological fields of excellence in host countries. The latter can be aimed either at consolidating or upgrading an existing technological strength of the MNC, or at extending and diversifying its competencies into new related technological fields.

In the last few decades, MNC activities have increased not only in their extent, but also in their intensity and variety (Pitelis and Sugden, 1999; Pitelis, 2000). The international dispersion of the creation of new technology and the change of innovatory strategies of MNCs make it all the more important to take into account the geographical concentration of MNC technological operations at a subnational level.

In fact, the change in MNC strategies towards a greater degree of cross-border coordination of their internationally dispersed operations requires an organisational structure that could not have been developed through purely arms-length market-based coordination between geographically separated units. As Dunning and Robson (1987) have effectively shown, transaction costs may shrink with the integrated governance of units, whatever the units are considered to be – either affiliates or different locations. However, the transaction costs approach, focusing basically upon benefits in terms of short-term efficiency and flexibility, fails to take into account the knowledge accumulation effects linked to the integration of innovative activities across geographically dispersed units. Dunning and Wymbs (1999) have demonstrated that the degree of multinationality is significantly associated with the perception that firms increase their global technological advantage from foreign sources. They pursue this aim by establishing integrated networks of affiliates, as a means of building a sustainable competitive advantage based much more on capabilities and dynamic improvements than on static efficiency factors. Through such networks, technology, skills and assets are transferred across national borders in a two-way direction – from the parent to subsidiaries and from affiliates to the parent company.

MNC networks, however, take a rather complex configuration, precisely because of the different types of agglomeration forces that shape spatial organisations. On the one hand, as seen above, there are general external economies and spillover effects which attract all kinds of economic activities in certain regions and determine, in the case of corporate integration, the localisation of new research units. These centripetal forces strengthen the inter-border intra-firm integration and the feedback of knowledge, expertise and information that occurs within networks of affiliates. On the other hand, sector-specific localisation economies intensify intra-border sectoral integration, implying local external networks between affiliates, indigenous firms and local non-market institutions. In both cases, by tapping into local knowledge and expertise, foreign affiliates gain a competitive advantage that can be exploited locally and/or transferred back to the parent company, enhancing its global technological competence. However, a geographical hierarchy of

Table 2.1 MNC networks for innovation

Type	Geographical direction	Innovation flows among units	Innovation strategy (Ghoshal and Bartlett, 1990)	Main impact
Intra-firm (corporate integration)	Cross-border	From parent to affiliates From affiliates to parent	Centre-for-global Local-for-global	On MNC and on both origin and host locations
Inter-firm (sectoral integration)	Intra-border	Between affiliates and indigenous firms	Local-for-local Local-for-global	On both MNC and host location
Inter-firm	Cross-border	Between parent and other firms	Global-for-global	On MNC

regional centres can be established, as a consequence of the interaction and the intensity of general external economies and localisation economies, which in turn depend upon the structural features of the regional system considered.

By mutating and adapting the classification proposed by Ghoshal and Bartlett (1990), it is possible to summarise the different patterns of knowledge flows backwards and forwards within and outside the MNC (see Table 2.1).

Internal (intra-firm) networks are established either in the case of a high centralisation of innovative activities in the parent company, which transfers technology, experience and knowledge to affiliates following an innovation pattern of Centre-for-global; or in the case of highly decentralised innovation undertaken by affiliates in different locations, which is subsequently transferred to the parent company and possibly applied to other units within the MNC, following a strategy of Local-for-global. While, in the first case, the impact on the host location may be adverse due to the competitive erosion of the domestic market base of indigenous firms – which leads to a reduction in the research potential of local firms – in the latter case (Local-for-global), the creation of innovation by affiliates is more likely to affect positively, through knowledge spillovers, the general innovation capacity of the region in which the affiliates are located.

External (inter-firm) networks provide intra-sectoral integration between foreign subsidiaries and local firms. In this case, the local character of innovation in the MNC's affiliate – which follows a Local-for-local pattern trying to tap into indigenous capabilities – might add substantially to the strength of the host region in which it is active. The technological specialisation of the host location is thus likely to be reinforced, as is the technological competence of the MNC, which absorbs sizeable corporate assets through its internal corporate network and the complementary Local-for-global strategy.

The choice of location by the MNC depends upon the number of regional centres and their relative position in the geographical hierarchy, and upon the extent to which the MNC has developed a strategy for technological diversification through tapping into specific competencies in a range of different regional centres of excellence (Cantwell, 1994).

Lastly, external networks can be established by the MNC parent through strategic alliances and collaborations with other large firms in selected areas of activity. The importance of such relationships for mutual exchanges of knowledge and information is increasing rapidly (Narula, 1999; Narula and Dunning, 1998; Narula and Hagedoorn, 1999; Archibugi and Iammarino, 2002), but since they do not depend upon geographically-specific characteristics, they will not be considered here.

It is worth pointing out that, from a conceptual point of view, the change in the way that MNCs manage their asset-augmenting cross-country activities is still perfectly framed and coherently explained by the eclectic (OLI, Ownership–Location–Internalisation) paradigm, which has been the leading explanation for the evolution of multinational operations over the past two decades. As Cantwell and Narula (2001) have effectively argued, globalisation has spurred the interactive dynamics between 'Ownership', 'Location' and 'Internalisation' advantages. On one side, as resulted from the above considerations, a more complex pattern of interdependence has emerged between 'O' and 'L' as, where the ownership advantages of the MNC and the attractiveness of the host region are strongest, the greatest potential for a strengthening of these advantages through the spillover effects of internationalisation is found. On the other side, 'I' has responded to the changing boundaries of the firm through the new integrated network organisation of innovative cross-border activities, as opposed to the old hierarchical organisational modes.[8] Globalisation has expanded firms' use of external resources to reduce, inter alia, innovation time spans, costs and risks, and to acquire greater flexibility in their operations (Hagedoorn, 1993).

To conclude, inter-border corporate integration and intra-border sectoral integration seem to strengthen technological linkages and specialisation between regions, especially where firms implement a rationalising strategy in order to adapt to a changing economic environment, such as the European Union during the 1990s (Cantwell and Dunning, 1991).

'Local' versus 'global': cumulative causation and regional hierarchies

It thus makes sense to assume that globalisation implies that location matters even more than in the past. The significance of the tendency of industrial innovation to agglomerate in certain regions on the one hand, and the emergence of a 'performance' type of MNC – identified by 'heterarchical' internal structure and innovation-based competitiveness (Dunning, 1993; Cantwell, 1992a, 1994; Amin and Tomaney, 1995) – on the other, tends to make the geographical polarisation of innovative activities stable and self-organising. Hence, as both globalisation and economic integration processes are likely to interact with the change of the MNCs organisation of innovative operations – spurring the rising function of local innovative contexts – we could argue that MNCs are to be considered as the key ring of the chain from global to local.

Increasing returns (of a dynamic type) and circular cumulative causation mechanisms have been the main ideas behind the evolutionary approach to the economic geography of innovative processes. As already argued, a crucial element in the model of the local accumulation of knowledge involves the attraction of outside resources, which may set off strong cumulative processes. The inflow of knowledge is driven both by actors from the outside attracted into the region and by local actors who try and tap into outside knowledge. Cumulative causation mechanisms might thus have been reinforced, giving rise to vicious and virtuous circles that depend strictly upon the sectoral points of strength and weakness of both the MNC and the regional innovation system.[9] The pertinent issue for the regional host economy in attempting to entice such high value added operations is to understand what renders a location attractive or 'sticky in such slippery space' (Markusen, 1996). Once the knowledge-seeking activity is located in the regional economy, 'each region finds itself increasingly integrated into an international division of labour for the development of new technological systems' (Cantwell and Piscitello, 1999, p. 19).

The 'competitive bidding' between European regional systems – in order to attract MNCs research and innovation activities – seems to have become increasingly tougher. In fact, the benefits of the global generation of innovation are not likely to be evenly spread between higher order regional centres of excellence. Furthermore, the risk of regional imbalances within national boundaries might also increase as a consequence of the fact that strong regional systems of innovation would become increasingly attractive, while backward regions would be further undermined by the strategies of MNCs.

As far as the latter point is concerned, we have stated above that location exerts a strong centripetal pull on the innovative activities of MNCs. However, the centrifugal forces that might offset the advantages of agglomerating in particular regions – such as the rising prices of locally available resources or other congestion effects – do not seem to have a large influence on location decisions of this kind. The typical arguments for convergence – based on assumptions such as the price–cost equalisation mechanism, homogeneity of firms and sectors, positive incentives to locate in the periphery, etc. – are not always applicable and it is hardly plausible that self-reinforcing regional growth (or decline) may be easily reversed by centrifugal forces stemming from conventional market mechanisms. Technologically declining regions, therefore, are not eligible as attractive locations for quality-seeking inward investment; although, if the latter occurs, there may be some benefits in terms of the revitalisation of past innovation capabilities through positive spillover effects (Cantwell, 1992a).

On the other hand, following the rationalisation of MNC innovation activity, stronger competition is likely to occur between technologically advanced locations, especially within an economically integrated area such as the EU. The relationship between the internationalisation of innovation and the competitiveness of local systems follows a circular pattern which – in the case of a virtuous circle – goes from the upgrading of local innovatory capacity to the increase of the share of research-related production, and from this to the improvement of competitive performances, setting in motion a positive interaction between foreign and indigenous research and production activity (Cantwell, 1992b).

The role of MNC networks for innovation turns out to be a function of the geographical hierarchy of regional centres – i.e. of the strategic importance of the host region and of the innovative dynamism of local competitors, suppliers and institutions. The sectoral composition of technological strengths, in fact, differs across regional centres, while the technological specialisation of foreign affiliates depends upon the rank of the regional location in the geographical hierarchy and upon its gradual change over time.

Arising from the above-mentioned differentiation of agglomeration economies, it is possible to distinguish between *higher order* and *intermediate* regional centres of technological excellence. Such centres, indeed, arise as a consequence of the interaction and the intensity of general external economies and localisation economies, which in turn depend upon the features of the regional innovation system considered. Clearly, the other extreme is that of *lower order* regions, i.e. technologically weak and backward regions that have an inadequate innovative base in order to compete with other locations and to be attractive for external flows of knowledge and technology. This differentiation has enabled us to distinguish between the form of potential knowledge spillovers and technological networks in operation between foreign-owned firms and their indigenous counterparts in different regions in Europe.

These interactions are more likely to further upgrade higher order regional locations, in which the Local-for-local strategy of MNC subsidiaries, and their capacity to incorporate backward and forward linkages in their external networks for innovation, aim at exploring local knowledge and expertise, which will be integrated to widen technological competence at the corporate level through the intra-firm network (Local-for-global). Indeed, when foreign research has a more pronounced exploratory nature, it is likely to be attracted by higher order cores, treating them as a source of general expertise and skills (Cantwell and Janne, 1999).[10] On the other hand, intermediate locations, with a narrower scope of technological advantage, are seen as sources of specific capabilities in some particular field and thus they might be negatively affected owing to the Local-for-local strategy of foreign affiliates, which follows a logic of exploitation of indigenous expertise, with the possible aim of out-competing local rivals. In other words, as the position of the region in the hierarchy falls, so the profile of technological specialisation of foreign-owned firms in that region becomes more closely related to the equivalent pattern of specialisation of indigenous firms in the same region. Conversely, a centre at the top of the hierarchy is more likely to attract a broad range of foreign innovative activities, as MNCs will generally try to extend their established lines of specialisation through intra-firm networks. Therefore, higher order locations should attract foreign research for their general reservoir of skills and resources, while centres further down are attractive more for their limited range of specialised expertise, thus bringing foreign and local technological profiles closer together.

Besides, it has also been pointed out that, by specialising according to the local strength in each location, MNC technological activity is broadened (Cantwell, 1992b). Instead, in the case of higher-order regions, the broadening of specialisation is one of the possible forms of incremental change in the composition of local innovation, since regional profiles may, in other cases, be reinforced and concentrated in their established areas of technological expertise.[11] In other words, only some higher order cores are able to adjust their profiles of specialisation to the highest technological opportunities over time, while others – which experience a slower process of convergence between old and new technologies – may end up gradually losing their competitiveness. The amount of spillovers that a region is able to attract depends upon the interactions within the whole regional system of innovation, which is constantly in motion. Hence, the process cannot be depicted in static terms: some regions will grow and others will decline through time. The location-specific and incremental nature of technological change might thus eventually imply the rise and the decline of technological poles within Europe.

Indeed, knowledge spillovers in higher order regions seem to operate mainly through exchanges in and around core technological systems, creating linkages between actors in quite separate alternative fields of specialisation. Such core systems appear to be rooted in the 'general purpose technologies' (GPTs) – such as, for instance, background engineering, mechanical methods, electronics and information and communication technologies (ICTs) – in which foreign-owned and indigenous firms' technological advantages appear to overlap in these higher-order centres. Empirical studies have demonstrated that MNC foreign affiliates account for an increasing share of all new technologies that are introduced in the multinational networks and that they are associated with a significantly higher probability of entry into new and more distantly related fields of technology, creating a long-term drift into new technological competence (Zander, 1997). These findings are consistent with the evolutionary view of the MNC, involving a gradual shift into new technological systems through the consolidation of international operations and the establishment of a network structure (Narula, 1995). When the latter occurs, international growth through time allows the MNC to leverage its accumulated experience and to smooth out the transition between major technological breakthroughs (Zander, 1997).

To summarise, the interaction between local and global processes of knowledge creation may spur regional gaps *within* a country – with agglomeration in centres of excellence (either higher order or intermediate) being strengthened and lower order backward regions experiencing further marginalisation – in addition to it being likely to entail a tougher competition between core regional systems *across* countries, in order to grasp the best growth opportunities offered by GPTs and innovation networks.

In the case of the EU, the globalisation of innovation through MNC networks has been comparatively stronger than in other economic areas. The removal of non-tariff barriers, the completion of the single European market and the recent attainments in the ultimate state of economic and monetary integration have spurred the reorganisation of operations of MNC affiliates located in the EU to a much greater extent than in the case of affiliates based outside the area. Cantwell (1992a) has shown that the degree of interdependency among geographically distinct units is relatively higher in Europe, where inter-firm networks and linkages between foreign affiliates and local firms turn out to be far more entrenched than in other areas of the world. The intra-area rationalisation of economic activities boosted by the integration process has thus given a strong impetus to globalisation, thereby strengthening the link between Local-for-local and Local-for-global MNC strategies.

Conclusions

The central aim of this book is to broaden the understanding of the crucial relationships between the globalisation of technological innovation by MNCs and regional systems of innovation in Europe. The conceptual framework behind our arguments is the Ownership–Location–Internalisation (OLI) paradigm, as we believe in its continued applicability (and adaptability) in the light of new developments related to the globalisation process.

The evolutionary view of firms' growth and technological change allows us to identify the major transformation brought about by globalisation, which, in the case of the MNC, consists of an increasing cross-border interdependence and integration of all kinds of operations, including those aimed at creating new knowledge and technology.

Such a process has been considered here in an economic geography perspective, as the increase of the extent, intensity and variety of MNC activities (organisational change) is associated with the growing interdependence of different regional systems (spatial change).

Our aim is thus to shed light – on the basis of original empirical evidence – on the dynamic interaction between ownership, location and internalisation advantages (or disadvantages) that underlie the growth of both the MNC and the regional system of innovation.

3 MNC technological activities and economic wealth

An analysis of spatial distribution in the European Union

Introduction

One of the crucial aspects of the ongoing globalisation of the world economy lies in the new modes of creating and diffusing new technological knowledge. The central role played by contemporary multinational corporations in such processes has been described in the evolutionary literature, stressing the metamorphosis of the MNC from the mere 'vehicle' of technical knowledge to the 'creator' of new technology. This has been seen as a key dynamic potential of modern MNCs, both for the evolution of the transnational firm as such and for the development of host locations. At the same time, the growing attention devoted by economic analysis to the phenomena of spatial concentration has provided increasing evidence of the highly bounded character of technology creation and spillovers, highlighting the implications for economic growth deriving from the beneficial interdependence between global creators of technology and regional and local innovation systems.

The aim of this chapter is twofold. First, we look at the spatial distribution of both the technological operations of MNCs and overall GDP across EU regions: in spite of the relevance of corporate innovation for economic growth, our knowledge of the locational patterns at the sub-national level is still very limited. Second, we obtain a representation of selected regional innovation systems as a means of illustrating some basic links between technological growth and systemic characters.

The chapter is divided into seven sections. The next section begins with a short summary of the relevant conceptual background, which is followed by the description of the data used in this book as a proxy for advanced technological capability, reported in the third section. An overall picture of the distribution and growth rates of both MNC technological activity and per capita GDP across 69 regions located in seven EU countries is provided in the section after. We then select 30 regions, the most meaningful in terms of our proxy for innovative activity, for a more in-depth analysis by technological sector and over time. In the fifth section, for the selected 30 EU regions, we first look for some classifying features on the basis of different economic and contextual indicators by means of principal component and cluster analyses;

we subsequently differentiate these groupings of regions in terms of attractiveness towards foreign innovative activity. The growth rates of particular sectors and the overall technological growth rate of each cluster of regions are then compared: some implications of the cross-regional technological strategies of MNCs for regional economic development are suggested in the concluding section.

Technological growth and regional convergence

A current general consensus that technological change is the most important source of dynamism in capitalist economic systems has brought about a great readiness to explore what is inside the 'black box'. Neo-Schumpeterian or evolutionary views – but now, increasingly, also mainstream economics – have been sharing the crucial assumption (of both Marx and Schumpeter) that capitalism is characterised, above all, by evolutionary turmoil linked to technological and organisational innovations (Freeman, 1994).

One of the topics tackled, after a considerable delay, in this field of research has been geographical agglomeration and regional development, almost completely neglected by Schumpeter himself and by those who first opened the 'black box'. This is somehow paradoxical, as evolutionary studies have extensively covered (since the late 1960s)[1] government technological and innovation policies, a theme in which the territorial dimension should have been considered as a fundamental variable.

However, more recently this gap has started to be filled in, as an increasing number of studies has suggested that localisation and regional clustering are major factors providing the basis for distinctive firms' performance, innovativeness and, ultimately, economic growth. Paraphrasing Nelson and Winter (1977, p. 46), 'to obtain a more solid understanding of innovation and what can be done to influence innovation, it is necessary to study in some considerable detail the process involved and the way in which institutions support and mould these processes'. The considerable detail explored here is the sub-national dimension and the distinctiveness of regional systems associated with corporate technological growth.

As previously pointed out, the evolutionary approach has shown that differences in technological growth and specialisation patterns are strictly dependent upon skills and capabilities, interactive learning, organisational modes and institutional settings, which are highly location-specific. That is to say, what happens inside the firm is fundamental, but the 'cluster effect' indicates that the immediate socio-economic environment around the firm plays a critical role in determining a successful competitive performance. Indeed, the same concept of technological paradigm implies a close link between technical progress, organisation and socio-economic institutions: by definition, any radical innovation brings about, to some extent, transformations in the organisation of markets, production and communities. Therefore, organisational and institutional change are inextricably associated with technological change; at the same time, distinctiveness, both institutional and technical, characterises evolutionary development of socio-economic systems (Foray and Freeman, 1993).

Furthermore, the features and the shifts of technological regimes are also likely to have a geographical dimension, thereby affecting the distribution of innovative and technological activities across space (Breschi, 2000). The balance between internal and external sources of knowledge varies not only across innovating actors, either firms or other organisations, but also within them over time. In fast-changing fields, innovation processes are critically informed by new developments occurring outside any individual firm. Particularly in such cases, therefore, technological progress benefits greatly from active participation in the technological community or context where new developments take place (Frost, 2001). Current technological opportunities affect the overall rate of regional technological growth, insofar as innovation flows will privilege, among core locations, those offering the best and fastest-growing breaks: the location of technologies activities needs, thus, to be understood as a dynamic process.

Yet, taking into account institutional diversity means adopting a comparative 'systemic' perspective: the interest in systems of innovation, and the recognition of their broad heterogeneity (even within national borders), has given rise to the problem of assessing the extent of technological and economic convergence across countries and regions. Following previous empirical evidence (see, for example, Fagerberg and Verspagen, 1996; Fagerberg *et al.*, 1997; Rodriguez-Pose, 1994, 1998; Caniëls, 2000),[2] some recent evolutionary modelling has actually pointed out that, contrary to the widespread belief and some economic theories, the impact of spatial proximity of the diffusion of technological innovation may be responsible for the reinforcement of core–periphery forces and regional divergence, especially in the presence of ongoing processes of economic integration (Caniëls and Verspagen, 2001).

On the other hand, regional diversity at the beginning of the third millennium cannot only be considered by itself. The comparative view necessarily calls for the global dimension of technological change, which is represented by the creation of new technology by multinational corporations. As Porter (1998) noted, 'paradoxically, the enduring competitive advantages in a global economy lie increasingly in local things – knowledge relationships, and motivation that distant rivals cannot match': *global* and *local* are intrinsically associated as never before.

As widely highlighted in the literature on multinationals, the accumulation of technological competence is a path-dependent process, being partly firm-specific and partly location-specific. Multinational corporations spread the competence base of the firm, and acquire new technological assets or sources of competitive advantage. Moreover, the strategic internationalisation of technological operations has indicated that decisions on 'what' and 'where' to internationalise are strictly related to the roots of the firm's competitiveness. An effective approach to the strategic management of technological functions entails the evaluation of the core technological competence, i.e. the set of knowledge, skills and capabilities that makes the firm's innovative capacity unique and original: the locational choice is part of the strategy and a central issue to optimise technological effectiveness and growth (Chiesa, 1995). For their part, indigenous firms benefit from local knowledge spillovers from MNCs, given the access of the latter to complementary streams of knowledge being developed in other locations. Consistent with the long tradition emphasising the key role played by backward and forward linkages as a vehicle of economic growth (from Hirschman, 1958, to Markusen and Venables, 1999), MNC technological experience has been increasingly seen as a fundamental ingredient of a cumulative process of development, as it has a positive and significant impact on the creation of knowledge linkages and of extensive networks of relationships with local firms endowed with complementary assets (Castellani and Zanfei, 2002). The presence of a number of leading foreign-owned companies tends to attract further knowledge, to stimulate spin-offs and to generate a positive cycle: once a region establishes itself as a technology hotspot, it can experience rapid and continuous growth. Overall regional knowledge stocks are thus very important, in so far as the cumulative nature of innovation will tend to make advantaged regions more advantaged compared with others in the next round of innovations, on the basis of the accumulated knowledge stock (Malerba, 1992; Beaudry and Breschi, 2000).

Yet, asset-augmenting and knowledge-seeking types of foreign investment, and the associated skills, expertise and competencies, are arguably of crucial importance as a catalyst for local growth: learning curve advantages are mainly people- and institution-embodied and regional systems may substantially gain from global corporations investing in innovation, technical knowledge and local human capital. On the other hand, it should be pointed out that the concentration of production and wealth in a certain location is not per se a sufficient condition to determine high technological growth. Innovative activities have often been proved to concentrate in locations where a market for technology and innovation has evolved more fully, somehow irrespective of the spatial distribution of production and income.

Technological innovation is, in general, more 'sticky' than production and this may be explained through the distinction – introduced by Henderson and Clark (1990) and developed within spatial systems by Phene and Tallman (2002) – between *component* and *architectural* knowledge. The first encompasses specific resources, assets, skills and technical systems that refer to particular constituents of the organisational system rather than to the whole. It ranges from technical (simple, tangible and tacit) to systemic (complex, intangible and tacit) component knowledge. Architectural knowledge is instead related to an organisational system as a whole which, through its institutional structure and routines, arranges the components for productive use (Phene and Tallman, 2002). Such architectural knowledge is cluster-specific, has a path-dependent and evolutionary nature and it is developed through relationships at both inter-firm and intra-community level. Thus, it provides a common framework through which the creation, adaptation, and diffusion of component knowledge is highly facilitated, raising local absorptive capacity – and therefore attractiveness – vis-à-vis that of other locations.

As already pointed out, localisation per se seems to account for knowledge externalities only to a certain extent: the combination of diverse kinds of knowledge into an interdependent economic and technological base needs, crucially, a plurality of sources and networking among these sources. The features of economic systems – and particularly their communication opportunities – play a major role in assessing the conditions of the production of new technology (Patrucco, 2001a; Antonelli, 2000). In this respect, for instance, urbanised and metropolitan regions have been proved to offer highly positive institutional contexts explaining the features of the collective dynamic of technological progress, due to the mix of a variety of complementing economic activities, science and technology infrastructures and communication and network mechanisms. On the other hand, regions with a strong industrial structure, composite and advanced knowledge-production basis and intense intersectoral externalities may provide the most suitable environment for technology creation and experimentation, as well as for the development of multilateral networks of dissimilar but complementary relations between global and local actors (Patrucco, 2001a, 2001b).

Although there has been a departure from the conventional economic approach – in which spatial factors shaping innovation were usually considered secondary (if not thoroughly negligible) – too little is still known about the regional scope with respect to the location of innovatory capacity in the global economy. Besides, the majority of empirical studies on knowledge externalities and their geographic boundness have dealt with the US case.[3] This is all the more surprising as a deep (and widening) process of economic integration, as is the case of the European Union, has apparently enormously bolstered the need to define the problems, and the policies aimed at solving them, in terms of centre/periphery economic convergence.

Patent data at the regional level

For the purpose of this book, patent data in the US are used to analyse the location of technological activity across space by the largest industrial firms in the world. The use of patents as an indicator of advanced technological capacity and ability to develop innovation is one of the most established and reliable methods of estimating innovative activities. Indeed, patents are not just a measure of outputs from R&D, but more a yardstick of wider innovative activity of firms. Indeed, in the words of Freeman – who defined patent statistics as a goldmine for empirical research – 'the recorded part of incremental innovation can be traced through technical journals, business histories and above all through patent statistics, which represent a unique long time series of inventive efforts on a worldwide basis' (Freeman, 1994, p. 476).

We certainly agree on the fact that 'we have a choice of using patent statistics cautiously and learning what we can from them, or not using them and learning nothing about what they alone can teach us' (Schmookler, 1966, p. 56).

The advantages and disadvantages of using patent statistics are well known in the literature (see, among others, Pavitt, 1988b; Griliches, 1990; Archibugi, 1992) and will not be rehearsed here. However, it is important to recall that, for large firms, like those covered in this book, patenting is more a mechanism to regulate an inter-firm exchange of technological knowledge than a monopoly device: in fact, most inventions of large firms are indeed patented, even in industries with a relatively low propensity to use patenting as a means of intellectual property protection (Cantwell and Barrera, 1998).

Problems arising in international comparisons can be overcome with the use of foreign patents in a common third country, so that all patents have undergone a similar screening process and international comparisons are therefore possible (Vertova, 1998, 2001). Furthermore, it is useful to bear in mind that the choice of US patenting is convenient since, historically, large firms are especially prone to patent their best quality inventions in the US market – the largest and the most technologically advanced market. It is therefore likely that our data reflect, over time, the patenting of inventions that have a significant commercial importance, as well as allowing for a meaningful analysis – based on common legal and institutional standards for comparison – of the territorial distribution of the technological operations of MNCs in the European Union.

The patent records used in this book are based on the patent database held at the University of Reading.[4] The data were obtained from the United States Patent and Trademark Office (USPTO) and cover all patents granted to large firms (both national and foreign) located in the regions of eight European countries (Belgium, France, Germany, Italy, the Netherlands, Sweden, Switzerland and the UK) over the 1969–95 period.[5] For our purpose, the use of patent records provides information on the address of both the inventor and the owner of the invention to which the patent has been assigned (from which we have derived the country of location of the parent firm through a consolidation of patents at the level of international corporate groups).

Each patent was classified into one of 56 technological sectors derived by mapping from the primary classification of the USPTO and organising patents into common groups (see Appendix 2(a) for the resulting 56 sectors).[6] Moreover, the sectoral classification of patents, in terms of the type of technological activity with which each patent is associated, as derived from the US patent class system, is distinguished from the main industrial output of the companies to which patents are assigned. Thus, our patent database also distinguishes large firms according to their primary field of production.

As said above, the company to which a patent has been assigned and the name and location of residence of the inventor responsible for the underlying invention are both recorded separately in the USPTO database. To facilitate a sub-national analysis of location, the data were regionalised according to the residence of the first-named inventor (i.e research facility responsible). This was achieved by attributing the location of the principal facility responsible for the innovation to an area code obtained from the Eurostat Nomenclature of Territorial Units for Statistics (NUTS95), which is the main source for comparable spatial data in the EU, providing a uniform breakdown of territorial systems. This classification is based on the institutional divisions in force in the member states, according to the tasks allocated to territorial communities, to the sizes of population necessary to carry out these tasks efficiently and economically, and to historical, cultural and other factors.[7]

The spatial distribution of MNC technological activity and GDP

The aim of this section is to present a mapping of the aggregate technological activity carried out by large multinational firms in the EU regions. The complete list of sub-national units considered here is reported in Appendix 1(a), which records names, corresponding NUTS levels and acronyms for the 69 regions belonging to our seven EU member states. The location-specific patent data are complemented through the use of other socio-economic indicators at the sub-national level provided by the EU database 'New-Cronos-Regio'. This has allowed us to build a map of MNC technological activity (patents per million of inhabitants) and GDP levels (per capita, expressed in purchasing parity standards) at the regional level, with reference to the first half of the 1990s.

First of all, in line with other recent empirical analyses (Caniëls, 2000; Paci and Usai, 2000a, 2001), Table 3.1 shows that the degree of concentration of technological activities – as measured by the coefficient of variation – across the EU7's regions appears to be quite high ($CV = 1.3$) and definitely higher than that of GDP ($CV = 0.26$).[8] More importantly, contrary to what was found by Paci and Usai (2000a), our data indicate that the regional agglomeration of the activity that underlies US patenting shows a tendency to increase over time, denoting, at first sight, the absence of a real convergence with reference to the spatial distribution of MNC technological activity.[9] The geographical concentration of technology varies considerably between countries: the highest coefficient is found, as expected, in Italy (1.54), where the degree of polarisation of industrial activities is among the highest in Europe and has not displayed a clear tendency to decline (Iammarino *et al.*, 1998). The lowest spatial concentration of technology is that of Belgium, the UK and Sweden, all showing a relatively high correlation between the concentration of MNC patenting and that of GDP levels; the highest correlation between the two variables is, anyway, that of France (0.95), where apparently the regional distribution of patents per million of inhabitants follows closely that of per capita GDP. In this respect, EU countries appear again to be rather differentiated,

Table 3.1 Regional dispersion of MNC technological activity (1991–5) and per capita GDP (1995)

	No. of obs. (regions)	Technological activity*(a) CV	GDP per capita (b) CV	Correlation (a–b)
Belgium	3	0.31	0.33	0.82
France	9	1.00	0.25	0.95
Germany	16	1.20	0.37	0.38
Italy	18	1.54	0.25	0.41
Netherlands	4	1.23	0.08	−0.09
Sweden	8	0.60	0.10	0.66
United Kingdom	11	0.55	0.11	0.69
EU7	69	1.30	0.26	0.34

Note
*USPTO patents per million of inhabitants

with Germany and Italy displaying much lower correlation coefficients, and the Netherlands even showing a negative correspondence between the two distributions.

In Figure 3.1 the same variables are standardised to the EU average, which in the case of 1995 GDP refers to the EU as a whole (EU15 = 100), while in the case of per capita MNC patents (1991–5) is the average of the seven countries considered (EU7 = 100).[10] In general terms, the geographical dispersion of MNC research is only weakly associated with the levels of economic wealth. Although, the impact of national systems of innovation (NSIs) appears to emerge quite clearly from our technological proxy, as in each country firms and other institutions are likely to interact to a different extent in generating and diffusing new technical knowledge, in principle at least, knowledge should spill over more easily across regions within the same country than across national boundaries. As can also be inferred from Table 3.1, Belgium, the UK and Sweden have a relatively even dispersion of regional MNC patenting, the latter two countries also with respect to the spatial distribution of per capita GDP. In other national cases, there seems to be an almost dualistic structure of MNC technological activities, providing an indication that NSIs are not always homogeneous entities. This is the case of Germany, the Netherlands and France, whose regions are highly differentiated with respect to the horizontal axis, a few being far more innovative than the EU average, while the others are positioned in rather low ranks. Yet, Germany is also highly scattered as far as GDP levels are concerned (with a group of regions, mainly the ex-East German Länder, at the bottom left of Figure 3.1), while the French regional 'outlier' with respect to GDP is the capital region (Île de France). The Netherlands are characterised by a relatively uniform distribution of economic wealth. The whole of Italy is, instead, below the EU average in terms of patents, but the country looks sharply divided with reference to per capita GDP.

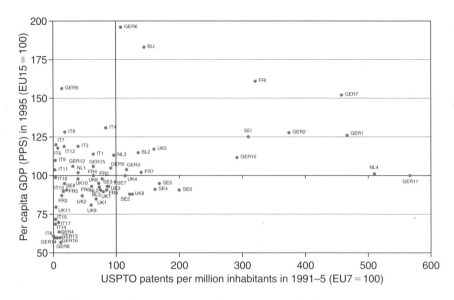

Figure 3.1 MNC technological activity and GDP in the EU regions.

Obviously, differences in industrial structures account for the bulk of technological differentials, particularly with the indicator used here, both at national and regional level. Emblematic is the Italian case, in which the relative 'firm dwarfism' – notoriously a prevailing feature of the national industrial structure – places the whole NSI below the EU average in terms of technological activities carried out by large firms, which are basically polarised in just two regions out of twenty.[11] This also underlies relative changes occurring in the overall time interval analysed: for instance, confronting the regional ranking in terms of US patent counts at the beginning (stock 1969–77) and at the end of the period (stock 1987–95), the Italian Sicilia shows the greatest improvement after that of the French Méditerranée, rising from the 60th to the 48th position largely as a consequence of the creation of the 'Etna Valley' and the considerable inflows of foreign direct investment by large electronics firms, which are likely to have boosted the regional propensity to patent as a whole in recent years.[12]

It is interesting to look at both the technology and economic wealth proxies in terms of growth, i.e. the percentage change of per capita GDP (in PPS) between 1978 and 1995 and the percentage change of US patents stocks between 1969–77 and 1987–95, always standardised to the EU average (Figure 3.2(a)). The same percentage variations relative to a shorter period – 1985 and 1995 for the GDP, and stock 1978–86 versus stock 1987–95 for patents – is reported in Figure 3.2(b), which also includes the Swedish regions for which GDP data at the sub-national level are not available prior to 1985.[13] One of the peculiar features of the regional mapping is the remarkable growth of MNC technological activities in the French regions between the end of the 1970s and the 1990s – higher than the EU7 for all of them but Île de France – which contrasts with a GDP growth lower than the EU average (again, except in the case of Île de France): this picture is almost unchanged in the shorter term 1985–95, although the growth of patenting slows down for a couple of regions. As already mentioned, the highest positive variation of MNC patents among all our EU regions is recorded in Mediterranée, which climbs the regional ranking of the indicator from the 34th position in the early 1970s to the 17th at the end of the period considered: such an outstanding performance may be largely ascribed to the government-pushed creation of innovative clusters, such as that of Sophia Antipolis, located on the French southern coast between Nice and Cannes. The UK regions manifest a variation of MNC patenting operations lower than the EU average (except for East Anglia), but at the same time showing less uniform patterns of growth with respect to GDP: the situation is not substantially altered when looking at the shorter run, in which the only remarkable improvement is that of Wales, whose technological operations – as well as those in Scotland – were spurred particularly by foreign investments in research.[14] In fact, although these regions – and particularly the area of 'Silicon Glen' in Scotland – have been rather successful in attracting foreign technological operations (thanks also to the attentive public support received since the late 1970s), this has somehow failed to stimulate the attraction of home-grown companies with advanced technological competence. Quite disappointing patterns of GDP growth are found across Swedish regions which, from 1985 to 1995, are all below the average; few of them record a positive change in patents stock between 1978–86 and 1987–95.[15] Both Belgium and the Netherlands register highly positive variations with respect to MNC patenting as well as to GDP, particularly since the second half of the 1980s: all regions in both countries are in the right upper quadrant of Figure 3.2(b), the only exception being Noord-Nederland, which shows the lowest dynamics of GDP among all geographical units observed. German and Italian regions display high economic growth with a few exceptions; with reference to US patenting, in the former case the dynamic picture confirms the dualistic structure of the German NSI, with (many) very fast-growing and (many) very slow-growing regions,[16] while in the case of Italy the mapping supports the relative weakness of the country as a whole with respect to large firms' presence. The only two Italian regions growing more than the EU average in terms of per capita MNC patenting are Liguria and Lazio (in the case of the latter, however, only with reference to the longer run), which, not surprisingly, are characterised by a relatively high presence of large-sized firms operating in scale-intensive and science-based industries and emerge – together with Lombardia and Piemonte – as the most R&D-intensive regions of the country (Evangelista *et al.*, 2002).[17]

To sum up, the above observations point to the relative diversity of EU systems of innovation in 1995, both at the regional and at the national level.

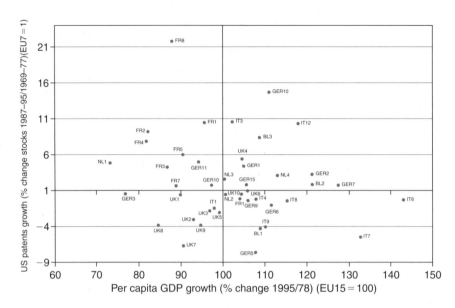

Figure 3.2a MNC technological growth and GDP growth in the EU regions, 1978–95.

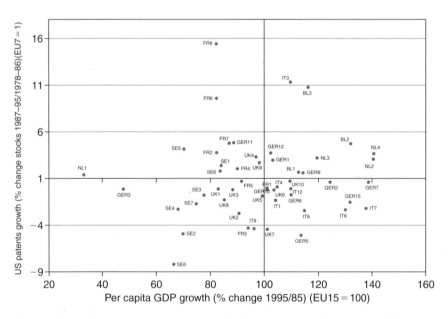

Figure 3.2b MNC technological growth and GDP growth in the EU regions, 1985–95.

The UK, Sweden and Belgium turn out to be, as far as MNC patenting is concerned, relatively homogeneous NSIs; however, only the regions of the latter can be identified as both technologically and economically dynamic. While Dutch regions display an outstanding economic uniformity, they are highly scattered with respect to technological activity, with Zuid Nederland being by far the strongest and the fastest-growing RSI, hosting the headquarters of Philips which, as is well known, has played a crucial role in shaping the Dutch NSI profile. Germany, Italy and France present a rather dualistic structure, being split into strongly innovative and technologically backward regions. This coincides with more scattered GDP levels and rates of growth. In Italy, however, the characters of the distribution of technological activities largely resemble those of an actual 'polarisation' (even taking into account the different NUTS level, i.e. NUTS2), confirming once again the huge regional imbalances of the national system.

MNC technological activity, regional cores and attractiveness

The analysis of the regional distribution of MNC technological operations at both sectoral level and over time cannot cover the whole set of our geographical units due to obvious limitations in the volume of patent counts. Therefore, we restricted the more detailed analysis of technological growth patterns to a selected number of regions, chosen on the basis of both technological size and foreign share of the overall regional MNC patenting. The 30 selected regions together represent 93.5 per cent of the total stock (1969–95) of US patents granted to large firms located in the seven EU countries covered by the University of Reading territorialised database,[18] and therefore they can be considered, in our perspective, as EU regional 'cores' of innovation (Appendix 1(b)).[19]

Counts of innovation (i.e. total US patents granted to large firms) normalised by the population are reported in Table 3.2, which shows in the last two columns the ranks of the 30 regions in terms of patents counts (absolute numbers) in 1969–77 and in 1987–95. The correlation coefficient between the two distributions at the level of all 69 EU regions is obviously very high (0.94), confirming the relative stability of the regional ranking on the basis of MNCs' patenting.

The further step was to look for some unifying features among the 30 regional cores on the basis of different economic and contextual indicators, as the aim was to obtain a representation of the technological dimension along with a more general view of the regional context, in order to identify possible connections between MNC technological patterns of growth and wider systemic features. The economic and contextual indicators are reported in Appendix 3. Clearly, comparing absolute numbers across regions ignores the fact that some regions are considerably larger than others: scale has obviously an impact on economic and systemic performance. Therefore, variables are

Table 3.2 US patents granted to large firms and ranks of patent counts in 1969–77 and 1987–95 for 30 EU regions

Regions	US patents 1969–95/ (millions of inhabitants)	Rank 1969–77	Rank 1987–95
Zuid Nederland	2,211.20	8	8
Hessen	2,046.07	6	6
Rheinland Pfalz	1,978.07	9	7
Bayern	1,761.71	3	2
Baden Württemberg	1,683.42	5	3
Île de France	1,492.48	4	4
Nordrhein-Westfalen	1,397.23	1	1
Stockholm-Östra Mellansverige	1,358.00	11	12
South East	925.69	2	5
West Midlands	804.80	7	18
North West	764.18	10	10
Hamburg	627.13	27	33
Centre Est	601.78	12	9
Flanders-Bruxelles	569.00	15	15
East Midlands	490.63	17	20
East Anglia	455.53	35	30
Niedersachsen	438.87	14	16
West-Nederland	436.13	16	13
Lombardia	416.47	13	11
Piemonte	399.49	20	23
North	386.11	25	29
Schleswig-Holstein	384.60	31	32
South West	380.25	22	21
Wales	328.31	23	36
Oost-Nederland	321.96	28	31
Yorkshire and Humberside	298.38	21	28
Bassin Parisien	264.11	19	14
Est	245.96	32	24
Méditerranée	210.88	34	17
Scotland	185.02	30	34

Note
Regions appear in descending order of US patents 1969–95 per million of inhabitants. Ranks refer to all 69 EU regions.

normalised either by economic size (GDP or employment) or by demographic size (population) of regions. In order to achieve a synthetic view of the 22 regional indicators, we applied factor analysis, a statistical technique commonly used to identify a small number of factors that can be utilised to represent geometric relationships among sets of many interrelated variables. As the variables considered here are quantitative, the method applied was the principal component analysis (PCA). The choice of the variables to be included in the PCA was made on the basis of the correlation matrix and the associated statistical tests; the evaluation of the appropriateness of the model and the factor extraction (through a stepwise and backward procedure) led to

Table 3.3a Principal component analysis: results

Correlation matrix for the 10 regional indicators included as active variables in the PCA

		denpop	unempl	agriemp	indemp	gdpcap	vaemp	r&dper	usptopat	airtraf	highedu
denpop	Pearson correlation	1	−0.063	−0.545	−0.294	0.690	0.591	0.206	0.034	0.487	0.557
	Sig. (2-tailed)		0.742	0.002	0.115	0.000	0.001	0.275	0.857	0.006	0.001
unempl	Pearson correlation		1	0.163	−0.345	−0.052	0.099	−0.177	−0.300	0.150	0.345
	Sig. (2-tailed)			0.389	0.062	0.785	0.603	0.349	0.108	0.429	0.062
agriemp	Pearson correlation			1	0.112	−0.389	−0.211	−0.282	−0.138	−0.583	−0.410
	Sig. (2-tailed)				0.557	0.034	0.263	0.131	0.466	0.001	0.025
indemp	Pearson correlation				1	−0.078	−0.030	0.063	0.234	−0.488	−0.444
	Sig. (2-tailed)					0.682	0.876	0.743	0.214	0.006	0.014
gdpcap	Pearson correlation					1	0.815	0.558	0.302	0.632	0.519
	Sig. (2-tailed)						0.000	0.001	0.105	0.000	0.003
vaemp	Pearson correlation						1	0.493	0.383	0.544	0.477
	Sig. (2-tailed)							0.006	0.037	0.002	0.008
r&dper	Pearson correlation							1	0.655	0.459	0.225
	Sig. (2-tailed)								0.000	0.011	0.232
usptopat	Pearson correlation								1	0.172	0.055
	Sig. (2-tailed)									0.363	0.772
airtraf	Pearson correlation									1	0.584
	Sig. (2-tailed)										0.001

Note

No. of obs. = 30.

Table 3.3b Principal component analysis: results
                Component matrix (two components extracted)

	Factor 1	Factor 2
Extraction sums of squared loadings		
Total	4.23	2.06
% of variance	42.28	20.63
Variables loadings		
denpop	0.76235	−0.16586
agriemp	−0.60788	0.01345
indemp	−0.30931	0.71346
unempl	0.04533	−0.67079
gdpcap	0.89292	0.15754
vaemp	0.81933	0.16346
r&dper	0.61496	0.53519
usptopat	0.36930	0.71557
airtraf	0.82404	−0.21449
highedu	0.71898	−0.42493

Tests
KMO Measure of Sampling Adequacy = 0.62
Bartlett's Test of Sphericity significant at 1%
The shading highlights by which of the two factors each variable is mostly represented.

the identification of ten active variables (see Tables 3.3(a), (b)) which determine the construction of the x and y axes – uncorrelated (orthogonal) and labelled according to the literature-based interpretation. The remaining 12 variables were introduced as illustrative variables, i.e. projected on the Cartesian plane but not included in the axes construction. This has thus allowed for a simple geometrical representation of both the original variables (indicators) and the individuals (30 regions) on a Cartesian plane.

The first principal component explains 42.3 per cent of the variance, while the second adds a further 21 per cent: the total estimated variance attributable to the first two factors is thus 63 per cent, which is a satisfactory result supporting the view that a two-factor model can be adequate to represent the data graphically.[20] The representation of the regions with respect to the factors extracted is shown in Figure 3.3. The x axis (factor 1) has been labelled 'Degree of urbanisation and contextual dynamism', since it is strongly characterised by the juxtaposition between the variables related to economic wealth and overall productivity (GDP per capita, valued added per employee) and indicators of urbanisation (population density, air traffic, higher education) on the positive (right) hand of the horizontal axis, and the share of employment in agriculture on the negative (left) one. Thus, the variables loadings suggest that the more we proceed in the positive direction, the more the regions are highly dynamic and urbanised systems, while scarcely populated, comparatively poorer regions with a low degree of urbanisation should be positioned towards negative values. The y axis (factor 2) has been cata-

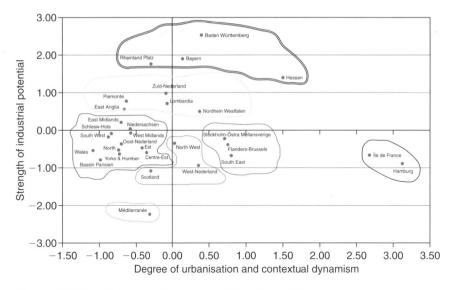

Figure 3.3 PCA and cluster analysis – plane of the selected EU regions.

logued as 'Strength of industrial potential', as it is marked on the upper bound by both the share of employment in manufacturing industry and patenting of large industrial firms, and on the lower bound by the rate of unemployment. Thus, positive values of the vertical axis are likely to represent strongly industrialised centres, while negative values suggest the presence of deindustrialising and stagnating areas.

The interpretation of Figure 3.3 is facilitated by cluster analysis (CA).[21] Seven regional clusters were identified on the basis of the two PCA factors. Each cluster is particularly characterised by some of the variables considered: the pseudo-*t* test and the levels of significance with reference to the mean of each variable in each regional cluster – as resulting from the CA – were used to label the grouping.

Cluster 1 is the most numerous, including 12 EU regions: six out of ten UK regions, together with some French systems, two east German Länder and one Dutch region. This group has been labelled 'medium industrial potential, scarcely urbanised regional contexts', as it is particularly characterised by a very low population density and a relatively significant weight of agriculture. Cluster 2 encompasses 'industry-based regions with medium–low degree of urbanization': the two Italian cores, East Anglia, Zuid Nederland and Northern Westfalen, all of them rather technology-oriented, both in terms of patents and R&D. The first two clusters have in common – although to different extents – relatively low degrees of openness (as proxied by the air traffic variable) and levels of enrolment in higher education below the average. Cluster 3, with three regions, includes essentially 'deindustrialising regions, with rather dynamic contextual conditions'. It is worth noticing that what brings Scotland into Cluster 3 (instead of being included in the first cluster, to which the region resembles more as far as economic wealth is concerned) are the considerable values of more contextual variables, such as air traffic and, especially, higher education. Cluster 4 gathers together three regional cores, basically 'service-driven and highly urbanised': the South East of England, Flanders-Brussels and the broad region of Stockholm-Östra Mellansverige. The prevailing features are a remarkable openness and the overall high level of economic wealth: the regions show, together with those of Cluster 7, the highest shares of services on total employment and a relevant innovative capacity, although represented relatively more by R&D indicators than by patenting activity (EPO or USPTO). Cluster 5 consists of only one region, Mediterranée, marked by the lowest population density, far above the average unemployment rate and the largest share of employment in agriculture. As mentioned above, the interpretation of clusters was supported by further information grasped from the illustrative variables not considered in the PCA: in the case of Mediterranée the character of a region 'mainly rural, with moderate systemic dynamism' is, for example, reflected by the female unemployment rate, by far the highest among all regions, even when considering the whole EU7; on the other hand, the region displays a rather good education level.

Cluster 6 includes 'industry-driven, technologically advanced manufacturing centres': all four regions are German industrial cores, principally featured by technological strength, as measured by both US patenting and R&D personnel; economic vitality emerges from the outstanding values of productivity and industrial employment. Conversely, this cluster shows, on average, some weakness in the systemic dynamism: the regions reveal a limited intensity of air traffic (with the exception of Hessen) and all score at the bottom with respect to the higher education indicator. The last group, Cluster 7, comprises two 'highly dynamic metropolitan contexts', namely Île de France and Hamburg. The two regions are marked primarily by astonishing levels of population density, economic wealth – both in terms of per capita GDP and productivity – higher education and openness; in contrast, the share of employment in industry is definitely tiny in both systems.

By means of the one-way ANOVA, complete with Tukey's HSD test, we checked to what extent the clusters of regions were related to 'attractiveness', as proxied by per capita foreign patenting activity (total stock 1969–95) located in each region (at 1995 population). This exercise added further elements to the analysis carried out here which, within its limits, provides rather interesting intuitions. First of all, the correlation coefficient was calculated between the clusters and our proxy for attractiveness: a significant coefficient (0.7) was found, confirming the supposition that the grouping of EU regions on the basis of our indicators reflected the distribution of foreign-owned technological activities. Moreover, it is interesting to note that the latter shows a significant correlation with per capita GDP in 1995 (the correlation coefficient is 0.8) indicating a positive association between attractiveness and economic wealth across regions: such a relationship is not observed for the overall patent stock 1969–95 (the correlation coefficient being, in this case, 0.3). The further step was to check whether, having allowed for cross-regional variance, cross-cluster variations do matter, supporting our expectation that the differentiation of the regional clusters is, to some extent, associated with foreign technological presence (i.e. variance *between* clusters prevails over variance *within* them). The results of the one-way ANOVA test are reported in Table 3.4(a).

The high value of F (6.75 significant at the 1 per cent level) is evidence against a null hypothesis, H_0, of equality of all population means, implying that cross-cluster variance of per capita foreign patenting matters more than intra-cluster variance (clusters are distinct and their differentiation is reflected by the proxy for attractiveness). However, a significant F does not allow us to establish any significant comparison between clusters, thus Tukey's test of Honestly Significant Difference (HSD) – which indicates which pairs of groups differ significantly at the 5 per cent level – is shown in Table 3.4(b).

Cluster 1, as expected, emerges as being significantly different from Clusters 4, 6 and 7 in terms of attractiveness towards foreign-owned research investments: regional capacity to pull foreign resources is definitely the feeblest among all groups. The other significant distinction is found between Clusters 2 and 7. In the latter case, although both groups reveal, on average, substantial levels of MNC technological activities, they appear to be sharply distinguished in their capacity to attract foreign research, with Cluster 7 far more attractive than Cluster 2. It is therefore possible to infer that regions showing similar economic-contextual environments exhibit a tendency to cluster together with regard to attractiveness, inward flows of foreign-owned technological resources, which are not only highly concentrated in a few regional clusters, but are also comparatively more attracted by agglomeration forces of the urbanisation type.

Table 3.4a One-way ANOVA: results
ANOVA (seven clusters)

Dependent variable = UsptoFORPAT69–95

	Sum of squares	df	Mean square	F	Sig.
Between groups	304078.8902	6	50679.81504	6.751	0.000
Within groups	172661.3455	23	7507.01502		
Total	476740.2357	29			

Note
Critical value of F (Prob. 0.01) for relevant degrees of freedom: 3.76.

Table 3.4b One-way ANOVA: results
Tukey's HSD test (six clusters†)

Multiple comparisons. Dependent variable: FOR6995

	(I) Cluster	(J) Cluster	Mean difference (I–J)	Std. error	Sig.	95% confidence interval Lower bound	Upper bound
Tukey HSD	1	2	−66.6148	46.1193	0.701	−209.7245	76.4948
		3	−81.5008	55.9278	0.693	−255.0467	92.0451
		4	−221.8808*	55.9278	0.007	−395.4267	−48.3349
		6	−198.2158*	50.0234	0.007	−353.4400	−42.9916
		7	−307.0708*	66.1747	0.001	−512.4131	−101.7285
	2	1	66.6148	46.1193	0.701	−76.4948	209.7245
		3	−14.8860	63.2751	1.000	−211.2308	181.4588
		4	−155.2660	63.2751	0.180	−351.6108	41.0788
		6	−131.6010	58.1219	0.248	−311.9552	48.7532
		7	−240.4560*	72.4908	0.031	−465.3972	−15.5148
	3	1	81.5008	55.9278	0.693	−92.0451	255.0467
		2	14.8860	63.2751	1.000	−181.4588	211.2308
		4	−140.3800	70.7437	0.381	−359.9001	79.1401
		6	−116.7150	66.1747	0.507	−322.0573	88.6273
		7	−225.5700	79.0939	0.084	−471.0010	19.8610
	4	1	221.8808*	55.9278	0.007	48.3349	395.4267
		2	155.2660	63.2751	0.180	−41.0788	351.6108
		3	140.3800	70.7437	0.381	−79.1401	359.9001
		6	23.6650	66.1747	0.999	−181.6773	229.0073
		7	−85.1900	79.0939	0.885	−330.6210	160.2410
	6	1	198.2158*	50.0234	0.007	42.9916	353.4400
		2	131.6010	58.1219	0.248	−48.7532	311.9552
		3	116.7150	66.1747	0.507	−88.6273	322.0573
		4	−23.6650	66.1747	0.999	−229.0073	181.6773
		7	−108.8550	75.0351	0.697	−341.6913	123.9813
	7	1	307.0708*	66.1747	0.001	101.7285	512.4131
		2	240.4560*	72.4908	0.031	15.5148	465.3972
		3	225.5700	79.0939	0.084	−19.8610	471.0010
		4	85.1900	79.0939	0.885	−160.2410	330.6210
		6	108.8550	75.0351	0.697	−123.9813	341.6913

Note
†Not performed for Cluster 5 because it has fewer than two cases
*The mean difference is sigmificant at the 0.05 level.

Technological growth patterns in EU regional systems of innovation

As stated before, a further aspect appears as relevant in examining the link between the 'global' and the 'local' dimension of technology creation: the innovative dynamism at the sectoral level and its connection with the overall growth of MNC research operations in the clusters of regions identified above. In other words, to what extent is the overall technological growth of regional groups related to the sectoral distribution of technological activities?

To give a preliminary answer to this question, and to add further elements to the debate on technological convergence among EU regions, we singled out technological classes that have shown the highest rates of technological growth at the worldwide level between 1969 and 1995, as a benchmark for technological dynamism or opportunities. The original 56 technological sectors were aggregated into 18 classes (see Appendix 2(c)): Table 3.5 reports their ranking at the world level in terms of growth between the first and the last period observed (1969–77 and 1987–95). Among the most dynamic technological classes, the only one displaying a tiny size in terms of patent counts is Nuclear reactors (7), which thus results in being much more concentrated in space than the other fast-growing classes (all far above the threshold of 20,000 patents at the world level). Not surprisingly, among the latter we find Office equipment (9) and Electrical equipment (8) – which include information and communication technologies (ICTs) – Pharmaceuticals (3), within which biotechnologies are encompassed, and Professional instruments (17); also Motor vehicles (10) and Non-metallic minerals (15) have recorded

Table 3.5 World US patents granted to large industrial firms

Tech18	Ranks of growth (1987–95/1969–77)	No. of patents
9	1	58,919
7	2	3,079
3	3	40,831
10	4	20,202
17	5	99,534
8	6	193,765
15	7	30,686
11	8	2,750
6	9	8,474
14	10	11,131
4	11	47,561
18	12	10,174
2	13	228,979
12	14	9,020
5	15	159,274
16	16	14,000
13	17	2,084
1	18	7,714

soundly positive variations over time, although they are slightly less significant in their absolute size.

Turning to the technological dynamism at the cluster level, the most meaningful indication emerges from the association, across regions, between the initial MNC patent stock (1969–77) and its growth rate between the first and the last period. The correlation coefficient is indeed neither positive (technological divergence) nor negative (technological convergence), but very close to zero: therefore, as a first approximation, it may be maintained that, over the 27 years observed, a 'steady technological differential' in overall MNC technological growth has characterised our sub-national units.[22]

As a matter of fact, among the fastest growing regions we find the whole of Cluster 6, at the top of the ranking with reference to patent stocks. Moreover, the four German cores show the highest positive variations in all the most dynamic technological classes, which account for substantial shares of regional patenting: Baden Württemberg and Hessen record both a significant size and growth even in the class of Nuclear reactors (7). Conversely, Cluster 1 is at the bottom of the scale with reference to the overall size of MNC technological activities and displays either negative or far below average increases of patents stocks. It is interesting to note that, among the 12 regions included in this cluster, those recording the worst technological performance over time have registered sharp drops, particularly in the fastest-growing classes, and most especially in Electrical equipment (8), Office equipment (9), Non-metallic minerals (15) and Professional instruments (17). The notable exceptions in Cluster 1 are the French regions: particularly in the case of Bassin Parisien and Est, the outstanding growth of MNC research operations coincides with a sectoral distribution that increasingly favours the most dynamic technological opportunities, especially classes such as Pharmaceuticals (3) and Electrical equipment (8).

In addition, in the other clusters, overall technological growth appears as closely related to that of patents in particular technological classes. In Cluster 4, the traditional EU centres of innovative excellence of Stockholm and the British South East have experienced an erosion of MNC technological activities and owe their negative growth rates to the weakening of fast-growing technological fields; particularly serious, in both regions, in Electrical equipment (8). As argued elsewhere, initial patterns of technological specialisation and institutional environments may be responsible for the lock-in trend, together with the service-driven character of these regional systems. The modest growth of the Flanders-Brussels region has to be almost entirely attributed to a sectoral distribution increasingly oriented towards the highly dynamic Pharmaceuticals (3) sector.

Cluster 7 exhibits negative technological growth: however, the two metropolitan systems show rather different patterns in the distribution of technological activities across classes, with Île de France more capable of achieving a faster process of convergence between old and new technological opportunities than Hamburg. In Cluster 2, which, overall, is the second most vital cluster in terms of both growth and sectoral distribution of MNC patenting, the only notable exception is recorded by the Italian Piemonte, where the negative rate of technological growth is largely ascribable to the losses in the broad classes which include ICT, namely Electrical equipment (8) and Office equipment (9). Cluster 3 is definitely identified as a declining group: apart from the modest strengthening of Scotland in both Pharmaceuticals (3) and Office equipment (9), the North West of the UK records a very disappointing technological performance both in aggregate terms and in fast-growing opportunities (the only exception is Pharmaceuticals); the growth of West Nederland is instead due to the rising weight of rather slow-growing technological classes, such as Chemicals (2) and Mechanical engineering (5).

Finally, it is worth mentioning that the only cluster highlighting a tendency towards convergence is Cluster 5, composed solely of Mediterranée. The region, characterised by features typical of relatively poor, non-industrial areas, has seen an enormous increase in its importance in the geographical strategies of (both nationally- and foreign-owned) multinational firms' research investments. As previously highlighted, the scientific park of Sophia Antipolis has made steady progress over the years, reaching a critical mass and only recently accelerating overall technological growth. The main technologies developed in the region are in medical and natural sciences (Pharmaceuticals) and electronic and advanced telecommunications (included in Electrical and Office equipment (8 and 9)). Public policy has been a critical driver here, and the whole cluster is the outcome of the explicit intention of the French government – as stated in the late 1960s – to aim at the creation of 'the great European city of science in the sun' (Dearlove, 2001). The attractiveness of the area towards foreign technological resources can be seen from our data – a number of leading big companies have established research laboratories in the region, including Siemens, Lucent Technologies, Compaq and SAP.[23]

To summarise, no real technological convergence is observed among the 69 regions belonging to the seven EU countries analysed here; on the contrary, some technological divergence emerges between the clusters of our 30 regional cores, with the group of 'industry-driven, technologically advanced manufacturing centres' being increasingly favoured by MNC locational choices regarding the creation of new technology, and 'medium industrial potential, scarcely urbanised regional contexts' falling, on average, further behind.

Conclusions

The descriptive analysis carried out above has given support to the idea that to treat the NSI as if it were a homogeneous socio-economic entity is no longer feasible. Our results have preliminarily indicated that the regional concentration of MNC technological activities seems to have increased over time, and that the risks of assuming homogeneity increase as the gap between the most technologically advanced RSIs and both backward regions and less dynamic innovation systems has become wider. Moreover, on the basis of the above picture it can be argued that the distribution of large firms' innovation among and within cluster appears to reflect, at least to some extent, economic and contextual features of EU regional systems. Some RSIs display rather fast MNC technological growth, while others – even traditionally strong innovative cores – experience a relative stagnation or decline: on the other hand, the highest degree of attractiveness towards foreign investment in research activities is found particularly in industry-driven clusters with fully evolved technological markets, or in some of the most prosperous metropolitan systems.

In spite of the caveats of our analysis – above all, the fact that we do not consider technological activities by companies other than the world's largest firms in defining the regional knowledge base – there are clearly several important implications in terms of tools and interventions for innovation and technological progress. We would like to mention just two broad points, one more concerned with macro-conceptual perspectives and the other underlying rather micro-oriented practices; both, we believe, need to be taken into account in the formulation of future technological and industrial intervention to sustain the development of the 'Europe of regions' and to promote research-conducive environments.

First of all, the characterisation of dynamic processes within the contemporary multinational firm suggests that the quite widespread host-location obsession with the MNC's footloose and crowding-out potential has become rather obsolete. As maintained by Pearce and Papanastassiou (2000), MNC technological operations – especially in the case of foreign-owned affiliates – are more than simply compatible with active public strategies for sustainable development that encompass the precepts of the new growth theory, i.e. technological progress, knowledge building and enhancement of human capital. To disregard MNC transition and its dynamic scope may lead to a myopic policy perspective, which fails to address the potential for mutual knowledge enrichment for both firms and regions, thus missing fundamental opportunities for local economic growth.

Second, as argued by Coronado and Acosta (1997), so far public efforts aimed at promoting regional technological growth have been likely to become a significant factor affecting growth, mainly if the original object was to support the increase of an already existing overall output of innovation activities, which – as shown above – displays a large spatial coincidence with the strength of the regional industrial potential. Notwithstanding the rise in the general level of NSI efficiency that such policies may surely attain, some forms of 'technological pragmatism' in public intervention might possibly give rise to vicious circles, spurring further interregional technological disparities and economic divergence. On the other hand, as pointed out more than a decade ago by Patel and Pavitt (1991), incentives aimed at creating or sustaining favourable local economic conditions are not sufficient to ensure a rewarding allocation of resources (by both local and foreign firms) to technological activities, the latter being definitely more sensitive to institutional factors than conventional market-driven investments. To stimulate a more diffused allocation of MNC technological functions, it is therefore not sufficient to devise policy tools similar to those used to foster conventional investments at the local level.

4 Geographical hierarchies of research locations in the European Union

Introduction

The nexus between global and local processes has been investigated quite extensively by the literature of recent years. As illustrated in the previous chapters, one crucial aspect of such a relationship lies in the creation and diffusion of innovation which, more than other economic processes, shows rather complex patterns of distribution across space.

Indeed, as emphasised by Dicken, ' "global" and "local" are not fixed scales; rather, they represent the extreme points of a dialectical continuum of complex mutual interactions' (Dicken, 1994, p. 103). As a consequence, neither the orthodox approach – which traditionally considers both the (multinational) firm and the local system as black boxes whose behaviours are determined by exogenous factors – nor an entirely endogenous perspective – which tends to explain structure and growth mechanisms as the result of purely internal forces – seem appropriate to investigate the issue 'global versus local'. Rather, the structure and behaviour of the two 'extreme points' need to be considered within the context of their increasing interdependence, including both endogenous determinants and exogenous variables relevant to the analysis.

As previously argued, in order to consolidate existing competencies, it is generally necessary for a firm to extend those capabilities into new related fields of production and technology, and across a variety of locations. The firm is thereby able to benefit from the dynamic economies of scope that derive from technological complementarities between related paths of innovation or corporate learning in spatially distinct institutionally settings or environments. In this perspective, MNCs spread the competence base of the firm and acquire new technological assets, or sources of technological advantage. For their part, indigenous firms benefit from local knowledge spillovers from MNCs, given the access of the latter to complementary streams of knowledge being developed elsewhere.

Evidence of tighter cross-border corporate integration of innovation coupled with heightened intra-border/inter-company exchange of knowledge renders it increasingly pertinent to investigate the precise nature and location of

MNC technological activities. As already highlighted, while such new structures for innovation are a natural consequence of the globalisation process, certain shocks have served to accentuate this process. As a result of closer European integration, greater interdependency among MNC units in the EU has provided us with a unique testing ground for analysing such phenomena.

The aim of the present chapter is to introduce the four country-studies examined in detail within the EU area, namely Italy, the UK, Germany and France. The basic premise of the existence of a hierarchy of research centres has been explored by examining the precise technological profile of both nationally- and foreign-owned firms located within regional centres of excellence in each of the four economies.[1] The following section offers an overview of the internationalisation of MNC technological operations, while the third section focuses, in a comparative perspective, on the four EU national systems of innovation relevant to the subsequent analysis. Section four reports on the methodological issues applied to identify the technological profiles at both national and regional level. The section after provides a comparative view of geographical agglomerations of large firms' research operations within national boundaries, and is followed by a brief conclusion on the 'national hierarchy' in the EU context.

The internationalisation of MNC technological activities: an overview

The international business literature postulates a number of explanations as to why technological activities might be located outside the home economy. In the early years of writing on the subject, much emphasis was placed upon the necessity of locating some lesser degree of R&D abroad to facilitate the localisation and adaptation of products to local tastes and requirements (Vernon, 1966). From the viewpoint of the firm, this was commensurate with the exploitation of existing technologies essentially developed at home. Empirical work that followed suggested instead that the internationalisation of R&D in large companies in the past was considerably greater than had at one time been supposed (on the basis of evidence of US MNCs in the early post-war period), but confirmed that such internationalisation was essentially motivated by dissimilarities in the implementation of technologies between home and foreign locations (see, inter alia, Cantwell, 1995). More recent contributions in this field reflect instead a shift in emphasis towards a new necessity for corporate strategy to focus on enhancing extant capabilities and creating new competencies within the firm (Cantwell and Piscitello, 2000). An increasing number of companies today look at cooperation across regional and departmental boundaries as an unavoidable strategic asset, and combine external expertise and know-how with that of top-performing research facilities worldwide (von Zedtwitz and Gassmann, 2002).

As mentioned in Chapter 2, the 'state of the art' on the international generation of innovation may be depicted as a trend towards increasing shares of

Table 4.1 Share of US patents of the world's largest firms attributable to research in foreign locations, organised by the nationality of the parent firm, 1969–95 (%)

Nationality of the parent firm	1969–77	1978–86	1987–95
US	5.4	6.9	8.3
Japan	2.1	1.2	1.0
Germany	11.7	13.2	19.0
UK	42.1	43.4	53.0
Italy	14.9	13.3	13.5
France	7.9	8.1	26.9
Netherlands	48.6	50.8	54.8
Belgium-Luxembourg	50.9	53.8	50.2
Switzerland	43.9	42.9	47.7
Sweden	19.1	27.5	36.5
Total European countries*	26.3	25.6	32.5
Total all countries**	10.3	10.7	11.3
Total excluding Japan	11.1	13.0	16.2

Source: Cantwell and Janne (2000).

Note
*EU15, Norway and Switzerland
**Total includes all the world's largest firms, some not presented separately in this table.

innovation generated outside the home country and integrated within the MNC. As shown in Table 4.1, although the share of US patents of world's largest industrial firms attributable to research undertaken in foreign locations (outside the home country of the parent firm) rose only modestly in the 1969–95 period, there is a wide disparity between different national groups of firms. Indeed, the reason for such a moderate increase is the rising share in total corporate patenting of Japanese and, to a lesser extent, Korean firms, which as yet are, on average, little internationalised in their technological development, and their greater contribution to the total has acted to pull down the global average of foreign share (Cantwell and Janne, 2000).

In fact, considering the total foreign share excluding Japanese firms, it rises much more strongly throughout the period, from 11.1 per cent in 1969–77 to 16.2 per cent in 1987–95. In the latter period, moreover, European parent firms show, on average, a share of patents granted for research located outside their home country of 32.5 per cent, indicating a much greater propensity to internationalise their innovatory capacity than firms of US origin (whose share over the same period is 8.3 per cent) or Japanese MNCs (1 per cent).[2] While relatively small European countries, such as the Netherlands, Belgium, Switzerland and Sweden, have, unsurprisingly, among the highest shares of technological activity abroad, countries such as France, Germany and, to a lesser extent, Italy, which used to have a somewhat more centralised approach, have moved to greater internationalisation of technological operations in the most recent years. British firms, as is well known, have been

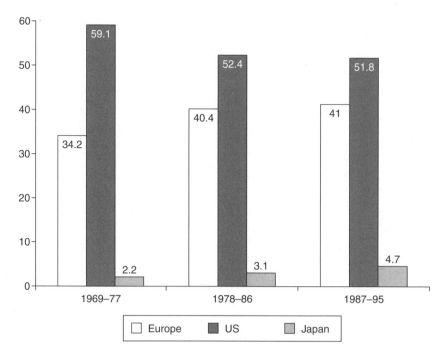

Figure 4.1 Patenting activity attributable to European-owned (EU15, Norway and Switzerland) research outside the home country by host area, 1969–95 (%).

amongst the most multinational in their organisation of technology creation, with over half (53 per cent) of their technological operations carried out abroad in the 1990s (Cantwell and Hodson, 1991).[3]

Yet, as emphasised in Chapter 2, the process towards the removal of non-tariff barriers, the completion of the European internal market and the achievement of the single currency has induced additional benefits and opportunities from greater specialisation and concentration in both produc-tion and innovative activities. The industrial restructuring brought about by the European integration has gone hand-in-hand with the globalisation strat-egies adopted by firms – especially large corporations – spurring interdepen-dence within firms and across locations and deepening the degree of agglomeration in the EU area.[4] As shown by Figure 4.1, the bulk of techno-logical activities carried out by European firms abroad is located in the US and in Europe. As highlighted by Cantwell and Janne (2000), the large share of European-owned research conducted in the US demonstrates that the much stronger propensity of European MNCs to internationalise their technological capacity is not simply the result of cross-border activity within Europe. On the other hand, the share of patents of European parent firms attributable to R&D undertaken within Europe rose substantially (from

34.2 per cent to 41 per cent) in the period considered, endorsing the presence of an 'integration effect' on the overall level of intra-area technological operations of European multinationals.

The European Union: some national features

Although the majority of multinational corporations continue to locate a large proportion of R&D in the home country, it is also widely recognised that MNCs are making increasing use of international networks for technology development to augment that generated in their home base (Cantwell, 1995; Fors, 1998; Dunning and Lundan, 1998; Kuemmerle, 1999; Cantwell and Piscitello, 2000). It is generally acknowledged that wide disparities in technological competencies exist across the economies of Europe (Verspagen, 1997; Paci and Usai, 2000a; Caniëls, 2000). Here we focus on four EU member countries – Italy, the UK, Germany and France – for which we have carried out more detailed studies at the sub-national level reported in the following chapters.

First of all, it is interesting to look at the geographical spread of R&D operations carried out abroad by the companies of each of the four national systems. As can be seen from Table 4.2, country specific characters are rather evident in terms of geographical orientation of outward research investments. The US is the most important location for German- and British-owned research abroad: however, while German firms have concentrated an increasing share of their foreign R&D operations in the US – somehow in contrast with the overall drift of European MNCs shown in Figure 4.1 – British firms have followed an opposite trend, with a rising share located in Europe (from 16.8 per cent to 26 per cent). Conversely France and, even more, Italy have the bulk of their foreign technological operations in Europe. Yet, while the share of research located in the 'Old Continent' is fairly steady over time for French-owned companies (above 50 per cent in all three subperiods), that of Italian companies has increased sharply from 28.7 per cent in 1969–77 to 68.5 per cent in 1987–95, with a corresponding withdrawal from the US, especially in the most recent years. The tendency towards a greater involvement in Japan is, instead, essentially due to the increasing technological presence of German and British firms. Thus, overall, British and German companies show widely globalised strategies encompassing facilities outside Europe; Italy is definitely more oriented towards a regionalised European restructuring; France is somehow in the middle, with almost equivalent shares of patenting from abroad located in Europe and in the US. This is consistent with the large variety of technology internationalisation paths among countries and firms pointed out by the most recent literature (Archibugi and Michie, 1995; Patel, 1995; Cantwell and Janne, 2000; Le Bas and Sierra, 2002; von Zedtwitz and Gassmann, 2002).

Table 4.3 reports on the distribution and penetration of foreign-owned innovative activity across the four economies. While the distribution figures

Table 4.2 Patenting activity attributable to research outside the home country by nationality of the parent firm and host area/country, 1969–95 (%)

Nationality of the parent firm	Host area/country								
	Europe			US			Japan		
	1969–77	1978–86	1987–95	1969–77	1978–86	1987–95	1969–77	1978–86	1987–95
Italy	28.7	34.6	68.5	67.9	64.2	29.3	2.7	0.0	0.0
UK	16.8	23.2	26.0	74.8	67.3	66.2	0.3	1.2	3.9
Germany	46.5	28.2	24.9	43.7	60.2	63.5	7.4	9.2	9.7
France	53.1	53.9	52.0	40.3	36.7	44.1	0.9	2.1	1.5

Source: adapted from Cantwell and Janne (2000).

Table 4.3 Distribution (D) and penetration (P) (%) of foreign-owned patenting
activity by host country, 1969–95

Host country	1969–72		1973–7		1978–82		1983–6		1987–90		1991–5	
	D	P	D	P	D	P	D	P	D	P	D	P
Italy	4.3	27.3	4.9	31.1	4.4	26.5	4.5	32.9	6.0	43.9	6.5	57.5
UK	29.3	27.7	26.8	30.8	25.0	31.3	22.6	36.0	21.0	35.4	21.2	45.2
Germany	27.0	16.3	30.2	15.6	31.8	15.2	35.6	18.8	33.5	18.1	28.9	17.4
France	13.2	24.2	14.9	24.7	14.5	24.0	14.2	25.1	14.9	27.1	15.6	28.9
Europe*	100.0	22.7	100.0	21.6	100.0	21.4	100.0	24.4	100.0	25.0	100.0	28.6

Source: Cantwell and Piscitello (1999).

Note
*EU15, Norway and Switzerland.

(D) highlight the attractiveness of the various locations against one another,
the penetration statistics (P) indicate the degree to which foreign-owned
activity has infiltrated the aggregate local innovative activity within each of
these economies.

In terms of distribution, the UK was the main host in Europe of foreign-
owned patenting activity in the early years, while, since the 1970s, Germany
has been the most attractive location. Italy is further behind, although
recording an increase in the proportion of foreign activity carried out in the
country since the mid-1980s. France displays an intermediate position, with a
rather stable share of foreign-owned patenting through time, although
increasing since the beginning of the 1990s. In terms of penetration – i.e.
percentage of foreign patenting compared with total patenting – the overall
proportion of foreign-owned research located in Europe has, on average,
increased over this time period with a noticeable rise in recent years (almost
29 per cent in 1991–5). While in the UK and Italy foreign-owned firms
constitute a substantial and rising proportion of aggregate MNC technological activity (with shares of 45.2 per cent and 57.5 per cent respectively in
1991–5), the same share in Germany is approximately 17 per cent at the end
of the period considered. In France, the share of foreign-owned firms compared with the overall total is 25.6 per cent for the 27 years as a whole: this is
consistent with other studies on the economic role of foreign affiliates,
which in fact place France in an intermediate position between the highly
globalised character of the research carried out in the UK and the historically
endogenously-based strength of German technological competencies
(Cantwell *et al.*, 2000).[5]

Looking at the shares of large firms' technological development in Europe
due to foreign-owned research according to the nationality of the parent
firm, Table 4.4 shows that, among the four EU economies, the two most
important locations for European-owned affiliates R&D facilities have been

Table 4.4 Patenting activity attributable to European-located foreign-owned research by host EU country and nationality of the parent firm, 1969–95 (%)

Host country	Nationality of the parent firm								
	Europe			US			Japan		
	1969–77	1978–86	1987–95	1969–77	1978–86	1987–95	1969–77	1978–86	1987–95
Italy	2.2	3.3	7.5	6.6	5.5	4.8	5.6	3.1	10.7
UK	17.1	13.8	10.9	35.9	32.4	30.8	8.6	30.2	65.7
Germany	30.2	38.4	32.9	28.7	29.7	29.9	20.2	53.1	10.7
France	16.8	16.8	17.2	12.7	12.3	13.6	3.0	3.1	1.7
Europe*	100.0	100.0	100.0	100.0	100.0	100.0	100.0	100.0	100.0

Source: adapted from Cantwell and Janne (2000).

Note
*EU15, Norway and Switzerland.

persistently Germany and France. Italy and the UK have followed opposite patterns, with Italy becoming more attractive over the 1969–95 period (from 2.2 per cent to 7.5 per cent), while the reverse applied to the UK (from 17.1 per cent to 10.9 per cent). Conversely, in the most recent years, the UK is definitely the favourite location for research carried out by Japanese firms in Europe (65.7 per cent of the European total in 1987–95), while Germany has declined sharply in its relative importance between the 1980s and the 1990s (the share dropping from 53.1 per cent in 1978–86 to 10.7 per cent in 1987–95). As far as US-owned research in Europe is concerned, the distribution by EU host country has remained fairly stable, with a declining relevance of the UK and Italy benefiting Germany and France.

Table 4.5 indicates the geographical composition of foreign-owned research carried out locally in each of the four NSIs and in Europe (i.e. total foreign-owned patenting in the country = 100). The increase in foreign participation in European technological activities – as emerged from the 'penetration' figures of Table 4.3 – has been primarily achieved thanks to the rising intra-European innovative activity of European firms: this is confirmed by the growing share of the latter in the four EU host countries considered. On the contrary, the relative importance of US companies has declined in all four host locations and in Europe as a whole (in the latter case, from 54.1 per cent to 43.7 per cent). Although Japanese-owned patenting is still rather tiny as a percentage of total foreign patenting in Europe, its share has increased over time, particularly in the UK and in Italy (representing, in 1987–95, 3.7 per cent and 2.1 per cent of total foreign research carried out in the two economies respectively).

In summary, while the tendency towards increasing shares of innovation generated outside the home country and integrated within the MNC is a general one, there is a remarkable variety in national patterns across the EU economies considered here. The UK appears definitely as the most 'globalised' in research strategies of MNCs, both nationally- and foreign-owned and for research carried out within and outside the national boundaries. Germany follows, despite its relative weak foreign penetration, while France and Italy appear to have been involved relatively more in a sort of 'Europeanisation' of R&D facilities, both inward and outward of national borders.

Finally, in terms of absolute size of large firms' patenting activity in the period 1969–95 as a whole, Germany, with 92,058 patents, has consistently accounted for the highest proportion (approximately 40 per cent) of patents granted by the USPTO to large firms located in the European Union, albeit this figure has declined since the mid-1980s. France, showing 28,106 patents, represents less than one third of the overall activity carried out in Germany, lags well behind the UK, with 35,219 patents, but is far above Italy, with only 7,040 (see Table 4.6).

Such observations generally support the presence of a ranking among European national innovation systems, reflecting their evolution over time and the different degree of openness of the national knowledge bases.

Table 4.5 Geographical composition of foreign-owned research by host EU country and nationality of the parent firm, 1969–95 (%)

| Host country | Nationality of the parent firm (%) | | | | | | | | |
| | Europe | | | US | | | Japan | | |
	1969–77	1978–86	1987–95	1969–77	1978–86	1987–95	1969–77	1978–86	1987–95
Italy	20.3	35.4	64.4	75.6	62.5	33.5	1.6	0.4	2.1
UK	26.6	27.3	27.9	69.8	69.0	63.9	0.4	0.8	3.7
Germany	45.1	53.8	57.2	53.6	44.7	42.1	0.9	1.0	0.4
France	51.0	55.2	60.3	48.2	43.5	39.0	0.3	0.1	0.1
Europe*	43.2	47.2	53.8	54.1	50.8	43.7	1.3	0.6	1.2

Source: adapted from Cantwell and Janne (2000).

Note
*EU15, Norway and Switzerland.

Technological specialisation profiles: methodological issues

One of the main drawbacks of using absolute numbers of patents is the difficulty associated with then making comparisons between the activity of heterogeneous areas of technological endeavour. Since the propensity to patent is higher in certain fields of activity (for example, pharmaceuticals), this poses potential problems when undertaking comparative analyses. However, this can be circumvented by employing the Revealed Technological Advantage (RTA) index, first applied in the country context by Soete (1987), and subsequently developed and extended to the analysis of company patterns by Cantwell (1989a, 1991, 1993) and Patel and Pavitt (1991). It is calculated in much the same way as the index of 'revealed comparative advantage', familiar from the literature on international trade (Balassa, 1965). In our case, the RTA is a proxy for technological specialisation and is calculated in the following way:

$$RTA_{ij} = (P_{ij}/P_{wj})/\Sigma_j P_{ij}/\Sigma_j P_{wj})$$

where

P_{ij} = number of patents granted in country/region i in technological sector j,

P_{wj} = number of world patents granted in technological sector j.

This shows that the RTA index of a country/region i in a particular technological sector j is given by the national/regional share of patenting in that particular sector divided by its share of patenting in all sectors. The index for a given country/region in a specified technology will vary around unity. An index greater than one indicates a relative technological advantage (or specialisation) whereas an index less than one points to a relative technological disadvantage (or despecialisation).[6] As the statistical methodology used in the country-studies reported in the following chapters requires unbiased RTA distributions, in order to reduce problems related to small patent counts – which can lead to biased distributions – conditions were imposed either at the level of regions' overall patenting activity or at the level of sectoral aggregation.[7] Here, it is worth mentioning that the introduction of different cut-off points is considered a sufficient condition for the construction of an unbiased RTA distribution, as demonstrated elsewhere (see Cantwell, 1991; Vertova, 1998).

Geographical agglomeration within EU national borders

Considerable sub-national differences exist across the four EU economies. Table 4.6 records the regional distribution of patenting activity by large firms located in each country over the 1969–95 period. In further support of the regional disparities and commensurate with the clustering activity thesis outlined in Chapter 3, very strong geographical agglomeration of patenting from innovative activity is found in three out of four EU countries (Cantwell *et al.*, 2000). In the case of both the UK and Italy, a very strong concentration of the overall technological activity carried out by large firms (both indigenous and foreign-owned) in the period 1969–95 is found in just a few regions. In the former country, the South East accounts for 47 per cent of the total, while large firms located in the North West and West Midlands represent an additional 26 per cent; in the latter economy, Lombardia accounts for 53 per cent of total patenting activity in Italy, with Piemonte providing a further 25 per cent. Geographical agglomeration also turns out to be outstanding in the French case: with reference to the main regional core, actually, it is the most pronounced in comparison with the other countries considered. In fact, more than 58 per cent of the overall patenting activity (in both foreign- and nationally-owned cases) is concentrated in Île de France, followed by Centre-Est, with almost 15 per cent, and Bassin Parisien, with slightly less than 10 per cent. On the contrary, in the German case, although agglomeration of innovation is also recorded, it is spread across a greater number of regions. Concentration is relatively strong in the regions of Nordrhein-Westfalen and Bayern, which together host 50 per cent of total large firm patenting over this period. Coupled with these regions in Germany, substantial agglomeration of innovative activity is also recorded in Baden Württemberg and Hessen: the four regions together record over 80 per cent of total MNC research in Germany.

Further differences are found when looking at the degree of geographical concentration of innovation by ownership. Yet, although innovative activities show a strong tendency to cluster in space, the extent of such a tendency may vary significantly and is rather context specific. While both foreign-owned and indigenous firms concentrate their research in the same region in the UK (South East), in France (Île de France) and in Italy (Lombardia), the same does not hold for Germany, where Nordrhein-Westfalen hosts the highest share of indigenous activity (29 per cent), but only represents the second most popular location for foreign-owned research after Baden Württemberg (with 31 per cent).[8]

The four economies are similar in that, even allowing for potential population and economic size, all record relatively high concentrations of innovative activity within their borders, which allows for a generic classification of 'core' regions (that is, those that host the highest proportions of patenting activity over time within each country).[9]

In the more detailed sectoral analysis, therefore, we have restricted our study to these regional centres of excellence.[10] It is interesting to note that, in all four countries, foreign-owned research appears to be relatively more dispersed outside the regional cores than that undertaken by the indigenous counterparts. In this respect, the most striking evidence is that of Italy:

Table 4.6 Regional breakdown of US patent grants to large firms, 1969–95 (% of each group's patent grants on national totals); population and output by region (1995)

	Percentage (%)				
	Indigenous	Foreign	Total	% Pop.*	% Output**
UK					
South East	40.2	60.8	47.1	30.6	35.7
West Midlands	16.4	3.6	12.1	9.1	8.1
North West	17.0	7.8	13.9	10.9	9.7
Others	26.4	27.8	26.9	49.4	46.4
Total UK	100.0	100.0	100.0	100.0	100.0
Total (absolute nos.)	23,404	11,815	35,219	58.4	785,697
Italy					
Lombardia	50.3	57.1	52.8	15.6	20.0
Piemonte	31.8	11.3	24.4	7.5	8.5
Others	17.9	31.6	22.8	76.9	71.5
Total Italy	100.0	100.0	100.0	100.0	100.0
Total (absolute nos.)	4,490	2,540	7,040	57.2	810,036
Germany					
Nordrhein-Westfalen	29.0	19.0	27.0	22.0	22.5
Bayern	25.0	14.0	23.0	15.0	18.8
Baden Württemberg	16.0	31.0	19.0	13.0	16.2
Hessen	13.0	14.0	13.0	7.0	11.2
Others	17.0	22.0	18.0	43.0	31.3
Total Germany	100.0	100.0	100.0	100.0	100.0
Total (absolute nos.)	76,535	15,523	92,058	81.5	1,420,439
France					
Île de France	58.3	58.2	58.3	18.9	28.4
Bassin Parisien	8.4	14.0	9.8	18.0	16.4
Centre Est	17.4	6.9	14.7	11.9	11.2
Others	15.9	20.9	17.2	51.2	44.0
Total France	100.0	100.0	100.0	100.0	100.0
Total (absolute nos.)	20,902	7,204	28,106	57.9	936,874

Source: Cantwell *et al.* (2000); Cantwell and Iammarino (2002).

Note
*Total population (millions)
**Gross value added (millions of euros).

Table 4.7 Sectoral dispersion (standard deviation) of technological specialisation, 1969–95

Region	Indigenous	Foreign
South East	0.81	0.69
West Midlands	1.08	0.97
North West	0.87	1.08
Total UK	0.47	0.49
Lombardia	1.10	2.10
Piemonte	6.40	1.60
Total Italy	2.10	1.20
Nordrhein-Westfalen	0.99	0.97
Bayern	0.62	0.98
Baden Württemberg	1.98	0.75
Hessen	1.60	1.28
Total Germany	0.60	0.66
Île de France	1.1	0.75
Bassin Parisien	0.79	0.77
Centre Est	1.0	0.75
Total France	0.64	0.56

Sources: Cantwell *et al.* (2000); Cantwell and Iammarino (2002).

foreign-owned firms locate approximately 68 per cent of their R&D in the two core regions of Lombardia and Piemonte, while 82 per cent of patenting by indigenous firms is located there. It is necessary to bear in mind, however, the differences in the degree of attractiveness of external resources that mark out the regional systems considered – already highlighted in the general picture given in Chapter 3 – which per se lend support, at least at first glance, to our hypothesis of the existence of a geographical hierarchy within the national boundaries.

Finally, looking at the sectoral dispersion of patenting at the country level, as measured by the standard deviation of the RTA index across the 56 technological fields of activity (Table 4.7), it appears that the technological advantage of firms (both foreign-owned and indigenous) located in the UK is by far the most widely dispersed at sectoral level with respect to their counterparts located in the other three countries. However, while the cross-sectoral variance of the RTA index for Germany and France does not diverge much from that observed in the UK, the Italian figures, albeit somewhat lower for the activity of foreign-owned firms located there, are in aggregate substantially higher relative to the other three EU economies. This confirms that, while the overall Italian pattern displays the characteristics of an *intermediate* research system (since both foreign-owned and indigenous firms are highly concentrated in their technological activities), the aggregate UK, German and French models correspond to *advanced* national research locations. As will be shown more in detail in the following chapters, the main explanation for this result is the smaller size of large firms' technological activity in Italy (and of large firms' overall presence in the country), given that there tends to be a good inverse relationship between technological size and the degree of technological specialisation (Archibugi and Pianta, 1992; Cantwell and Santangelo, 2000).

Conclusions

What generally emerges from the comparative analysis of MNC technological features across and within countries is a kind of rank within the EU area, first of all at the level of national system of innovation.

This variety in the geographical agglomeration of technological activity offers a unique testing ground for our analysis of foreign-owned research location and indeed provides a number of interesting observations on the globalisation of MNC technological operations. As pointed out in Chapter 2, the main premise to be tested is that regional agglomerations of technological knowledge and capabilities in the EU attract FDI in R&D to a different extent and with a different sectoral spread, according to a geographical hierarchy of regional centres. The precise research location chosen by a MNC will therefore depend upon the number of regional centres available, their positioning in the geographical hierarchy and the degree to which the MNC has developed a strategy for new technological combinations and/or diversification through tapping into specific competencies across a range of centres. The following country-studies constitute a significant contribution to the analysis of sub-national innovative activity across the EU and represent a crucial base for the formulation of a future EU-wide technology policy that aims to foster regional systems through the promotion of inward FDI in technological innovation. The next chapters document the characteristics of the hierarchies of regional research centres that exist within and across the EU countries.

5 Multinational corporations and the Italian regional systems of innovation*

Introduction

From the discussion carried out above, it becomes quite clear that foreign investment in innovation has as much a regional scope as it has a national one. In particular, recent trends in the European Union support the conjecture that a comparative analysis at the sub-national scale is the most appropriate way to identify the effects of the globalisation of technology. Therefore, we have tried to devise a more suitable and detailed geographical unit of analysis, in order to throw some new light on the circumstances that give rise to geographical agglomeration and increasing interactions between MNCs' research location and regional systems of innovation.

The important issue for our purpose, actually, is not so much the precise delimitation of the 'local' or 'regional' location in geographical terms, as to make it clear that it is a geographical space characterised by a certain coherence based on common behavioural practices linked to local institutions and culture (including technological culture), industrial structure and corporate organisation (Saxenian, 1994).[1]

As argued previously,[2] the hypotheses to be tested here, as well as in the following three chapters, are that the regional location of innovative activities by MNCs conforms to a geographical hierarchy of centres, and that the composition of technological specialisation differs between these centres. Accordingly, the technological specialisation of foreign-owned affiliates in each region depends upon the position of that region in the locational hierarchy. In particular, we hypothesise that, as the position of the region in the hierarchy falls, so the profile of technological specialisation of foreign-owned firms in that region becomes more closely related to the equivalent pattern of specialisation of indigenous firms in the same region. Conversely, a centre at the top of the hierarchy is more likely to attract a broad range of foreign innovative activities, as MNCs will generally try to extend their established lines of specialisation through intra-firm networks. Therefore, higher order locations should attract foreign research for their general reservoir of skills and resources, while centres further down are attractive more for their limited range of specialised expertise, thus bringing foreign and local technological profiles closer together.

The empirical investigation – aimed at testing the relationship between the foreign-owned and the indigenous company profiles of technological specialisation in regional centres ranked according to the geographical hierarchy – is carried out by using patents granted to the world's largest industrial firms classified by the host region in which is located the research facility that is responsible for the relevant technology.[3]

This chapter is divided into four parts. After the introduction, the second section explores the general features of the location of foreign research in the Italian case by using patents arranged by the host Italian region. The third section provides a preliminary attempt to test the relationship between foreign-owned and indigenous firms' profiles of technological specialisation in the selected Italian regional systems, while the final section presents some concluding remarks.

The location of MNC technological activities in the Italian regions

The regionalisation of the University of Reading patent database has brought to light interesting insights on the geographical location of the innovative activities of MNCs in the Italian case, which would not have been captured by the usual analysis at the aggregate (country) level.

Confirming the results of previous empirical studies on Italian technological innovation at regional level (Cesaratto *et al.*, 1993; Silvani *et al.*, 1993; Breschi and Mancusi, 1997; Iammarino *et al.*, 1998; Breschi *et al.*, 1999), the territorial distribution of innovation generated in the affiliates of MNCs turns out to be highly polarised in just two regions – namely Lombardia and Piemonte. Therefore, we focused our attention on these two regional cores, for which the 'Schumpeterian hypothesis' seems to hold on the basis that the average firm size in Lombardia and Piemonte, which is higher than the national average, is associated with a relatively greater propensity to generate new technologies in-house and to commit to formal R&D activities (Iammarino *et al.*, 1998).[4] The capacity to attract external resources shows that general external economies and spillovers have been at work in the two regions, giving rise to the well known dichotomy of the Italian innovation system; that is, on the one hand the two regional cores, and on the other SME-based regional systems (such as Veneto and Emilia) more oriented towards engineering and design-based process innovations carried out by local firms and where the degree of attraction of external research, as proxied by the patent indicator used here, is very low. This broadly supports the fact that the traditional north–south economic divide in Italy does not give full account of the spectrum of regional patterns in the case of technological innovation.

Indeed, Piemonte and Lombardia can also be labelled as regional cores for innovation on the basis of other indicators available. In fact, as the survey on technological innovation in the Italian manufacturing industry (undertaken in the wider EU framework of the Community Innovation Survey – CIS) pointed out, in the first half of the 1990s, 44 per cent of all Italian innovative firms was located in the two regions, and more than 50 per cent of total national costs for innovation was spent in Lombardia and Piemonte. Interestingly, the CIS survey also revealed that these two regions are the most internationalised regions in terms of both technological receipts and R&D carried out on behalf of foreign customers, showing at the same time rather different geographical orientations of research linkages, i.e. more connected with the EU in the case of Lombardia, strongly US-oriented in the case of Piemonte (Iammarino *et al.*, 1998, 1999). More generally, technological collaborative relationships and linkages between the business sector and university and research institutions are indeed far more entrenched in these two regions than anywhere else in Italy, even in comparison with other relatively R&D-intensive regions (such as Lazio or Liguria). As shown elsewhere, the Italian case illustrates that proper regional systems of innovation are found only in a few well-defined areas, while in most regions systemic interactions and knowledge flows among different actors are simply too sparse and weak to reveal the presence of systems of innovation (Evangelista *et al.*, 2002).

Turning to our indicator, Table 5.1 reports the shares of US patents of the largest Italian firms attributable to research located in Piemonte and Lombardia relative to that which these firms located in Italy as a whole, and the equivalent regional shares for the research of foreign-owned firms by technological sector in the period 1969–95.[5]

As already emphasised, the geographical agglomeration of innovation is striking: more than 77 per cent of the total research activity of large firms is concentrated in these two regions. As also pointed out in Chapter 4, foreign-owned research located in Italy appears to be relatively more dispersed than the research carried out by Italian firms: for foreign-owned firms, the aggregate share of the two regional cores is 68.4 per cent, while for indigenous firms it is as high as 82 per cent. However, the capacity to attract externally-owned innovation activity differs markedly between the two regional systems, supporting, at least at first glance, our hypothesis of the existence of geographical hierarchies. While Lombardia accounts for 57.1 per cent of the total Italian-located research of foreign affiliates (above the indigenous company share of 50.3 per cent), the equivalent share in Piemonte is only 11.3 per cent, much lower that the regional share of patents granted to the largest Italian firms (31.8 per cent).

The sectoral distribution of patents demonstrates interregional differences to an even greater extent. The key to the sectoral codes used in Table 5.1 is given in Appendix 2(a). In many sectors, the large firm (Italian + foreign) total for the two regions (Piemonte + Lombardia) accounts for almost all the innovative activity carried out by such firms in the country as a whole. However, in Lombardia, the regional share of patents attributable to the research of foreign firms is higher than the equivalent share for large Italian firms in most sectors. In some sectors in particular – such as, for example, Mechanical calculators and typewriters (30) or Office

Table 5.1 Shares of US patents of the largest Italian firms attributable to research in Italian regions relative to Italy as a whole, and the equivalent regional shares for the Italian-located research of foreign-owned firms, by technological sector, 1969–95 (%)

Sectors	Regions						Piemonte + Lombardia total
	Piemonte			Lombardia			
	Italian firms	Foreign firms	Total	Italian firms	Foreign firms	Total	
3	36.5	11.1	33.7	43.2	22.2	41.0	74.7
5	9.4	6.4	8.2	68.6	66.4	67.7	75.8
6	66.7	1.7	3.4	33.3	4.3	5.1	8.5
7	26.7	7.1	21.9	59.3	32.1	52.6	74.6
9	8.5	2.2	7.5	66.7	38.7	62.0	69.5
11	15.0	1.4	10.6	67.6	73.2	69.4	80.0
12	3.3	2.2	2.9	80.8	85.7	82.7	85.6
13	50.9	10.6	32.4	21.8	27.7	24.5	56.9
14	41.0	19.1	32.1	37.0	45.6	40.5	72.6
16	17.9	5.9	14.8	49.5	41.2	47.3	62.1
17	33.0	42.4	37.2	50.5	38.8	45.2	82.4
18	14.3	1.9	3.3	42.9	54.7	53.3	56.7
20	54.8	11.4	39.8	23.8	40.9	29.7	69.5
25	3.6	1.1	2.3	42.9	96.7	71.0	73.3
28	21.3	18.9	20.4	67.0	22.6	51.0	71.4
29	56.8	57.4	57.0	23.2	23.8	23.4	80.4
30	95.9	12.1	82.2	2.4	87.9	16.3	98.5
33	61.8	7.3	32.0	29.4	80.5	57.3	89.3
34	68.8	6.7	54.0	18.8	60.0	28.6	82.5
38	38.8	20.1	26.6	56.5	62.6	60.5	87.1
39	62.3	4.9	33.0	24.6	68.8	47.2	80.1
40	62.5	1.1	6.3	37.5	73.6	70.5	76.8
41	71.5	4.8	39.5	17.5	81.7	48.3	87.8
42	54.4	69.2	55.6	32.7	15.4	31.3	86.9
49	9.2	16.0	10.1	80.4	20.0	71.9	82.0
50	14.3	6.9	12.5	40.7	75.9	49.2	61.7
53	53.7	7.7	43.2	38.4	51.6	41.5	84.7
56	6.9	0.0	6.3	58.6	40.0	57.1	63.5
Total Tech 56	31.8	11.3	24.4	50.3	57.1	52.8	77.2

equipment and data processing systems (41) – the strong geographical agglomeration in the region holds only for foreign affiliates (87.9 per cent and 81.7 per cent in these sectors respectively), while the research carried out by Italian MNCs considered in the sample (respectively 2.4 per cent and 17.5 per cent of the national total) has apparently gone mainly to other regional locations. Conversely, the geographical concentration of foreign-owned research in Piemonte is substantial and higher than that of Italian firms, except in a few sectors – namely Metal working equipment

Table 5.2 Foreign shares (foreign-owned companies' percentage of total patents granted to large firms for local research in Italy), by sector and region, 1969–95

Sectors	Regions		Italy
	Piemonte	Lombardia	
3	3.6	5.9	10.8
5	31.8	40.1	40.9
6	50.0	83.3	97.5
7	8.0	15.0	24.6
9	4.9	10.6	16.9
11	4.1	33.8	32.0
12	29.4	39.6	38.3
13	15.2	52.0	46.1
14	24.1	45.6	40.5
16	10.3	22.4	25.8
17	51.4	38.8	45.2
18	50.0	90.6	88.3
20	9.8	47.4	34.4
25	25.0	71.2	52.3
28	33.3	16.0	36.1
29	34.9	35.3	34.7
30	2.4	87.9	16.3
33	12.5	76.7	54.7
34	2.9	50.0	23.8
38	49.6	67.7	65.4
39	7.5	74.4	51.1
40	16.7	95.5	91.6
41	5.8	81.1	47.9
42	10.1	4.0	8.1
49	22.2	3.9	14.0
50	13.3	37.3	24.2
53	4.1	28.5	22.9
56	0.0	5.6	7.9
Total 56	16.7	39.1	36.1

(17), Other general industrial equipment (29), Internal combustion engines (42) and Rubber and plastic products (49). A noticeable case is that of Photographic chemistry (6), in which the combined foreign share located in the two regions accounts only for 6 per cent of total foreign-owned corporate patents in this field in Italy, and the local concentration of foreign research is negligible in both cases.

Turning to the shares of total patents granted to large foreign-owned firms for local research, Table 5.2 shows that the highest contribution of foreign research to the regional total is once again recorded in Lombardia (39.1 per cent for the period 1969–95), confirming the attractiveness of the region relative to both Piemonte, with a foreign share of less than 17 per cent and, to a lesser extent, the country as a whole (whose foreign share is 36.1 per cent).

The sectoral picture again emerges as rather different between the two regional cores. Foreign shares of regional and national patents lower than the average are found in some chemicals sectors, with the most notable exception of Photographic chemistry (6), for which the contribution of foreign research to the sectoral patenting activity is very high in all cases – 50 per cent for Piemonte, 83.3 per cent for Lombardia and 97.5 per cent for the country as a whole. It is useful to recall that, although the foreign share in this sector is relatively high for both the regions considered (Table 5.2), the sector turned out to be the least concentrated in the two regional cores (Table 5.1). Other examples of relatively small foreign shares in all three cases are found in chemical and allied equipment (16), Internal combustion engines (42), Other instruments and controls (53) and Other manufacturing (56). On the contrary, many of the sectors identified as types of electrical equipment show foreign shares much higher than the average, both in Lombardia and in the country as a whole – for instance Semiconductors (40), for which research is due almost entirely, in both areas, to affiliates of foreign multinationals. The only noteworthy discrepancy between Italy and Lombardia is in Mechanical calculators and typewriters (30), in which the regional patenting activity is attributable almost entirely to foreign affiliates (88 per cent), although foreign-owned firms represent a tiny proportion of national patents in the sector (16.3 per cent) and one of the lowest foreign shares in Piemonte (2.4 per cent). In the latter region, the sectors for which the shares of research attributable to foreign firms register the highest values are generally to be found in the broad group of mechanical engineering and machinery – for example, Metal working equipment (17), Paper making apparatus (18), Other specialised machinery (28), Other general industrial equipment (29) – and in Electrical devices and systems (38). The foreign share in Piemonte is high, relative to the low values for both the country as a whole and Lombardia, for Rubber and plastic products (49).

Thus, it emerges that the sectoral distribution of foreign-owned companies' shares of regional and national research activity shows a greater correspondence between Lombardia and Italy, while in the case of Piemonte it seems to indicate more focused sectoral patterns. It should be recalled that the narrower sectoral spread of the foreign geographical concentration and shares of research in Piemonte has also to be understood in relation to its high degree of productive specialisation in some particular sectors in the broad industrial groups of mechanical engineering and electrical equipment, for which the region has been labelled, in relative terms, a mono-specialised region. On the other hand, Lombardia appears to have a much wider sectoral spread of production specialisation – as also reflected in the composition and competitiveness of regional exports – including, along with traditional industries, some science-based industries and a consistent number of firms specialised in the mechanical area (Evangelista *et al.*, 2002).

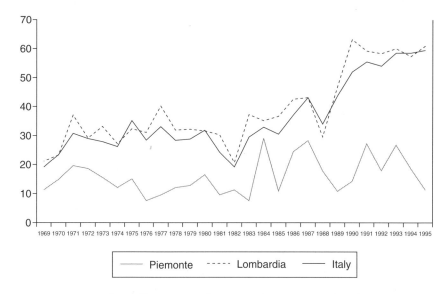

Figure 5.1 Foreign shares (foreign-owned companies' percentage of total patents granted to large firms for local research in Italy) by year and region, 1969–95 (%).

Figure 5.1 reports the evolution over time of the foreign shares for the 56 sectors as a whole. It emerges clearly that – in line with the observations reported in Chapter 4 – the foreign proportion of total research undertaken in Italy by large firms has increased markedly over the 27 years considered here, reaching the highest values at the end of the period. This pattern seems to be shaped by that of Lombardia, which has recorded a remarkable growth of foreign innovative activities, particularly since the second half of the 1980s, which led, in 1995, to a foreign share of 61.4 per cent, three times larger than that in 1969. Conversely, the foreign share of regional patents in Piemonte shows a much more unstable trend, actually finishing with a marginally lower share in the final year than in 1969.

In general terms, the above picture seems to confirm, at least in the Italian case, that the location of technological activities of foreign-owned MNCs tends to be strongly agglomerated at a sub-national level. This is evident particularly in Lombardia, regardless of sectoral specificities, whereas in Piemonte the geographical concentration of foreign affiliates' research seems to follow distinctive sectoral patterns. Moreover, the strong attractiveness of Lombardia is also demonstrated by its high foreign share of total regional patents, which is increasing over time more than it is for the whole country. As argued above, the economic geography approach suggests that the attractiveness of regional locations is determined by general economies of scale, which lead to regional concentration, and by highly sector-specific localisation economies. We can therefore establish, on the basis of a different interaction between agglomeration forces in different regional systems, a geographical hierarchy of regional centres in Italy.

Lombardia can be considered, from both the geographical and the sectoral perspectives, a *higher order* location at the top of the scale, strongly attracting a broad range of foreign-owned technological activities because of the general characteristics of its regional system of innovation. Piemonte comes next, with much lower values of both geographical concentration within its boundaries and foreign shares of regional patenting and, as an *intermediate* research location, it seems to be more attractive for some specific sectoral features of the regional technological potential. The other Italian regions, although with some differences among them, are definitely behind, both in terms of domestic innovative activity and even more in terms of the absolute level of foreign-owned research that they are able to attract.

Technological specialisation and the regional hierarchy in Italy

The RTA index has been calculated for both Italian- and foreign-owned firms in the two regional cores, Piemonte and Lombardia, and in Italy as a whole for the period 1969–95. As explained in Chapter 4, the index gives a measure of the performance of (nationally-owned or foreign-owned) firms in a region in one particular sector relative to their world performance.

Table 5.3 reports the RTA values by region and sector. In line with what has been said above, the technological advantages of both Italian and foreign-owned firms in Piemonte, relative to Italian and foreign-owned firms in Lombardia and in Italy, are more narrowly concentrated at sectoral level. It should be noted that, in sectors such as Metal working equipment (17), Other general industrial equipment (29), Mechanical calculators and typewriters (30) and Internal combustion engines (42), for which local firms in Piemonte record a high specialisation both in technology and in production, foreign affiliates also show a very strong geographical concentration of their research (see Table 5.1).[6] Indeed, as already pointed out, it is useful to remind ourselves that the productive structure of Piemonte is still heavily dominated by the automobile industry – namely the Fiat group – and by a large number of specialised firms producing related pieces of equipment and components (Balcet, 1999; Balcet and Enrietti, 2002). This would support the expectation that in Piemonte – defined as an intermediate regional core – the attraction of foreign resources is likely to be motivated by the willingness of MNCs to tap into sectoral-specific local expertise and to increase their own technological advantage in some particular technological fields.

As far as Lombardia is concerned, the technological specialisation of Italian and foreign-owned firms overlaps to a lower extent. In particular, Italian firms show revealed comparative advantages mostly concentrated in the broad group of chemicals and pharmaceuticals, in which foreign-owned research also appears to have a technological advantage.[7] As for Piemonte, in these

Table 5.3 RTA (Italian and foreign firms) relative to the world by sector and region, 1969–95

Sectors	Regions					
	Piemonte		Lombardia		Italy	
	Italian firms	*Foreign firms*	*Italian firms*	*Foreign firms*	*Italian firms*	*Foreign firms*
3	1.828	0.337	1.371	0.133	1.596	0.343
5	0.264	0.615	1.216	1.268	0.893	1.092
6	0.064	0.321	0.020	0.159	0.031	2.084
7	0.688	0.298	0.965	0.265	0.819	0.471
9	0.481	0.123	2.378	0.437	1.793	0.645
11	0.844	0.179	2.409	1.911	1.793	1.491
12	0.195	0.405	2.990	3.057	1.862	2.039
13	0.805	0.716	0.218	0.368	0.504	0.761
14	1.110	1.753	0.634	0.827	0.862	1.036
16	0.737	0.420	1.292	0.581	1.314	0.806
17	1.233	6.503	1.193	1.179	1.189	1.735
18	0.101	0.504	0.192	2.893	0.226	3.021
20	1.780	0.964	0.490	0.687	1.035	0.959
25	0.337	0.560	2.561	9.862	3.008	5.824
28	0.843	2.101	1.681	0.499	1.262	1.258
29	1.598	4.277	0.412	0.350	0.896	0.842
30	34.561	4.252	0.540	6.097	11.483	3.964
33	0.632	0.450	0.190	0.979	0.326	0.695
34	1.543	0.233	0.266	0.415	0.715	0.395
38	0.692	3.387	0.638	2.082	0.568	1.900
39	1.303	0.528	0.326	1.478	0.666	1.228
40	0.176	0.176	0.067	2.226	0.090	1.728
41	1.164	0.355	0.180	1.206	0.518	0.843
42	3.716	2.083	1.411	0.092	2.174	0.340
49	0.834	1.187	4.636	0.294	2.903	0.838
50	0.281	0.215	0.506	0.468	0.626	0.353
53	1.328	0.281	0.601	0.373	0.787	0.412
56	0.283	0.000	1.522	0.139	1.307	0.199
Total Tech 56	1.000	1.000	1.000	1.000	1.000	1.000

sectors – such as Chemical processes (5), Other organic compounds (11), Pharmaceuticals and biotechnology (12) and also Textile and clothing machinery (25) – the geographical distribution of foreign technological activity is highly concentrated in the region. On the other hand, foreign affiliates also have an RTA greater than one in a number of sectors related to electrical equipment – such as Electrical devices and systems (38), Other general electrical equipment (39) and Semiconductors (40) – and to office equipment (30, 41); whereas the Italian large firms in the region appear to be substantially despecialised.[8] Therefore, foreign innovative activities in Lombardia, although heavily concentrated in the region from a geographical perspective and with a high contribution to regional innovation, seem to coincide with the technological expertise of local firms only in a limited number of sectors, basically in chemicals and pharmaceuticals (5, 11 and 12) and in Textile and clothing machinery (25), which represent points of strength in the productive and export specialisation pattern of local firms.[9]

It is worth noting that, as far as Italy as a whole is concerned, the match between the technological specialisation of Italian firms and that of foreign affiliates is relatively more pronounced, as in the case of Piemonte. The overlap is particularly evident for Other organic compounds (11), Pharmaceuticals and biotechnology (12), Metal working equipment (17) and in some sectors of specialised industrial equipment (25, 28) and Office equipment (30). However, in some Electrical equipment sectors (38, 39, 40), the specialisation of foreign-owned firms does not correspond to an Italian technological advantage.

In order to test further our hypothesis that the technological specialisation of foreign-owned subsidiaries in each region is associated with the position of the region in the geographical hierarchy, a simple regression analysis was carried out. However, before going into the regression model, it is worth looking at the correlation matrix between the RTA indices (Table 5.4), which provides some additional insights on the characteristic features of the regional and national innovation systems.

The relevant point that emerges from Table 5.4 is that the specialisation patterns of Italian firms in Lombardia and Italian firms in Piemonte are not correlated – i.e. the regional hierarchy in Italy is associated with distinctive patterns of regional specialisation. However, the Italian national system as a whole can be understood as a composite of these two distinctive regional systems, as confirmed by the significant correlation found between the RTA of Italian firms in the regions and in the country as a whole (although the coefficient is much higher for Piemonte than for Lombardia).

Accordingly, in the period 1969–95, two geographical levels were taken into consideration in the cross-section regression analysis: first of all, the hypothesis was tested at regional level for Piemonte and Lombardia, then for Italy as a whole. In the former case, a log-linear model was assumed, since the distribution of the RTA index for the two regions is skewed because of the relatively small numbers of patents in each of them, showing the existence of lognormality, which is not the case for the country as a whole. Indeed, the standard assumption of this methodology is that the regression is linear, which is valid if the cross-sector index approximately conforms to a normal distribution. However, as discussed more extensively in Cantwell (1991), if the sample of patents is really insufficiently large, an artificially high degree of dispersion in the index is very likely to be found, as is the case of the two regions considered here. This is what tends to lead to a skewed distribution, rather than any property of the RTA index itself. Thus, for the two regions, the sectoral distribution represented by the RTA conforms more closely to a lognormal than a normal distribution, so taking a logarithmic rather than a linear functional form in such cases improves the values of

Table 5.4 RTA correlation matrix

	RTAFF	RTAFFLO	RTAFFPI	RTAITF	RTAITFLO	RTAITFPI
RTAFF	1	0.8390 (0.000)***	0.1532 (0.260)	0.3245 (0.015)**	0.0068 (0.960)	0.3000 (0.025)**
RTAFFLO		1	0.0962 (0.481)	0.4236 (0.001)***	0.1002 (0.463)	0.3456 (0.009)***
RTAFFPI			1	0.3191 (0.017)**	-0.431 (0.753)	0.3758 (0.004)***
RTAITF				1	0.3819 (0.004)***	0.8957 (0.000)***
RTAITFLO					1	-0.0444 (0.745)

Notes
56 cases / 2 tailed significance
**Significant at 5%
***Significant at 1%

Legend:
RTAITF: RTA of Italian firms in Italy
RTAITFPI: RTA of Italian firms in Piemonte
RTAITFLO: RTA of Italian firms in Lombardia
RTAFF: RTA of Foreign firms in Italy
RTAFFPI: RTA of Foreign firms in Piemonte
RTAFFLO: RTA of Foreign firms in Lombardia.

the *t*-statistic on β. The regression was run across all the 56 technological sectors (j).[10]

$$\ln RTA_{FFPIj} = \alpha + \beta \ln RTA_{ITFPIj} + \varepsilon_j \tag{5.1}$$

$$\ln RTA_{FFLOj} = \alpha + \beta \ln RTA_{ITFLOj} + \varepsilon_j \tag{5.2}$$

$$RTA_{FFj} = \alpha + \beta RTA_{ITFj} + \varepsilon_j \tag{5.3}$$

The regressions give an indication of whether the RTA index of foreign firms is correlated with the RTA index of Italian large firms; the significance of the estimated slope coefficient provides a sign of the correlation over the period 1969–95 as a whole. Furthermore, the period was broken down into 1969–82 and 1983–95 in order to test the validity of the hypothesis at the two different geographical levels over time. Arguably, according to the concept of globalisation of innovation as defined in Chapter 2, such a process is likely to have taken off, especially from the 1980s onwards, mainly in response to the deepening of the European economic integration process after the announcement of the Delors' Plan. Thus, we might expect our hypothesised relationship to become stronger through time. In this latter case, we adopted a Granger notion of sequential causality, and the regressions were run for 47 technological sectors. The reason for having a smaller number of sectors in the lagged cross-section model is that, when we subdivided the period 1969–95, we dropped all the technological sectors with an overall number of patents less than 600 in the world total in both 1969–82 and 1983–95. The purpose was to avoid the inclusion of sectors with a relatively low propensity to patent at the world level. Thus, we have

$$\ln RTA_{FFPIjt} = \alpha + \beta \ln RTA_{ITFPIjt-1} + \varepsilon_{jt} \tag{5.4}$$

$$\ln RTA_{FFLOjt} = \alpha + \beta \ln RTA_{ITFLOjt-1} + \varepsilon_{jt} \tag{5.5}$$

$$RTA_{FFjt} = \alpha + \beta RTA_{ITFjt-1} + \varepsilon_{jt} \tag{5.6}$$

where j refers to the 47 sectors of technological activity, t refers to the period 1983–95 and $t-1$ to 1969–82. The regressions show whether the RTA index of foreign MNCs at time t is correlated with the RTA index of Italian MNCs at the earlier period in time $t-1$.

In the case of Piemonte (see Table 5.5), the profile of technological specialisation of foreign-owned firms is closely related to the equivalent pattern of specialisation of indigenous firms in the region. This supports our hypothesis that an *intermediate* regional research centre attracts firms more for its limited range of specialised expertise, which foreign research try to tap into. This is also valid when looking at the regression over time.

The case of Lombardia is, instead, rather different (Table 5.6). Here, the

Table 5.5 Results of the regressions for Piemonte

Results of the regression $lnRTAFFPI_j = \alpha + \beta lnRTAITFPI_j + \varepsilon_j$

	Coefficient	Standard error	T-ratio[Prob]
$lnRTAITFPI_j$	0.5409	0.10928	4.9496[0.000]***
Intercept	0.1500	0.09122	1.6446[0.105]
R2	0.3120		

Absence of heteroscedasticity χ^2 (DF = 1)	0.58788[0.443]
No. of observations	56

Results of the regression $lnRTAFFPI_{jt} = \alpha + \beta lnRTAITFPI_{jt-1} + \varepsilon_{jt}$

	Coefficient	Standard error	T-ratio[Prob]
$lnRTAITFPI_{jt-1}$	0.4049	0.1213	3.3299[0.002]***
Intercept	0.2708	0.1094	2.4740[0.017]**
R2	0.1970		

Absence of heteroscedasticity χ^2 (DF = 1)	0.01007[0.920]
No. of observations	47

Notes
**Significant at 5%
***Significant at 1%.

specialisation of foreign-owned firms does not depend on the technological advantage of Italian firms, since there might be other factors bringing foreign firms into the region – such as, for example, spillovers due to the high concentration of technological and productive activities, infrastructures, financial facilities, etc. This seems to suggest that a region at the top of the geographical hierarchy, such as the *higher-order* Lombardia, attracts a broad range of foreign-owned firms, generally extending their lines of specialisation while drawing on the local source of general capabilities and on other characteristics of the regional innovation system.

Finally, the combination of the two regional systems give us a picture of the overall Italian model (Table 5.7), which is closer to the case of Piemonte (although, as expected, in Piemonte the relationship between the technological advantages of foreign and Italian firms is more robust than in the country as a whole), as the specialisation of the foreign and Italian firms matches for the overall period and, even more, through time.

Conclusions

In this chapter we have attempted to investigate the relationships between foreign MNCs and regional systems of innovation in the Italian case. In line with most empirical studies on national and regional innovation systems in

Table 5.6 Results of the regressions for Lombardia

Results of the regression $lnRTAFFLO_j = \alpha + \beta lnRTAITFLO_j + \varepsilon_j$

	Coefficient	Standard error	T-ratio[Prob]
lnRTAITFLO$_j$	0.11146	0.1585	0.7032[0.484]
Intercept	0.4294	0.1058	4.0580[0.000]***
R2	0.0090		
Absence of heteroscedasticity χ^2 (DF = 1)		0.76238[0.383]	
No. of observations		56	

Results of the regression $lnRTAFFLO_{jt} = \alpha + \beta lnRTAITFLO_{jt-1} + \varepsilon_{jt}$

	Coefficient	Standard error	T-ratio[Prob]
lnRTAITFLO$_{jt-1}$	0.1682	0.203	0.8288[0.411]
Intercept	0.3954	0.1337	2.9558[0.004]***
R2	0.1970		
Absence of heteroscedasticity χ^2 (DF = 1)		2.4508[0.117]	
No. of observations		47	

Notes
**Significant at 5%
***Significant at 1%.

the country, the two regions of Lombardia and Piemonte represent the technological heart of Italy for both national and foreign research. The full range of links and interactions forming the skeleton of a regional system of innovation is plainly visible in both regions, where technological linkages between firms, and between firms and public and private research institutions, are far more structured than in the rest of the country.

The Italian case is particularly helpful in describing the implications for public policy of the crucial link between the 'global' and the 'local' dimension of technology creation. It confirms that the presence of a good scientific and technological infrastructure and of diffused networks of technological services, along with an active role of regional innovation policies, are crucial determinants of the local attractiveness towards global technological flows. Although the two regional systems differ quite considerably in their technological and industrial profile – being thus positioned at different levels of our locational hierarchy – they are indeed a clear illustration that innovative patterns diverge, not only according to the specific strategies and technological performances of firms, but also according to the relevance of the systemic interactions and to the presence of the contextual factors favourable to innovation that were mentioned in the previous chapters.

The comparative lack of innovation policies aimed at improving and upgrading the infrastructural conditions – rather than at providing generic

Table 5.7 Results of the regressions for Italy

Results of the regression $RTAFF_j = \alpha + \beta RTAITF_j + \varepsilon_j$

	Coefficient	Standard error	T-ratio[Prob]
RTAITF$_j$	0.2268	0.0900	2.5207[0.015]**
Intercept	0.8786	0.1732	5.0724[0.000]***
R2	0.1052		

Absence of heteroscedasticity χ^2 (DF = 1)	0.049296[0.824]
No. of observations	56

Results of the regression $RTAFF_{jt} = \alpha + \beta RTAITF_{jt-1} + \varepsilon_{jt}$

	Coefficient	Standard error	T-ratio[Prob]
RTAITF$_{jt-1}$	0.2578	0.0899	2.8679[0.006]***
Intercept	0.7155	0.1917	3.7318[0.000]***
R2	0.1540		

Absence of heteroscedasticity χ^2 (DF = 1)	0.2599E-4[0.996]
No. of observations	47

Notes
**Significant at 5%
***Significant at 1%.

financial support – underlines the Italian incapacity to diffuse innovation from the (highly concentrated) cores to the (highly widespread) periphery according to the life cycle of technology, and thus to reduce the well-known historical imbalance that characterises the country.

6 Multinational corporations and the UK regional systems of innovation*

Introduction

Despite the highly internationalised nature of the UK economy and the globalised character of the research carried out in the country (as well as outside it by UK firms) – as already pointed out in Chapter 4 – somehow surprisingly little is known at the regional level with respect to the geographical dispersion of technological activities within the country, despite this dispersion's undoubted influence upon inter-regional growth rates across sectors.[1]

The first aim of this chapter is to look at the geographical distribution of innovative activities carried out by large industrial multinational corporations, both local and foreign, in the UK regions. This might help identify the basic factors underlying regional differences that have characterised the country for over half a century, and particularly in the most recent decades. The second goal is to examine whether the concentration of technological activity by foreign affiliates is correlated to the concentration of the same activity carried out by local firms. The assumption is that regional agglomerations of knowledge and capabilities attract foreign direct investment (FDI) in R&D to a different extent and with a different sectoral spread, depending upon the position of the region in a locational hierarchy, which can be established both within and across national boundaries.

This chapter is divided into five sections. After the introduction, the second section explores some general regional features and the geography of the location of innovation of both indigenous and foreign large firms in the UK regions. An attempt is also made to compare MNC regional technological profiles with the scientific specialisation of publicly-funded research in each region. Our effort to test the relationship between foreign-owned and UK multinationals' technological profiles, in order to clarify the concept of 'regional hierarchy' across EU regions, is reported upon in the third section; finally, section four presents some concluding remarks.

The location of MNC technological activities in the UK regions

The regionalisation of the University of Reading patent database has been extended to cover the case of the United Kingdom.[2] The UK case differs substantially from the Italian one, both in terms of the magnitude of the phenomenon under investigation and in terms of the kinds of government policies adopted to support regional attractiveness.[3] Figures 6.1 to 6.3 report, with reference to the year 1995 – which is the last year of the period considered in the Reading database – some selected indicators by region.

Not surprisingly, all the indicators point rather clearly to the strong polarisation of innovative activities in the South East of England, even relative to the demographic size of the region (almost 30 per cent of total population) and its economic weight (35 per cent of national value added in 1995). Indeed, a number of studies – using different measures of local innovation and technological activities – have pointed out the strong concentration of (indigenous) innovation in the South East, providing evidence of the fact that significant innovations are more likely to be introduced into the South East regional context than elsewhere in the UK (see, among others, Harris, 1988; Thwaites and Wynarczyk, 1996; Cosh and Hughes, 1996; Keeble and Bryson, 1996; Keeble, 1997). Thwaites and Wynarczyk (1996), in particular, have shown that the innovative performance of the South East is related to elements of macro and corporate culture and of the *modus operandi* of firms located in the region.

In terms of R&D personnel employed in the business sector (Figure 6.1), the South East represents 42 per cent of the total, followed by the North

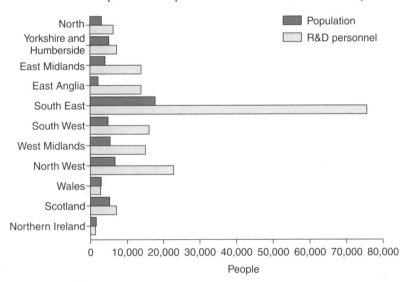

Figure 6.1 Population (000s) and R&D personnel (absolute numbers) by UK region, 1995.

Source: Eurostat (1995).

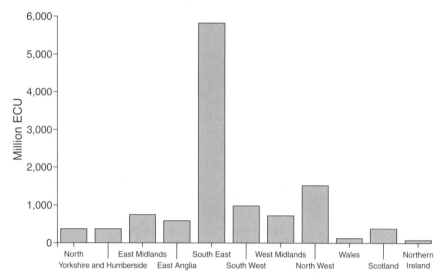

Figure 6.2 R&D expenditure by UK region, business sector, 1995.

Source: Eurostat (1995).

West, with 13 per cent, and the South West (9 per cent), while the concentration of R&D expenditure of the business sector (Figure 6.2) in the South East reaches 49 per cent of the national expense. The indicator of technological output (Figure 6.3) presents a more evenly spread territorial distribution with regard to all European Patent Office (EPO) requests, of which the South East accounts for 34 per cent and the North West over 15 per cent, but the share of patents granted in 1995 by the USPTO to large corporate inventors in the South East is over 52 per cent, followed by the North West (11 per cent) and the West Midlands (8 per cent).[4]

Regional gaps arise not only in existing technological stocks and relative size, but also in dynamic terms, endorsing the view of a widening of regional differences within the country. Indeed, Chatterji and Dewhurst (1996), estimating a model using nominal GDP per capita by NUTS2 region over the period 1977–91, have shown that the UK counties (and regions) tend to diverge relative to the GDP per capita of Greater London (South East).[5] As already stated, it has been shown that differences in innovative capabilities across European regions – which are even more pronounced than at a purely country level – account for a good deal in explaining divergent trends in economic growth (Fagerberg and Verspagen, 1996). Insofar as globalisation spurs agglomeration in regional centres, the tendency toward divergence might thus be reinforced. It should be noted, however, that the fact that regional inequalities in technological innovation increase with the level of geographical breakdown is not surprising. This is the consequence of the tendency of economic and, to an even greater extent, innovative activities to agglomerate,

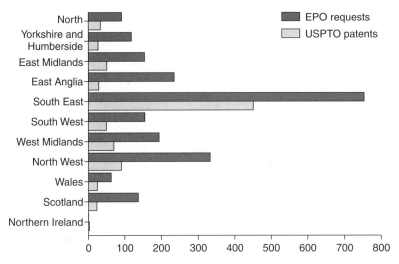

Figure 6.3 EPO requests and USPTO patents by UK region, 1995.

Sources: Eurostat (1995) and University of Reading database.

and of forces that concentrate key-functions in core centres, such as Greater London in the UK, driving out other activities with lower value added content. At a high level of geographical aggregation (namely the country level), such differences often average out (Dunford, 1996).

Turning more specifically to the geographical distributions of innovation generated by large firms, Table 6.1 reports, for the whole period 1969–95, the shares of US patents (relative to the UK as a whole) of both the largest

Table 6.1 Shares of US patents of both the largest UK firms and the UK-located foreign-owned firms, attributable to research in UK regions relative to the UK as a whole, 1969–95 (%)

Regions	UK firms	Foreign firms	Total
North	4.0	2.3	3.4
Yorkshire and Humberside	4.4	3.9	4.3
East Midlands	6.3	4.5	5.7
East Anglia	1.5	5.3	2.7
South East	40.2	60.8	47.1
South West	5.7	4.2	5.2
West Midlands	16.4	3.6	12.1
North West	17.0	7.8	13.9
Wales	2.4	3.4	2.7
Scotland	2.0	4.0	2.7
Northern Ireland	0.1	0.3	0.1
Total UK	100.0	100.0	100.0

Note
Any discrepancies are due to rounding errors.

UK-owned firms and the largest UK-located foreign-owned firms, attributable to the research of each group located in the UK regions.

As already highlighted, the geographical agglomeration of innovation is remarkable: more than 73 per cent of the total research activity carried out by large firms in the UK is concentrated in three regions, namely the South East, with 47.1 per cent of the total, the North West (13.9 per cent) and the West Midlands (12.1 per cent). Foreign-owned research appears to be even more singularly concentrated than that of UK firms, with 60.8 per cent of total research undertaken by foreign-owned affiliates located in the South East (well above the indigenous company share of 40.2 per cent). Both the North West and West Midlands, though, exhibit regional shares definitely higher for indigenous companies (17 per cent and 16.4 per cent of the total respectively) than for foreign-owned firms (7.8 per cent and 3.6 per cent of the total UK-located research of foreign-owned affiliates).

However, it is interesting to note that, contrary to what is observed in the Italian case, the capacity to attract externally-owned innovation activity seems to be relatively higher in regions that show the lowest overall shares. This is particularly the case of East Anglia, with a share of foreign-owned patents almost quadruple the equivalent for UK-owned firms (the regional share of research of foreign-owned affiliates is 5.3 per cent, compared with 1.5 per cent for indigenous firms), but a similar proportionately greater attraction of foreign-owned research also occurs in the most peripheral regions of the UK outside England, i.e. Wales, Scotland and even Northern Ireland (whose regional share of the overall total is anyway negligible).

It is worth mentioning here the role played by region-specific public science externalities, which may be proxied by Research Council Grants to higher education institutions (HEIs), funded through the government's Office of Science and Technology (OST). Universities and other HEIs are the main providers of basic research and much of the strategic research carried out in the UK. The role played by the government in strengthening the regional science base and maximising its contribution to economic performance – by providing the core general funding – is therefore crucial in shaping the pattern of local attractiveness towards external resources. Figure 6.4 shows the regional shares of research grants for the period 1994–7, confirming once more the primacy of the South East, with 40 per cent of total grants, followed by Scotland (12.4 per cent), the North West (8.6 per cent) and East Anglia (8.4 per cent). The attractions of the science base in Scotland and East Anglia may help to explain how the technological efforts of foreign-owned firms are relatively more drawn to these regions than the spatial distribution of indigenous corporate R&D would suggest. Particularly in the case of Scotland, government efforts to improve the wealth-creating potential of basic research – giving rise to positive spillovers – may help explain the relatively higher share of foreign-owned technological development located in the region.

The high geographical concentration of innovation generated in MNCs compels us to restrict our analysis at a more detailed level to the three regions

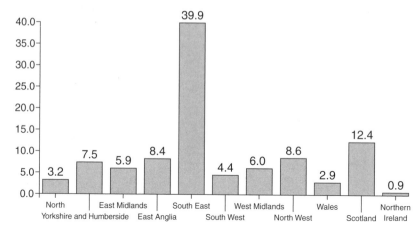

Figure 6.4 Government research grants to higher education institutions by region, 1994–97 (percentage of the UK total).

Source: Higher Education Statistics Agency.

mentioned above, i.e. the South East, the North West and the West Midlands, since the absolute number of patents granted in the other regions is too low for meaningful statistical analysis. It is necessary to bear in mind, however, the differences in the degree of attractiveness of external resources, already highlighted, which mark out these three regional systems as against all others in the UK, and thus lend support, at least at first glance, to our hypothesis of the existence of an internal geographical hierarchy.

The sectoral distribution of patents demonstrates interregional differences to an even greater extent. Table 6.2 reports the foreign shares by sector and region (foreign-owned firms' percentage of total patents granted to large firms for research located in the region).[6] As expected, Table 6.2 shows that, for the period 1969–95, the highest contribution of foreign research to the regional total is recorded in the South East (43.3 per cent), which is significantly above the national average (33.5 per cent). The other two regions are far less relatively attractive – with foreign shares accounting for almost 19 per cent of regional research in the North West and 10 per cent in the West Midlands.

The most pronounced and consistent contribution of foreign-owned research to the regional total is found, in the case of the South East, in sectors identified as various categories of electrical equipment, such as Semiconductors (40), Image and sound equipment (36), Other electrical communication systems (34), Telecommunications (33) and Electrical devices and systems (38). As for the country as a whole, the foreign share is also above average in all these sectors, but in the same macro-sector, the other two regions show foreign shares significantly higher than the average only in Image and sound equipment (36) and, for the North West, in Semiconductors (40).

Table 6.2 Foreign shares (foreign-owned firms' percentage of total patents granted to large firms for local research in the UK) by sector and region, 1969–95

Sectors	Regions			United Kingdom
	South East	West Midlands	North West	
1	14.6	13.3	35.7	20.7
3	35.1	18.5	32.8	23.2
5	40.1	12.6	19.9	31.5
6	87.9	60.0	54.3	80.0
7	48.2	13.2	22.3	38.5
9	27.6	6.9	18.4	28.8
11	42.4	11.1	18.9	34.4
12	43.3	47.2	26.2	41.5
13	39.0	23.6	22.5	28.5
14	58.3	18.3	11.2	40.1
16	33.3	27.4	25.0	29.6
17	45.4	16.2	6.1	32.1
20	49.5	20.8	21.6	44.4
23	65.2	6.8	33.3	50.0
25	25.9	0.0	38.5	37.6
28	45.7	18.3	31.4	38.2
29	27.6	3.9	20.2	16.0
33	51.4	4.5	15.4	44.8
34	59.3	10.1	14.3	47.8
35	34.6	16.7	0.0	31.5
36	61.8	28.6	50.0	58.4
37	33.1	4.9	14.3	28.3
38	50.3	6.2	9.7	37.3
39	46.7	3.6	6.0	27.7
40	74.4	11.1	57.9	62.1
41	56.7	8.8	20.0	49.9
42	24.4	3.6	33.3	17.6
49	17.6	4.8	6.5	15.9
50	35.4	13.2	4.8	23.1
51	25.0	0.0	3.0	17.9
53	41.9	15.0	15.9	33.3
56	44.5	2.6	8.1	28.4
Total Tech 56	43.3	10.0	18.8	33.5

Foreign shares of regional and national patents are significantly below average in all cases in Synthetic resins and fibres (9), Rubber and plastic products (49), and Coal and petroleum products (51). In contrast, some examples of relatively large foreign shares in all regions and in the country as a whole are found in Photographic chemistry (6) – in which the contribution of foreign research to the sectoral patenting activity is particularly remarkable in the South East (88 per cent) and in the UK total (80 per cent) – and in Pharmaceuticals and biotechnology (12).

As expected, and in line with what is observed for Lombardia in Italy,[7] the sectoral distribution of foreign-owned companies' shares of regional and national research activity shows a greater degree of correspondence between the South East and the UK than between the UK as a whole and any other individual region. Indeed, such higher order regions have a greater overall volume of activity spread across a wider representation of the fields of innovation that characterise a country as a whole. This might be illustrated with reference to the cases of Mining equipment (23), Office equipment and data processing systems (41) – both of which show a foreign share over 50 per cent of either regional or national total research – and Miscellaneous metal products (14), in which the core region and the country as a whole have foreign shares well above the average.

The other two regions, as in the case of Piemonte in Italy, seem to indicate more focused and locally specific sectoral patterns in the distribution of foreign participation in local research. In particular, in the West Midlands, foreign-owned research makes a substantial contribution in Pharmaceuticals and biotechnology (12), in which field the foreign share for both the country as a whole and the North West is also above average, and in the broad industrial groups of metals and metallurgy – i.e. Metallurgical processes (13) and Miscellaneous metal products (14) – and mechanical engineering – i.e. Chemical and allied equipment (16), Metal working equipment (17) and Assembly and material handling equipment (20). Technological innovation in mechanical engineering also receives a particularly high contribution by foreign-owned affiliates in the North West, although it appears principally directed to sectors such as Mining equipment (23), Textile and clothing machinery (25) and other Specialised machinery (28) – a different set of engineering fields from those in which foreign-owned firms are most active in the West Midlands. However, it is worth noting that these two regions manifest foreign shares that are well above average in some sectors for which the South East and the UK instead show relatively low values, such as (for the North West) Food and tobacco products (1) and Inorganic chemicals (3). A noteworthy discrepancy between the North West and the other cases illustrated is in Internal combustion engines (42), in which foreign-owned affiliates account for one-third of regional patenting activity, substantially above foreign participation in research in this field in other UK regions.

Figures 6.5 and 6.6 report the evolution over time of, respectively, the UK-owned and foreign-owned firms' total numbers of patents and the foreign shares for the 56 sectors as a whole by region. From Figure 6.5, it emerges clearly that the number of patents granted in the US to UK-owned firms has been on a continually declining trend, and has seen a sharp downturn since the end of the 1980s. By contrast, the number of patents granted to foreign-owned firms for research carried out in the UK has remained fairly stable, which has led, by the end of the period considered, foreign-owned affiliates to overtake indigenous firms in the absolute magnitude of technological effort that they undertake in the country.

The foreign proportion of total research performed by large firms in the South East (Figure 6.6), having been stable for most of the period, has

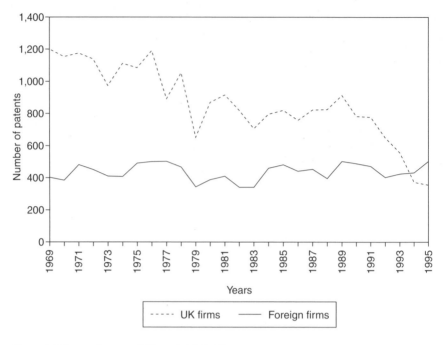

Figure 6.5 Patents by year, UK total, 1969–95.

increased markedly in recent years, reaching the highest values (over 70 per cent) at the end of the period. This pattern is also evidently driving that of the country as a whole, which in 1995 recorded a foreign share of approximately 60 per cent, more than double the equivalent share in 1969. This is due mainly to the decline of indigenous innovative activities, which is observed more markedly at the country level than for any of the three particular regions considered. The foreign share of regional patents in the West Midlands and the North West shows, in both cases, a greater fluctuation, increasing moderately over the period 1969–95 as a whole, with some sharp decreases in the mid-1980s for the West Midlands and at the beginning of the 1990s for the North West. However, both regions end with shares in the final year that are about three times bigger than those registered in 1969.

In general terms, the above picture seems to confirm – in the UK case as in Italy – that the location of technological activities of foreign-owned MNCs tends to be strongly agglomerated at a sub-national level. In a pattern that also matches the dominant role of Lombardia in Italy, foreign-owned technological development in the UK is concentrated in the same major region (the South East) that has served as the main pole of attraction for the equivalent activity of indigenous firms. Indeed, foreign-owned innovative

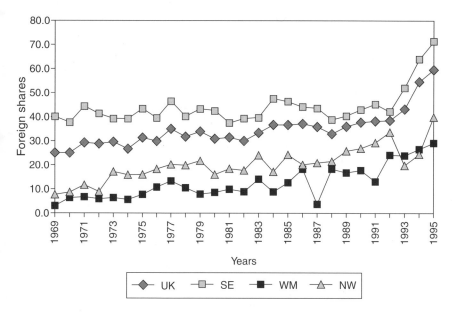

Figure 6.6 Foreign shares (% of total patents) by year and UK region, 1969–95.

activities are even more concentrated in the South East than is domestically-owned innovation, as demonstrated by the high foreign share of total patents in that region.

Moreover, it might be possible to interpret the remarkable decline in the patenting activity of UK-owned firms from their home base either by a narrowing of UK corporate technological specialisation, or by the renewed increase in the internationalisation of research by UK-owned companies in the early 1990s from already high levels (Cantwell and Harding, 1998). Allied to a further relocation of UK-owned corporate research abroad as an explanation of why foreign-owned firms have overtaken local firms as creators of technological innovation, might be the form taken by newer inward asset-seeking investment, namely the acquisition of UK firms by foreign MNCs. In other words, some of the relative shift in the patenting activity from UK to foreign MNCs may simply reflect a change in the ownership of R&D facilities through acquisition.[8]

Technological specialisation and the regional hierarchy in the UK

To investigate the characteristics of the profiles of technological specialisation of foreign-owned and local firms we have used the Revealed Technological Advantage (RTA) index calculated for both UK-owned and foreign-owned firms in the three regions – the South East, the North West and West Midlands – and in the UK as a whole for the period 1969–95.

Table 6.3 reports the RTA values by region and sector and it can be compared with Table 6.4, which shows the Revealed Scientific Advantage (RSA) index by scientific sector and region. The latter index has been built on an

Table 6.3 RTA index (UK and foreign firms) relative to the world, by sector and region, 1969–95

| Sectors | Regions | | | | | | United Kingdom | |
| | South East | | West Midlands | | North West | | | |
	UK firms	Foreign firms	UK firms	Foreign firms	UK firms	Foreign firms	UK firms	Foreign firms
1	2.742	0.616	0.416	0.576	0.556	1.336	1.707	0.884
3	0.648	0.458	0.555	1.134	0.949	1.999	0.947	0.565
5	0.870	0.765	0.867	1.122	1.299	1.397	0.998	0.909
6	0.230	2.198	0.024	0.323	0.185	0.950	0.205	1.620
7	0.659	0.804	0.368	0.501	4.159	5.159	1.297	1.610
9	0.747	0.373	0.372	0.248	1.452	1.417	0.823	0.659
11	1.306	1.262	0.187	0.210	2.459	2.484	1.196	1.240
12	3.480	3.482	0.115	0.925	2.084	3.206	1.997	2.807
13	0.751	0.630	1.424	3.948	0.641	0.804	1.061	0.839
14	0.678	1.245	1.573	3.172	0.768	0.421	0.966	1.281
16	0.899	0.587	0.541	1.833	0.749	1.080	0.911	0.759
17	0.617	0.671	1.540	2.671	0.599	0.169	0.944	0.882
20	0.541	0.694	0.606	1.426	0.403	0.481	0.603	0.956
23	0.184	0.452	1.154	0.759	0.163	0.352	0.596	1.180
25	0.342	0.157	2.220	0.000	0.647	1.748	1.539	1.837
28	1.089	1.200	1.398	2.824	0.727	1.442	1.206	1.475
29	1.279	0.639	5.209	1.883	0.527	0.575	2.080	0.783
33	0.978	1.354	0.471	0.202	0.238	0.187	0.732	1.177
34	0.930	1.778	1.080	1.096	0.706	0.509	0.806	1.460
35	3.464	2.406	0.230	0.413	0.177	0.000	1.740	1.582
36	0.575	1.219	0.057	0.206	0.055	0.239	0.321	0.894
37	1.956	1.267	1.066	0.496	0.213	0.153	1.130	0.884
38	0.852	1.131	1.167	0.691	0.729	0.340	0.808	0.952
39	0.575	0.661	1.349	0.457	0.762	0.212	0.762	0.579
40	0.343	1.307	0.421	0.473	0.101	0.603	0.310	1.008
41	0.482	0.826	0.323	0.279	0.239	0.259	0.367	0.723
42	1.354	0.573	2.301	0.778	0.100	0.217	1.141	0.483
49	1.185	0.332	3.550	1.596	1.541	0.463	1.736	0.649
50	0.689	0.495	0.636	0.868	2.330	0.504	1.010	0.602
51	1.230	0.538	0.159	0.000	0.545	0.074	0.903	0.390
53	1.123	1.064	0.647	1.024	0.549	0.450	0.946	0.935
56	1.032	1.085	0.975	0.237	0.865	0.330	1.267	0.994
Total Tech 56	1.000	1.000	1.000	1.000	1.000	1.000	1.000	1.000
Standard deviation	0.807	0.685	1.080	0.974	0.868	1.078	0.470	0.485

Table 6.4 RSA index relative to the UK, by scientific field and region, 1994–7

Sectors	Regions		
	South East	West Midlands	North West
Medical Sciences	1.365	0.557	0.487
Pharmacy, Pharmacology and Biosciences	0.880	0.763	0.797
Chemistry	0.751	1.180	1.153
Physics	0.951	1.307	1.577
Agriculture and Forestry	0.513	0.000	0.000
Earth, Marine and Environmental Sciences	1.032	0.336	1.168
General Sciences	0.005	0.000	0.458
General Engineering	0.949	2.233	0.212
Chemical Engineering	1.072	2.840	0.607
Mineral, Metallurgy and Materials Engineering	0.885	2.271	1.422
Civil Engineering, Architecture and Planning	0.780	0.833	1.574
Electrical, Electronic and Computer Engineering	1.047	0.772	1.094
Mechanical, Aero and Production Engineering	0.923	0.820	1.405
Other Technologies	0.588	0.000	3.456
Mathematics	0.724	0.959	1.111
Information Technology and Systems Sciences	0.659	0.634	1.032
Catering and Hospitality Management	0.653	0.000	0.000
Business and Management Studies	0.804	2.396	2.054
Geography and Social Studies	1.217	1.473	0.738
Librarianship, Communication and Media Studies	0.198	0.076	1.093
Language Studies, Humanities and Creative Arts	0.969	0.510	1.160
Total	1.000	1.000	1.000

Source: Higher Education Statistics Agency (HESA).

equivalent basis using the values of Research Grants to HEIs awarded by the government in 1994–7 classified by the location of each HEI and by the scientific field of activity, and it gives an account of the scientific special-isation of publicly-funded research in each region relative to the UK as a whole.

First of all, the overall picture seems to indicate that the technological advantages of both the nationally-owned and foreign-owned firms in the South East and in the country as a whole are more widely dispersed at the sectoral level than in the other two regional cases (the cross-sectoral variance in the RTA index is lower for the South East or the UK than it is for either the West Midlands or the North West). In both the South East and the UK as a whole, the technological specialisation of foreign-owned affiliates over-laps most with that of local firms in the areas of Pharmaceuticals and biotech-nology (12) and Special radio systems (35). In the latter sector, the fact that foreign shares appear to be well below the average in both cases suggests a point of strength of local technological innovation. Looking at scientific advantages (Table 6.4), the South East turns out to be rather specialised in medical sciences and electrical, electronic and computer engineering, while regional public research is relatively weak both in pharmacy, pharmacology and biosciences and in information technology and system sciences. This helps to suggest the form of local linkages between science and the development of corporate technological competencies. In other words, foreign MNCs are probably much more attracted by the university general expertise in some broader and related scientific areas – such as medical sciences with respect to pharmaceuticals and biotechnology – rather than by specific capabilities in their own immediate field of expertise. The latter may well be preferably developed and strengthened 'in house' in large firms, and thus funded to a much greater extent by the private sector through commercial research, as well as through the international linkages of the MNC (cross-border corporate integration, which also provides indirect links to the best university research in the biosciences themselves on a worldwide basis).

Other examples of a comparative advantage of local firms in the core region and in the country as a whole are found in Other organic compounds (11) and Other specialised machinery (28). The South East alone attracts foreign research in sectors such as Illumination devices (37), Other instruments and controls (53) and Other manufacturing and non-industrial (56), while the country as a whole shows a greater matching between indigenous and foreign firms in Cleaning agents and other compositions (7), in all of which the foreign technological contribution turns out to be substantial.

As far as the other two regions are concerned, the technological specialisation of both local and foreign firms is more concentrated within broad industrial groups. In the West Midlands, local firms show a strong comparative advantage in metals and metallurgy – i.e. Metallurgical processes (13) and Miscellaneous metal products (14) – and mechanical engineering – i.e. Other specialised machinery (28) and, particularly, Other general industrial equipment (29) – in which foreign-owned affiliates are also relatively specialised. The latter sector, with the most remarkable value of the RTA, is indeed one of the traditional points of strength in the regional production structure, and despite the attraction of foreign-owned research in this field (a RTA value above one), the foreign share of the total regional research carried out in the sector has remained low. The same comment applies to another sector conventionally indicated as strong in the regional pattern of production specialisation linked to traditional engineering and motor vehicles, namely Rubber and plastic products (49), in which foreign-owned firms also show a technological advantage but have failed to achieve a high foreign share of local activity. Moreover, it is interesting to note that, in the case of the West Midlands, the high values of the RSA index in both general and chemical engineering and mineral, metallurgy and materials engineering, confirm a remarkable specialised engineering expertise in publicly-funded research, which however is not found for mechanical engineering as such. This supports our earlier hypothesis that the relationship between private (foreign) and public basic research is not as direct as might be expected, and operates more through scientific fields that are related and complementary to the specific sector of technological specialisation of the MNC (the most immediate knowledge for which is likely to be generated directly from within large firms).

Turning to the North West, the sectoral concentration of comparative advantages turns out to be the greatest for both indigenous and foreign-owned firms. The region shows a clear focus of strength in chemicals – i.e. Chemical processes (5), Cleaning agents and other compositions (7), Synthetic resins and fibres (9), Other organic compounds (11) – and in Pharmaceuticals and biotechnology (12), the latter being an area of technological advantage in the UK as a whole.[9] Also in this case, the RSA index shows a regional scientific specialisation in chemistry and physics, while indicating a relative despecialisation in pharmacy, pharmacology and biosciences, which shows once more that the kind of matching between privately- and publicly-funded research occurs more at the level of complementary sectors of science and technology rather than between directly similar fields of expertise, with clear implications for regional policy aimed at encouraging linkages and spillover effects. It should be recalled that the narrower sectoral spread of foreign-owned and locally-owned research in the North West has to be understood in relation to its historically high degree of productive specialisation in textiles and clothing, from which the region's specialisation has shifted over time towards chemicals, through the development of synthetic fibres (it is worth noting that the largest research facilities of ICI are based in the region). This seems to be reaffirmed by the small foreign share of patents in Synthetic resins and fibres (9) despite a high foreign-owned RTA value, while in Textile and clothing machinery (25), and Other specialised machinery (28), foreign-owned affiliates show both high contributions to regional research and comparative technological advantages (whereas large local firms appear to have since undergone a process of despecialisation).

It is worth mentioning that the correlation coefficients between the RTA indices of different regions provide some additional insights into the characteristics of the regional and national systems of innovation. The relevant point that emerges is that the specialisation patterns of both UK-owned and foreign-owned firms in the three regions are not significantly correlated – i.e. the regional hierarchy, in this case, turns out to be associated with distinctive patterns of regional specialisation. As expected, the UK national system as a whole can be understood as a composite of the three regional systems, as confirmed by the significant correlation found between the RTA of UK-owned firms in each of the regions and in the country as a whole (the highest coefficient, as expected, is found for the South East).

In order to test our hypothesis that the composition of technological specialisation of foreign-owned affiliates in each region follows more closely the equivalent pattern of specialisation in indigenous companies in intermediate compared with in higher-order regions, a simple regression analysis was carried out for the period 1969–95. In accordance with the two territorial units considered in the analysis (regional and national), two geographical levels were taken into consideration in the cross-section regression analysis. First of all, the hypothesis was tested at regional level for the three regions (in equation (6.1) the relevant subscript i = South East, West Midlands or North West), and then for the UK as a whole (equation (6.2)). In the former case, a logarithmic transformation of the index was used, since the distribution of the RTA index in each regional case is skewed because of the smaller numbers of patents at the regional level, creating a pattern closer to lognormality than to normality, unlike for the country as a whole.[10] The regression was run across all the 56 technological sectors (subscript j).

$$\ln RTAFOR_{ij} = \alpha + \beta \ln RTAUK_{ij} + \varepsilon_{ij} \qquad (6.1)$$

$$RTAFOR_j = \alpha + \beta RTAUK_j + \varepsilon_j \qquad (6.2)$$

First of all, in both the core region – i.e. the South East – and the UK as a whole, the specialisation of foreign-owned firms does not depend on the technological advantage of indigenous firms (see Table 6.5).

For the South East, this result is analogous to our findings for Lombardia in the Italian case, suggesting that regions at the top of the geographical hierarchy, such as the South East and Lombardia in the UK and Italy respectively, attract the development efforts of a broad range of foreign-owned firms, generally extending their own lines of domestic specialisation by drawing on the general capabilities to be found locally in the leading centre of all-round excellence. This is all the more true in the case of Greater London, whose dynamism in terms of technological and productive activities

Table 6.5 Results of the cross-sectoral regressions of foreign-owned RTA on indigenous RTA in the UK as a whole, and in the three UK regions

	UK	*South East*	*West Midlands*	*North West*
RTAUKj[a]	−0.100	0.154	0.447**	0.791***
	(−0.691)	(−1.518)	(−2.200)	(−5.061)
Intercept	1.088***	−0.524**	−2.125***	−1.239**
	(−6.241)	(−2.589)	(−3.520)	(−2.646)
LM Diagnostic Statistics				
Serial correlation	0.104[0.747]	0.388[0.533]	0.109[0.742]	0.588[0.443]
Heteroscedasticity	0.014[0.906]	0.038[0.845]	0.026[0.872]	1.231[0.267]
No. of observations	56	56	56	56

Notes
a For the three individual regions the regression was run in logarithmic form, the independent variable thus being $\ln RTAUK_{ij}$.
**Significantly different from zero at 5%
***Significantly different from zero at 1%

(particularly services), general infrastructure, financial facilities, etc., goes without saying. Moreover, it has been shown that local firms based in the South East region are much more open to external networks, whether through competition or through collaboration, not only in comparison with other UK regions, but also with other European locations (Keeble, 1997). Therefore, it might be argued that the spillover effects due to a high concentration of productive and innovative activities apply over a broader range in this region, which may thus be labelled as a *higher order* location in the geographical hierarchy, both within the UK and even in a European context. On the other hand, the overall UK model, unlike the Italian case, resembles the model of its core region, suggesting a kind of attractiveness towards foreign resources based on general technological competencies and infrastructural supports (in terms of degree of openness to foreign investors, business climate, corporate and enterprise culture, language, etc.) offered by the country as a whole. In contrast, the Italian model was closer to the case of an intermediate national system of innovation, attracting foreign-owned research over a narrower range on a more sector-specific basis.

The West Midlands and the North West show, instead, a rather different picture. Here, the profile of technological specialisation of foreign-owned firms is closely related to the equivalent pattern of specialisation of indigenous firms in both regions. In the case of the North West, the relationship between the two technological profiles seems to be particularly strong (the coefficient is significant at the 1 per cent level), as suggested by our earlier discussion of the detailed composition of the RTA indices. This is consistent with our hypothesis that *intermediate* regional centres, such as also applies to Piemonte in Italy, attract the innovative activities of foreign MNCs for their specific set of specialised expertise that can be accessed by asset-seeking foreign-owned affiliates. By locating research facilities in such regions, aligned with sectoral-specific local strengths, foreign MNCs may be able to upgrade their own technological capabilities in some particular technological fields.[11]

Conclusions

In a rapidly globalising economy, and particularly in the face of a process of economic integration such as that occurring in the EU, regions forge an increasing number of linkages with other locations, within and across national boundaries, through the technological activities of integrated parts of MNC networks that the regions have managed to attract.

The first attempt to analyse the UK case has provided further support for the hypothesis that the pattern of MNC networks for innovation conforms to a hierarchy of regional centres, whose composition differs between industries. Accordingly, the technological specialisation of foreign-owned affiliates in different regional locations depends upon the position of the region in the hierarchy. Moreover, without any intervention to influence the broad forces of globalisation, the strong geographical concentration of innovation might bring about a further marginalisation of backward regions, excluding them from the possibility of entering the locational hierarchy.

The growing interdependence between local and cross-border innovative activities requires a search for a more macro-systemic approach to the organisation of technological resources and capabilities. Therefore, a refocusing of regional and industrial policies to develop and improve local technological competence to attract and retain development efforts that contribute a locally specific source of innovation to international networks, seems to have become central to the agenda of the 'Europe of the regions'. The analysis of the regional position in the hierarchy and the understanding of the strategic behaviours of MNCs – increasingly guided by the aim of capturing the synergies offered by combining different local contexts – may help promote a more even distribution of the creation and diffusion of knowledge, providing the basis for a new phase of regional development in Europe.

7 Multinational corporations and the German regional systems of innovation*

Introduction

This chapter seeks to examine the proposition that, in line with trends else-where recorded in the European Union, a substantial concentration of large firm technological activity is evident in Germany. Such agglomerations, in turn, highlight the potential for inter-firm technological communication at such locations. By analysing the precise technological composition of such concentrations, and in particular the incidence of overlap between foreign and indigenous firm research activity, we test the hypothesis that there exists a geographical hierarchy of regional research centres across Europe. As in the previous chapters, undertaking this analysis for large firms located in Germany serves to inform us of this economy's position in the European hierarchy.

The chapter is organised as follows: the next section examines the owner-ship and technological distribution of patents granted by the USPTO to large firms researching in Germany over the 1969–95 period. A regional analysis of innovative activity is presented in the third section, where the relationship between foreign and indigenous technological profiles is examined and tested. The potential for inter-regional technological interaction between firms is also analysed in this section, while the fourth section concludes by summarising the main findings in the German case.

The location of MNC technological activities in the German regions

Germany presents us with a particularly good testing ground for inter-firm technology transfer as it has traditionally secured the highest percentage of utility patents granted by the USPTO to firms and inventors located in Europe.[1] During the 1969–95 period, 82 per cent of total patents granted to large firms based in Germany resulted from research located in just four of the 16 Bundesländer. These core regions within the German innovation system are Nordrhein-Westfalen, Bayern, Baden Württemberg and Hessen.[2] It is worth reminding ourselves that the latter three regions – together with

Rheinland-Pfalz – were grouped, according to the analysis carried out in Chapter 3, in the cluster named 'industry-driven, technologically advanced manufacturing centres', while Nordrhein-Westfalen was included in the cluster 'industry-based regions with medium–low degree of urbanisation'; both clusters revealing substantial levels and growth rates of MNC research activities compared with the rest of the EU.

Both foreign and German-owned research (79 and 83 per cent respectively) is almost evenly dispersed across these four regions, highlighting the geographical agglomeration of both foreign and indigenous innovation in this economy. Comparing this picture against population and industrial employment statistics, we find that, while patenting activity is far more concentrated than population across these regions,[3] it is relatively close to the regional distributions of industrial employment in the cases of Nordrhein-Westfalen and Baden Württemberg. In contrast, innovative activity is far more concentrated than industrial employment in Bayern and Hessen.

The evolution of this agglomeration is traced by dividing the data into two time periods – 1969–82 (or t_1) and 1983–95 (or t_2). As emerges from Table 7.1, both regional shares in the national total and foreign/indigenous shares in each group's total have changed considerably over time. While research undertaken in Nordrhein-Westfalen continues to account for the highest proportion of patents granted to all large firms located in Germany, the number of patents attributed to research in this region declined by two percentage points in the second time period. This is in marked contrast to the pattern recorded in Baden Württemberg, where the share of total patenting (German-owned + foreign-owned) increased by 2.6 percentage points. The latter region continues to host the largest percentage of patents granted to foreign firms located in Germany, while Nordrhein-Westfalen hosts the greatest proportion of patents granted to indigenous firms. This contrasts substantially with the previously observed patterns in the UK and Italian cases, where both foreign and indigenous activity was concentrated in the same regions. This differing pattern for Germany, we believe, can be explained by considering the type of technological activity associated with Nordrhein-Westfalen. This region is the traditional home of the German chemical/ pharmaceutical industry and continues to record substantial technological advantage for indigenous firms that base their research there. This strength is further reflected in the research profiles of the universities and research institutes located in the region (Blind and Grupp, 1999, p. 461).

Coinciding with the results obtained for the UK case in Chapter 6, it is interesting to note that the ability to attract foreign research innovative activity was higher in a number of regions that show low overall shares of patenting activity. Most noticeable in this respect is Niedersachsen. It played host to a significant amount of foreign activity during the entire 1969–95 period. Despite the fact that the relative positioning of this region in national terms declined during the second period, foreign activity in this region actually recorded a dramatic increase (representing 30 per cent of total regional

Table 7.1 USPTO patent grants to large firms located in Germany by region, 1969–82 (t_1) and 1983–95 (t_2)

Region	% of total grants					
	Indigenous		Foreign		Total	
	t_1	t_2	t_1	t_2	t_1	t_2
Nordrhein-Westfalen	29.4	27.8	19.5	18.6	27.9	26.0
Bayern	23.9	25.0	14.9	12.9	22.5	23.0
Baden-Württemberg	15.4	17.0	28.4	33.8	17.4	20.0
Hessen	13.5	12.1	13.5	14.2	13.5	12.5
Niedersachsen	3.9	2.8	4.5	5.6	4.0	3.3
Rheinland-Pfalz	8.5	9.9	4.2	5.4	7.8	9.1
Others	5.4	5.4	15.0	9.5	6.9	6.1
Germany	100.0	100.0	100.0	100.0	100.0	100.0

patenting activity in t_2). Potentially, this could be due to congestion effects in the core regions.

Table 7.2 records the shares of US patents of the largest German firms attributable to research located in the regions relative to that which they located in Germany as a whole, and the equivalent regional shares for the research of foreign-owned firms by technological sector in the period 1969–95.[4] This serves to highlight the regional preferences of indigenous/foreign firms across particular technological sectors. Approximately 95 per cent of the total research activity of large firms was concentrated across these six regions over the 1969–95 period, with particular concentration taking place in the four larger Länder as highlighted above. These top four regions accounted for more than 70 per cent of total activity in all but two sectors – Agricultural chemicals (4) and Image and sound equipment (36).

Focusing upon regional patterns of concentration, results point to a very high concentration (greater than 50 per cent) of aggregate activity in the Transport technologies (42, 43 and 47) in Baden Württemberg, Chemicals (9) in Nordrhein-Westfalen, Electronics (sectors 34 and 40) and Photographic equipment (52) in Bayern. While research concentration is relatively low in the other regions, the regional averages are outstripped in a number of technologies. Hessen and Rheinland-Pfalz, for example, host an above average concentration, inter alia, in Chemical technologies (6, 7, 10, 11, 12), and Niedersachsen is high in the Electrical and transport technologies (33, 34, 36 and 41, 42, 43, 47).

Defining a substantial concentration of activity as occurring if more than 25 per cent of each group's total patents is located in one region, it is interesting to note that an overlap of foreign/indigenous regional concentration occurs in a number of sectors. In Baden Württemberg, for example, both

Table 7.2 Shares of US patents of the largest German firms attributable to research in German regions relative to Germany as a whole (G), and the equivalent regional shares for the German-located research of foreign-owned firms (F), by technological sector, 1969–95 (%)

Sector	Baden-Württemberg			Nordrhein-Westfalen			Bayern			Niedersachsen			Hessen			Rheinland-Pfalz		
	F (%)	G (%)	Tot (%)	F (%)	G (%)	Tot (%)	F (%)	G (%)	Tot (%)	F (%)	G (%)	Tot (%)	F (%)	G (%)	Tot (%)	F (%)	G (%)	Tot (%)
3	7.5	6.5	6.6	33.3	42.7	42.0	5.0	14.5	13.4	24.2	2.0	4.0	9.2	22.3	21.0	10.8	9.8	9.9
4	50.0	7.3	10.0	1.4	43.1	40.5	5.7	6.1	6.3	12.9	0.5	1.3	8.6	8.3	8.0	4.3	28.0	26.7
5	31.4	6.6	9.9	27.6	32.0	31.5	10.2	27.6	24.2	5.3	2.1	2.5	14.0	16.3	16.0	3.0	11.1	10.0
6	25.4	3.4	5.5	7.7	44.2	40.9	4.2	11.5	13.6	0.0	0.1	0.1	53.5	24.8	27.5	1.4	14.6	13.4
7	19.0	4.8	6.0	21.6	45.2	43.0	15.2	11.7	10.9	9.5	2.0	2.7	16.9	22.3	21.9	4.8	10.7	10.1
9	24.6	3.8	5.0	19.4	53.7	51.8	19.2	9.4	8.9	3.2	2.9	2.9	23.3	11.6	12.0	3.0	17.1	16.2
10	77.0	2.9	8.0	2.7	40.5	38.0	9.5	6.2	13.9	1.4	0.4	1.4	2.7	33.6	31.6	2.7	15.5	14.7
11	32.5	7.1	8.9	8.1	42.1	39.8	36.8	6.9	6.5	7.5	1.3	1.8	8.3	19.8	19.0	2.3	19.3	18.0
12	44.9	10.2	12.9	6.8	38.1	35.6	15.6	9.9	14.9	18.1	0.8	2.2	5.0	20.0	18.8	2.9	11.8	11.1
13	32.1	10.6	13.9	17.0	31.2	28.9	17.3	31.7	30.7	2.2	5.0	4.5	19.9	13.9	14.8	4.0	3.3	3.4
14	15.5	30.8	24.5	35.5	18.1	25.0	7.8	21.3	15.1	4.2	10.0	7.6	22.5	9.2	14.7	9.6	4.8	6.8
16	28.8	10.2	13.2	29.6	36.2	35.0	7.8	22.1	18.8	5.7	2.3	2.8	15.4	8.9	9.9	3.2	7.7	7.0
17	22.0	12.8	15.0	17.4	49.0	40.6	40.1	16.9	14.1	1.8	3.3	2.9	12.2	8.4	9.5	3.3	3.6	3.5
20	27.1	16.4	19.0	31.8	24.9	26.9	7.9	28.3	20.9	8.9	5.4	6.4	6.4	13.3	11.5	3.9	3.0	3.3
25	32.1	7.8	18.5	12.9	23.4	18.8	6.3	45.8	25.9	2.5	3.0	2.8	15.3	3.0	8.5	3.6	3.9	3.7
26	32.2	2.8	5.8	5.1	1.3	1.7	3.4	43.9	43.6	0.0	2.1	1.9	44.1	37.4	38.0	1.7	9.5	8.7
28	25.6	22.6	23.7	22.4	32.3	29.0	8.3	20.1	13.8	2.8	4.7	4.1	21.2	8.7	12.8	10.9	4.6	6.6
29	16.7	44.0	37.0	16.8	16.8	16.9	9.7	24.2	19.1	10.6	4.0	5.6	26.5	5.6	10.7	14.7	2.1	5.1
31	28.1	43.5	41.6	7.9	9.5	9.0	6.1	35.4	31.9	4.4	2.8	3.0	35.1	3.8	7.8	14.0	1.9	3.5
33	49.4	3.9	17.0	6.7	3.5	4.5	28.4	68.7	48.8	2.2	13.2	10.0	4.4	2.6	3.0	0.4	1.6	1.3
34	47.2	22.1	28.8	4.1	4.3	4.0	16.1	56.1	58.9	6.7	7.8	7.4	6.2	4.0	4.6	3.1	0.9	1.5
36	39.7	6.0	17.8	4.3	3.0	3.5	14.2	40.6	28.9	7.0	10.0	8.9	7.8	20.8	16.0	0.9	2.4	1.8
37	29.2	27.2	27.8	36.0	1.1	10.0	6.3	50.0	41.9	1.6	3.7	3.1	7.9	9.4	9.0	1.2	0.4	0.6
38	36.2	16.3	21.0	13.5	5.0	7.0	18.7	57.4	43.8	2.6	3.7	3.4	12.5	3.9	6.0	2.1	0.9	1.2
39	42.9	23.5	27.0	22.0	8.5	11.0	9.3	44.9	42.9	1.5	2.4	2.3	14.9	9.0	10.0	2.7	3.8	3.6

40	51.6	17.6	25.9	2.7	2.6	2.6	14.3	74.2	62.6	2.2	0.7	1.1	4.9	2.2	2.9	4.9	0.3	1.4
41	53.9	22.6	32.6	3.8	4.5	4.0	9.7	52.3	37.2	4.4	5.5	5.2	12.0	7.4	8.8	1.2	3.2	2.6
42	8.1	76.5	74.8	32.3	4.9	5.6	8.1	9.8	12.2	1.6	6.7	6.5	38.7	0.5	1.5	6.5	0.8	1.0
43	8.6	68.5	55.8	27.6	4.6	9.5	5.5	15.4	12.8	2.5	7.6	6.5	45.4	0.7	10.0	9.8	0.7	2.6
47	42.0	54.4	51.7	19.8	8.9	11.0	5.6	21.3	16.7	3.1	11.6	9.6	19.1	0.5	4.8	4.3	1.3	2.0
49	12.2	5.3	6.5	43.0	37.6	38.7	17.4	18.8	15.9	2.9	10.2	8.9	13.4	12.0	12.0	8.1	10.4	10.0
50	29.0	5.8	10.2	43.3	33.0	35.0	13.1	20.1	17.7	2.5	3.9	3.6	9.2	18.8	17.0	4.1	15.3	13.2
52	71.2	13.7	20.4	1.6	2.9	2.7	4.8	64.6	58.8	0.8	0.6	0.6	10.4	12.8	12.6	1.6	2.6	2.4
53	32.6	25.2	26.9	18.0	8.9	10.9	9.8	44.2	34.7	3.7	3.6	3.6	4.8	9.6	8.6	2.8	2.7	2.7
56	32.8	3.6	5.5	34.3	53.8	52.7	4.5	28.4	26.6	1.5	2.5	2.5	14.9	5.8	6.4	1.5	3.3	3.2
Tot Tech 56	31.0	16.0	19.0	19.0	29.0	27.0	14.0	25.0	23.0	5.0	3.0	4.0	14.0	13.0	13.0	5.0	9.0	9.0

foreign and indigenous firms record substantial concentration in Instruments and controls (53), Other transport equipment (47), Illumination devices (37) and Power plants (31). Similar concentrations are found in Nordrhein-Westfalen in Chemical technologies (3 and 5), Equipment technologies (16 and 20) as well as Rubber and plastic products (49), Non-metallic mineral products (50) and Other manufacturers (56). Bayern and Hessen also record substantial agglomeration – the former in Telecommunications (33), and the latter in Photographic processes (6) and Printing and publishing (26). Such patenting concentrations are absent in both Niedersachsen and Rheinland-Pfalz.

Focusing upon foreign firm activity, we note a very high concentration (again, greater than 50 per cent of total patents) in Baden Württemberg in the Chemical (4 and 10) and Electronics fields (33, 40, 41 and 52). Because the regional concentration of foreign research in these technologies does not coincide with that of their indigenous counterparts – and following the definition of hierarchical centres presented in the previous chapters – this tentatively suggests that Baden Württemberg may be classified as a higher order research centre. Foreign firms may have been (at least initially) attracted to this region because of the dynamic small- and medium-sized enterprise, or *Mittelstand*, sector. This region boasts a highly developed capacity for networking under the umbrella of a very mature and successful system of innovation (Cooke and Morgan, 1994).[5] This may help to explain the high foreign concentration rates in this region. Alternatively, the fact that indigenous research within such technologies is located in close geographical proximity (in neighbouring Bayern) may however suggest that the location decisions of foreign companies in these technologies were actually conditioned by the extant knowledge base of indigenous firms, albeit in the bordering region. For instance, patenting by German-owned firms located in Bayern is substantial in electronics technologies. This, in turn, may point to the ease of inter-firm communication across regional borders in Germany.

The contribution of foreign research at the regional level is reported in Table 7.3. This is calculated by extracting foreign presence from the total regional patenting performance. As expected, foreign firm presence is most pronounced in the research output of Baden Württemberg, where it accounts for 28 per cent of the total. As noted above, substantial foreign patenting also occurs in Niedersachsen, where 24 per cent of the total is attributed to the research efforts of large foreign firms. Relative to the national average, small foreign shares in the regional totals are found in just under half of the technological areas – most noticeably in the chemical sector whose research is concentrated in Baden Württemberg and Niedersachsen.

Focusing upon total foreign firm activity within specific technologies, we note a substantial contribution (over 40 per cent) in the Textile and clothing machinery (25) and Miscellaneous metal product (14) technologies. In addition, activities of this group make up over 20 per cent of the total recorded in the Electrical (34, 36, 37, 38, 40 and 41), Mechanical (17, 20, 28 and 29) and Transport technologies (43 and 47).

Table 7.3 Foreign firm share by technological sector and region, 1969–95 (%)

Sector	Regions						
	Baden W.	Bayern	Hessen	Ndr.-West.	Niedersac.	Rhd. Pfalz	Germany
3	10.6	3.4	4.0	7.4	55.8	10.0	9.3
4	32.4	6.2	6.7	0.2	64.0	1.0	6.5
5	41.8	5.3	11.5	11.5	27.0	3.9	13.1
6	42.9	3.6	18.0	1.7	0.0	0.9	9.2
7	28.9	11.7	7.2	4.7	32.8	4.4	9.3
9	29.4	11.7	11.6	2.3	6.8	1.0	6.1
10	65.5	10.0	0.6	0.5	73.0	1.0	6.6
11	25.9	29.1	3.1	1.5	30.0	0.9	7.2
12	27.7	12.1	2.1	1.5	65.6	2.0	8.0
13	35.5	9.0	20.6	9.0	7.0	17.7	15.4
14	26.0	20.4	63.1	57.9	22.8	58.0	41.2
16	34.3	6.2	24.3	13.1	31.8	7.0	15.7
17	39.3	47.1	35.2	11.8	16.9	25.0	27.5
20	38.6	9.6	15.5	32.7	38.0	33.0	27.7
25	76.5	9.8	80.0	30.3	39.0	41.9	44.2
26	55.9	0.9	11.6	30.0	0.0	1.9	10.1
28	34.6	16.2	53.2	24.5	21.5	52.0	32.0
29	10.9	11.4	60.4	24.3	46.0	69.0	24.4
31	8.7	2.5	58.0	11.0	18.5	51.6	12.9
33	83.8	14.5	40.8	43.5	6.5	10.0	29.1
34	43.8	9.5	36.4	25.8	24.0	54.5	26.7
36	78.3	15.9	16.9	44.1	27.0	16.7	35.1
37	27.7	4.3	23.0	91.9	13.0	50.0	26.3
38	42.0	9.6	51.0	46.7	18.8	44.0	24.6
39	29.1	4.4	27.0	36.7	12.0	13.8	18.5
40	48.5	5.8	42.3	25.0	50.0	84.6	24.5
41	52.8	8.0	43.2	28.1	27.0	15.0	32.0
42	0.3	2.1	66.7	14.6	0.6	16.7	2.5
43	3.3	8.8	94.9	61.6	8.0	80.0	21.3
47	18.4	7.1	7.1	7.2	91.0	39.5	22.7
49	32.3	16.0	18.7	19.1	5.6	13.9	17.2
50	52.9	12.9	10.0	22.9	12.8	5.8	18.5
52	39.9	0.9	9.4	6.7	14.0	7.0	11.4
53	26.5	5.8	12.1	36.0	22.0	22.0	21.8
56	39.3	1.1	15.4	4.3	4.0	3.0	6.6
Tot Tech 56	28.2	10.2	18.1	11.9	23.7	9.6	16.7

At a regional level, a very high foreign contribution (greater than 90 per cent) is recorded in Motor vehicles technologies (43) in Hessen, Illumination devices technologies (37) in Nordrhein-Westfalen and Other transport equipment (47) technologies in Niedersachsen.

Technological specialisation and the regional hierarchy in Germany

To examine further the relative specialisation patterns of foreign and indigenous patenting activity, the Revealed Technological Advantage (RTA) indices were calculated and the results are reported in Table 7.4.

In terms of overall positioning within this country, it can be seen that foreign firms enjoy technological advantage in 14 of the 35 technological sectors under study. This advantage is most prominent in the mechanical technologies, with a particularly high specialisation (RTA > 3) recorded in the Textile and clothing machinery (25) sector. Indigenous firms record a technological advantage in 15 sectors, demonstrating a noticeable specialisation in the historically strong chemical technologies. At a regional level, strong specialisation in these technologies is found in Nordrhein-Westfalen, Hessen and Rheinland-Pfalz. The highest RTA (3.1) is recorded in the Bleaching and dyeing technology (10). At an aggregate level, a strong overlap in the technological specialisation of local and non-local MNCs occurs in the Mechanical (17, 26, and 29) and Transport sectors (43 and 47).

While the aggregate or national figures demonstrate little difference in the degree of sectoral concentration of foreign and indigenous firms' technological advantages, results at the regional level diverge from this finding. With the exception of Bayern (standard deviation = 0.62), indigenous firms are, in general, more concentrated in fewer technologies than their foreign counterparts. This is particularly so in the case of indigenous firms located in Baden Württemberg and Hessen (and to a lesser extent Rheinland-Pfalz). Given that recent evidence suggests an inverse correlation between the standard deviation of the cross-sectoral RTA distribution and the overall size of innovative activity (Cantwell and Fai, 1999; Cantwell and Bachmann, 1998) this result is surprising. The indigenous German sector is, on average, five times larger than the foreign sector yet more regionally specialised, which highlights the very strong regional focus and importance of regional specialisation for indigenous German firms.

Turning to the issue of regional technological advantage, it is clear that indigenous firms located in the Baden Württemberg region reveal a very strong technological advantage in the Transport technologies (42, 43 and 47). As noted above, indigenous firms reveal a very narrow sectoral spread of technological advantage in Hessen (Chemicals and pharmaceuticals, especially 10, 11 and 3), Baden Württemberg (Transport) and Rheinland-Pfalz (Chemicals, particularly 4, 10 and 11). While, in Bayern, their technological advantage spans practically all technologies, in Niedersachsen – with the exception of transport technologies – they hold few other advantages (the exception is indeed Other general industrial equipment (29)).

Foreign firms located in the Baden Württemberg region record their advantage in the broad electronics and mechanical fields – especially in Textile and clothing machinery (25) and in Telecommunications (33) – and account for an average of approximately 50 per cent of total regional patent grants in these technologies (see Table 7.3). As highlighted above, any attempts to explain such specialisation patterns in terms of the extant large firm indigenous advantage in these sectors (and implied potential for intra-sectoral, inter-firm knowledge exchange) would therefore appear to be rather futile.

Examining the correlation coefficients between the RTA indices across the regions, it is apparent that there is little correlation between indigenous and foreign-owned regional technological specialisation profiles. Despite the aggregate result however, there are a number of cases in which similar specialisation patterns exist between the two groups of firms. Both foreign and indigenous firms are specialised in Other transport equipment (47) in Baden Württemberg and Niedersachsen for example, Other general industrial equipment (29) in Nordrhein-Westfalen and Niedersachsen, Metal working equipment (17) in Nordrhein-Westfalen and Printing and publishing (26) in Hessen. As a general conclusion, however, results suggest that there are very distinct patterns of specialisation between foreign and indigenous firms across the six German regions.

The national indigenous research activity appears to be the composite of that undertaken in Rheinland-Pfalz, Nordrhein-Westfalen and Hessen, as highlighted by the significant correlation that exists between indigenous firms researching in these regions and in the country as a whole. In the case of foreign activity, all regions conform to the national pattern with the exception of the technological innovations carried out in Niedersachsen.

As discussed so far, in the case of Germany, patenting activity is concentrated in six Bundesländer. To ascertain the status of these regions in the research centre hierarchy, the methodology employed in the previous two chapters was followed and a simple regression analysis was undertaken. The first hypothesis tested was that the aggregate patenting activity of foreign firms in Germany was dependent upon the technological specialisation of indigenous firms (equation (7.1). This hypothesis is then tested for each of the six regions.

$$RTA_{fj} = \alpha + \beta\, RTA_{dj} + \varepsilon_j \qquad\qquad (7.1)$$

where RTA_f = Revealed Technological Advantage of foreign-owned firms (f) located in Germany.

RTA_d = Revealed Technological Advantage of indigenous domestically-owned firms (d) located in Germany.

$j = 1, \ldots 56$ technological sectors.

This model was then extended to ascertain the relationship between foreign and indigenous firm research at regional level (equation (7.2)). Because there is a possibility that certain technologies will attract a relatively lower number of patents at regional level, an artificially high degree of dispersion in the

Table 7.4 RTA index (German and foreign firms) relative to the world, by sector and region, 1969–95

Sector	Regions													
	Baden W.		Ndr.-West.		Bayern		Nieders.		Hessen		Rld. Pfalz		Germany	
	F	G	F	G	F	G	F	G	F	G	F	G	F	G
3	0.18	0.63	1.36	1.92	0.26	0.83	3.50	0.61	0.48	2.37	1.71	1.41	0.76	1.44
4	1.26	1.10	0.06	3.01	0.32	0.54	1.97	0.24	0.47	1.36	0.71	6.26	0.66	2.23
5	0.76	0.45	1.15	1.00	0.55	1.10	0.78	0.47	0.75	1.20	0.48	1.11	0.76	1.00
6	0.34	0.19	0.18	1.13	0.12	0.37	0.00	0.03	1.57	1.50	0.12	1.19	0.42	0.82
7	0.39	0.40	0.75	1.73	0.68	0.57	1.17	0.53	0.75	2.02	0.64	1.31	0.64	1.22
9	0.41	0.41	0.56	2.67	0.71	0.60	0.33	0.99	0.86	1.36	0.33	2.73	0.53	1.59
10	2.83	0.62	0.17	3.95	0.77	0.77	3.32	0.27	0.22	7.76	0.66	4.86	1.14	3.12
11	0.74	0.89	0.32	2.42	1.86	0.51	1.04	0.53	0.42	2.70	0.35	3.56	0.74	1.84
12	0.95	1.04	0.25	1.79	0.72	0.59	2.31	0.27	0.23	2.22	0.41	1.78	0.66	1.50
13	0.75	0.57	0.68	0.77	0.89	1.01	0.31	0.86	1.02	0.82	0.61	0.27	0.74	0.80
14	0.96	1.14	3.78	0.31	1.07	0.47	1.59	1.20	3.07	0.37	3.93	0.27	1.95	0.55
16	0.84	0.68	1.48	1.10	0.50	0.86	1.01	0.48	0.99	0.64	0.61	0.75	0.92	0.97
17	1.42	0.92	1.93	1.63	5.71	0.72	0.71	0.77	1.73	0.66	1.41	0.39	2.03	1.06
20	1.25	0.83	2.51	0.58	0.80	0.84	2.48	0.89	0.65	0.74	1.20	0.22	1.44	0.75
25	3.85	0.50	2.66	0.69	1.67	1.72	1.80	0.62	4.05	0.21	2.83	0.37	3.78	0.94
26	1.24	0.41	0.34	0.09	0.29	3.74	0.00	0.97	3.73	5.92	0.43	2.02	1.20	2.14
28	1.59	1.26	2.40	0.83	1.14	0.66	1.05	0.85	2.90	0.53	4.50	0.38	1.97	0.83
29	0.95	0.05	1.65	1.51	1.21	0.74	3.69	5.77	3.32	0.33	5.54	0.61	1.80	1.10
31	0.73	3.23	0.35	0.32	0.35	1.54	0.70	0.68	2.01	0.30	2.43	0.21	0.84	1.09
33	1.97	0.16	0.45	0.07	2.49	1.65	0.54	1.72	0.39	0.12	0.12	0.10	1.26	0.60
34	1.25	0.67	0.19	0.06	0.94	1.00	1.08	0.76	0.36	0.13	0.54	0.04	0.84	0.45
36	1.23	0.14	0.23	0.03	0.97	0.58	1.31	0.78	0.53	0.55	0.18	0.08	0.98	0.36
37	1.07	1.17	2.26	0.02	0.51	1.27	0.35	0.51	0.64	0.44	0.29	0.03	1.15	0.63
38	1.34	0.78	0.86	0.11	1.53	1.62	0.58	0.56	1.02	0.20	0.52	0.06	1.17	0.70

39	1.13	1.15	0.99	0.19	0.54	1.30	0.24	0.38	0.86	0.48	0.47	0.27	0.83	0.72
40	1.19	0.53	0.11	0.04	0.73	1.32	0.31	0.07	0.25	0.07	0.75	0.01	0.73	0.44
41	1.24	0.46	0.15	0.04	0.49	0.63	0.61	0.37	0.60	0.17	0.18	0.10	0.72	0.30
42	0.07	10.40	0.47	0.31	0.15	0.79	0.08	2.91	0.72	0.07	0.36	0.17	0.26	2.00
43	0.46	5.69	2.53	0.18	0.65	0.75	0.80	2.03	5.33	0.06	3.47	0.08	1.67	1.22
47	2.38	4.43	1.93	0.33	0.70	1.02	1.07	3.02	2.39	0.05	1.62	0.15	1.78	1.20
49	0.37	0.32	2.22	1.06	1.15	0.68	0.53	2.00	0.88	0.80	1.62	0.94	0.95	0.90
50	0.80	0.30	2.04	0.77	0.80	0.60	0.42	0.64	0.56	1.04	0.75	1.15	0.87	0.75
52	1.01	0.64	0.04	0.06	0.15	1.76	0.07	0.09	0.32	0.65	0.15	0.18	0.45	0.68
53	1.25	1.46	1.19	0.24	0.83	1.51	0.86	0.67	0.40	0.61	0.70	0.23	1.21	0.85
56	0.46	0.30	0.82	2.04	0.14	1.38	0.13	0.67	0.46	0.52	0.14	0.40	0.45	1.21
Tot Tech 56	1.00	1.00	1.00	1.00	1.00	1.00	1.00	1.00	1.00	1.00	1.00	1.00	1.00	1.00
Standard Deviation	0.75	1.98	0.97	0.99	0.98	0.62	0.98	1.09	1.28	1.60	1.35	1.42	0.66	0.60

RTA indices is encountered (Cantwell, 1991). To overcome the potentially skewed distribution, a log transformation is taken:

$$\ln RTA_{fij} = \alpha + \beta \ln RTA_{dij} + \varepsilon_{ij} \tag{7.2}$$

where $i = 1, \ldots 6$ regions and $j = 1, \ldots 35$ technological sectors.

Results from this analysis were weak and it was impossible to reject the null hypothesis. This suggested the absence of a relationship between foreign patenting activity and that of indigenous firms.

By dividing the data into the two separate time periods – 1969–82 and 1983–95 – the second hypothesis is tested. This hypothesis rests on the assumption that the patenting activity of foreign firms in the second period (t) was dependent upon that of indigenous firms in the first time period $(t-1)$ (equation (7.3)).

$$RTA_{fjt} = \alpha + \beta RTA_{djt-1} + \varepsilon_{jt} \tag{7.3}$$

This was then extended to the six regions:

$$\ln RTA_{fijt} = \alpha + \beta \ln RTA_{dijt-1} + \varepsilon_{ijt} \tag{7.4}$$

Results obtained from these regressions were again statistically insignificant. All regression outputs coincide with the reported findings for Lombardia in the Italian case (Chapter 5) and the South East in the UK case (Chapter 6), suggesting that the six German regions are positioned at the top of the geographical hierarchy, i.e. they can be labelled *higher order* regions. These regions attract the research activities of foreign firms, which do not appear to be correlated to the extant activity of indigenous firms in equivalent technologies. As highlighted above, however, it is possible that a linear relationship exists in certain technological sectors.

In analysing the relationships between private and public research in Germany, Beise and Stahl (1999) suggested that co-location at a regional level was not such an important factor in the development of such linkages. It seems that 'within Germany, distance did not matter much for high technology firms. Apart from start-ups, it might be argued that German R&D performing companies lose their dependence on local research institutions' (Beise and Stahl, 1999, p. 411). Such results support prior work in this area – among others, Fromhold-Eisebith (1992); Beise and Spielkamp (1996); Grotz and Braun (1997). In addition, these results concur with results reported using US data. Mansfield (1995) and Mansfield and Lee (1996) demonstrate that firms located in the US are more reluctant to support research at a college or university 1,000 or more miles away than if it were less than 100 miles. Given that the greatest distance in Germany (from Nouth east to South West) is approximately 600 miles, and coupled with the very well established infrastructure, such results are perhaps unsurprising.

Whether, and to what extent, the same apparent irrelevance of regional borders is found when firms engage in inter-firm technological interaction has been little explored in the literature. To offer a preliminary investigation of such an important issue, we extend the regression analysis to analyse the potential for inter-regional technological communication between firms. We regress the second period (*t*) foreign technological specialisation in each region on two independent variables. These are (i) indigenous firm specialisation in region *i* in the first time period (*t* − 1) and (ii) foreign firm specialisation in region *i* in the first time period (*t* − 1):

$$\ln\text{RTA}_{fijt} = \alpha + \beta \ln\text{RTA}_{dijt-1} + \chi \ln\text{RTA}_{fijt-1} \tag{7.5}$$

Results from this exercise are reported for a 10 per cent significance level and can be seen in Figure 7.1.

In almost all cases, foreign firm research activity in the second period is determined by foreign research in the first period.[6] This result further supports the finding that profiles of corporate technological specialisation remains fairly stable over time (Cantwell, 1993; Patel and Pavitt, 1998).

From Figure 7.1 it is apparent that the activity of foreign-owned firms located in Germany between 1982–95 (i.e. F_t), is significantly related to indigenous counterparts in different regions over time. Whether, and to what

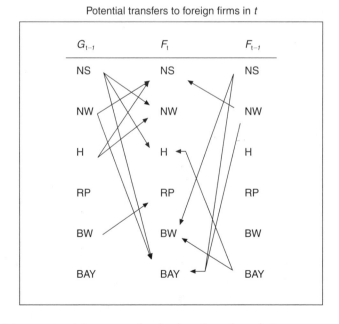

Figure 7.1 Inter-regional, intra-sectoral technology flows through time.

degree, such similarities are reinforced through inter-regional communication between the firms cannot be confirmed from this analysis. We tentatively suggest, however, that if intra-sectoral communication occurs between indigenous and foreign firms in Germany, then the highest incidence of such activity is likely to be observed amongst firms located across different regions.

While a plethora of potential interactions is evident from these results, a number of interesting observations can be made. Looking at the interaction that emanated from indigenous firms that are located in Nordrhein-Westfalen and Hessen, for example, we see that potential transfer occurs from these firms to foreign firms that are located in bordering Niedersachsen. Examining the changing technological advantage for these firms through time (i.e. RTA indices for t and $t-1$), it is clear that inter-firm interaction is likely to occur within the Chemical and pharmaceutical technologies (3, 7, 11, and 12). This suggests the importance of locating close to the bordering indigenous chemical/pharmaceutical cluster in Nordrhein-Westfalen. While location within the cluster itself may be too costly (due to, inter alia, congestion effects), the foreign firms' ability to access indigenous expertise and know-how (however difficult) appears as a potentially important element in their decision to base their chemical/pharmaceutical research in Germany. In addition, it is interesting to mention that potential inter-regional interaction within the foreign group of firms over time is far more varied than that recorded for the indigenous group. This again confirms the very strong regional focus detected above for indigenous firms and perhaps points to locational difficulties encountered by the relatively later established non-native companies.

Conclusions

This chapter sought to examine the location decisions of foreign-owned innovative activity in Germany and to classify the German regions within a locational hierarchy. This in turn enabled us to ascertain the potential for inter-firm interaction at the regional level across the 56 technologies. The degree to which the technological research activity of foreign and indigenous firms overlapped was investigated by examining their patenting activity over the 1969–95 period. The results demonstrated that activities located across the various regions differed greatly, with each group of firms driving regional advantage in different technological sectors. An OLS regression analysis was carried out to ascertain whether, and to what degree, foreign firm research was related to the existing knowledge base of domestic firms. Results from this exercise led to the classification of the six regions as being higher order research locations. This, in turn, suggests that limited intra-regional, inter-firm communication takes place in the same technological sector, and knowledge spillovers in higher order regions seem to operate mainly through exchanges in and around core technological systems. Relationships then form between actors in otherwise quite separate alternative fields of specialisation.

Such core systems appear to be rooted in the background engineering, mechanical methods and electronics technologies – sectors in which foreign-owned and indigenous firms' technological advantages appear to overlap in these higher order centres.

In acknowledging the highly developed research and transportation infrastructure in Germany, we revised our model to test for potential for technology interaction taking place in the same technological sector but across regions. Substantial inter-regional overlap was found between the technological specialisation of these two groups of firms, suggesting that foreign firms' location decisions may have been determined by the existing knowledge base of indigenous firms within certain technologies, albeit in different regions. The very mature infrastructure within this country may facilitate inter-regional interaction within certain technological fields.

8 Multinational corporations and the French regional systems of innovation

Introduction

As previously seen, it is widely accepted that the organisation of innovative activities can no longer be illustrated simply on the basis of concepts such as the dichotomy of market-hierarchies and the transaction costs mechanism being fundamental explanations of the internalisation/externalisation of capabilities, functions and assets. Indeed, it has been increasingly observed the emergence of the trend for MNCs to establish internal (intra-firm) and external (inter-firm) networks for innovation – network that are characterised by different levels of *territorial* and *social* embeddedness with reference to the location that hosts them. Furthermore, it has been shown that MNC affiliates abroad have assumed a predominant role in an increasing proportion of all the most advanced technologies. The interpretation given is twofold: on the one hand, the ceaseless relevance of local innovation processes as reservoirs of different technical expertise in the globalisation era, and, on the other, the outgrowth of an 'organisational capital' that allows the integration of several related technological competencies across geographically dispersed units (Zander, 1997).

This chapter presents an analysis of the location patterns of multinational firms' innovative activities in France. The chapter is divided into four sections. The following section briefly – compared with the three previous national case studies – presents the geographical distribution of innovative activities of large firms, both indigenous and foreign-owned, across the French regions in the period 1969–95. The third section documents the characteristics of the hierarchy of regional research centres in France, by testing the relationship between the profiles of local technological specialisation in foreign-owned and French firms. As we have suggested, differences in the regional capacity of attraction of high value added activities serve as a prerequisite to unveiling the potential technological communication (or technological spillovers) that may be in existence within these regions and, indeed, across EU national boundaries. Finally, the fourth section highlights the main peculiarities and the conclusions drawn from the case in question.

The location of MNC technological activities in the French regions

In the case of other major EU member states – namely the UK, Italy and Germany – our empirical results supported the thesis that the geographical distribution of technological innovation is highly concentrated within these economies. There are, however, significant cross-regional variations in the sectoral distribution of technological activity, which point to a very clear dichotomy, between *higher order* and *intermediate* research centres, in the nature of interaction between local and international corporate innovation exchanges. As illustrated in the third section of this chapter, such a dichotomy turns out to be less clear-cut in the case of the French regional cores, where the geographical concentration is confirmed, but the overall regional profiles of technological specialisation seem to be influenced more by the local expertise in particular leading technologies. Ultimately, this is a reflection of the highly centralised structure of the national innovation system and of the pervasive State involvement in technology creation.

While, in the case of an intermediate location, knowledge in specific technological fields is accessed and injected into the multinational network, affiliates located in higher order centres can enjoy a broader range of spillovers from the local environment.[1] However, while there is evidence that much of the technology developed abroad by large firms lies in their core areas of strength (Petel and Vego, 1999), MNC research in foreign locations is also increasingly associated with a higher probability of entry into new and more distantly related fields of technology. Such knowledge-seeking activity is undertaken to help define the future directions in the evolution of the corporations' sources of competitiveness (Pearce, 1999).

Drawing upon the previous results for Italy, the UK and Germany,[2] it is useful to summarise the main findings as follows.

- *Country differences*: in absolute terms, the UK was the main host in Europe of foreign-owned patenting activity in the first part of the last century, up to 1969; while, since the 1970s, Germany has been the most attractive location (albeit declining since the mid-1980s). Italy is further behind, although recording an increase in the proportion of foreign activity carried out in the country since the mid-1980s. In terms of penetration – i.e. the share of foreign patenting in total national patenting – while foreign-owned firms in the UK and Italy constitute a substantial and rising proportion of aggregate activity, the same share in Germany is approximately half that of the UK and Italy. Such observations generally support the presence of a ranking among European national innovation systems, reflecting their evolution over time and the different degree of openness of national knowledge bases.
- *Geographical concentration*: in the case of both the UK and Italy, a very strong concentration of the overall technological activity carried out by

large firms (both indigenous and foreign-owned) in the period 1969–95 is found in just a few regions; in the German case, in contrast, innovation is spread across a greater number of regions. Further differences are found when looking at the degree of geographical concentration of innovative activities by ownership. While both foreign-owned and indigenous firms concentrate their research in the same region in the UK (the South East) and Italy (Lombardia), the same does not hold for Germany, where Nordrhein-Westfalen hosts the highest concentration of indigenous activity, but only represents the second most popular location for foreign-owned research, after Baden Württemberg. This suggests that, although innovative activities show a strong tendency to cluster in space, the extent of such a tendency may vary significantly and is rather context-specific.

- *Regional hierarchies*: looking at the technological specialisation across the subnational economies, a very clear dichotomy between higher order and intermediate research locations does emerge. In the South East region of the UK, Lombardia in Italy and all six German regions, statistical support was found for the thesis that it is not because of the existing indigenous technological specialisation that these regions attract foreign-owned firms. Technological activity of foreign-owned and indigenous firms in these regions is typically broad ranging in nature and extends across a spectrum of technologies. Indeed, knowledge spillovers in higher order regions seem to operate mainly through exchanges in and around core technological systems. Relationships then form between actors in otherwise quite separate alternative fields of specialisation. Such core systems appear to be rooted in the 'general purpose' technologies (GPTs) such as background engineering, mechanical methods and electronics technologies – sectors in which foreign-owned and indigenous firms' technological advantages appear to overlap in these higher order centres. On the contrary, results for the other Italian and British regions suggest the presence of intermediate research locations. Technological specialisation profiles of foreign-owned firms were found to be closely correlated with those of indigenous technological expertise so that knowledge spillovers are likely to be intra-sectoral in nature. This is consistent with the hypothesis that intermediate regions attract the innovative activities of foreign-owned MNCs because of a very particular set of sectorally-specific expertise on offer in these regions. By basing research facilities in such locations, foreign-owned MNCs may be able to upgrade their own technological capabilities in particular technological fields, which may be subsets of their own major areas of technological interest (Cantwell *et al.*, 2000).

As in the previous case-studies, the geographical unit of analysis used to explore the French case is based upon the comparable NUTS level (NUTS1).[3]

Figures 8.1 and 8.2 provide some selected indicators by region – relative to the end of the period to which our database on US patents refers – in order

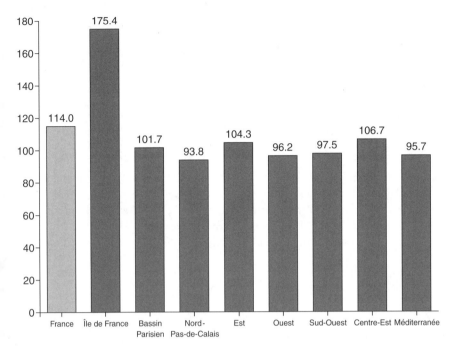

Figure 8.1 French regions, GDP per inhabitant, 1996 (EU15 = 100).

Source: Eurostat (1999).

to give a picture of the relative size of the French regions. At a first glance, Île de France appears to be the only region well above the national average for almost all indicators; as highlighted in Chapter 3, its economic relevance is also leading when compared with the EU average – the index of GDP per capita in 1996 being much higher than the base (EU15 = 100, EU15 refers to the 15 EU countries). More generally, the most economically advanced areas are certainly those around the capital region, the centre and the centre-east of the country, which show a GDP higher than the EU average (Figure 8.1).

Looking at innovation in general terms, according to the National Innovation Survey, the most innovative areas are identifiable within the southern and eastern belt of Île de France (within the Bassin Parisien region) – where the greatest concentration of innovative firms was found by the Survey – while the north west and the south of the country appear to be lagging behind. Such a difference in the geographical spread of innovative activities is mainly attributed to the regional industrial structure – i.e. the industrial sectors most represented in the eastern part of France are those in which SMEs show a relatively stronger propensity to innovate – and to the effects of local policies for research and technological development (Ministère de l'Industrie, 1994).

As shown in Figure 8.2, even accounting for demographic and economic size, both in terms of R&D expenditure (as a percentage of GDP) and of R&D personnel (as a percentage of active population), Île de France drives up the national figure: 3.3 per cent against 2.4 per cent in the case of the former indicator, and 2.3 per cent against a national average of 1.5 per cent with respect to the latter.[4] It should be noted that, in absolute terms, the highest R&D expenditure among all EU regions (at the comparable geographical level) is indeed that of Île de France: more than €11,400 million in 1995 (the same figure, for example, for the South East of the UK was approximately €6,000). Moreover, the French capital region is at the top of the ranking of EU regions that are both wealthy (per capita GDP above the EU average) and innovative (R&D as a share of GDP above the EU average) (Eurostat, 2000).

The EU indicator for technological output suggests an even greater geographical polarisation of innovation. In 1996, the number of patent applications submitted to the European Patent Office (EPO) – always expressed relative to the regional demographic weight – was 210 for Île de France, fol-

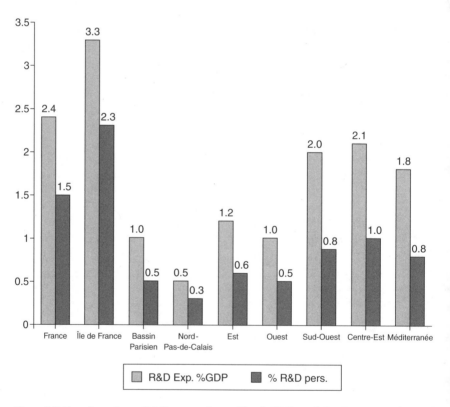

Figure 8.2 French regions, R&D expenditure (% of GDP) and R&D personnel (% of active population), 1995.

Source: Eurostat (1999).

Regions	Concentration		Diversification	
	Consolidating the leading fields of specialisation	*Falling further behind the leading fields of specialisation*	*Slipping back from the leading fields of specialisation*	*Catching up with the leading fields of specialisation*
South East UK	1, 3, 7, 25, 30	2, 5, 8, 10, 11, 16, 17, 21, 24, 26, 27, 29	*6, 15, 18, 19, 20, 22, 23, 28, 32*	*4, 9, 12*, 13, 14, *31, 33*
Lombardia	7, 14	5, 12, 15, 17, 24, 25, 26, 33	2, 3, 6, 10, *16*, 23, 27, 28, 30	1, 4, 8, *9, 11*, 13, *18, 19, 20, 21, 22, 29, 31, 32*
Baden Württemberg	15, 26, 27	2, 13, 21, 22, 25	16, 18, 24, *31, 32*	*1, 3, 4, 5, 6, 7, 8, 9, 10, 11, 12, 14, 17, 19, 20, 23, 28, 29, 30, 33*
Île de France	2, 5, 7, 9, 15, 16, 25	3, 6, 8, 11, 12, 17, 21, 22, 28, 29, 31	*18, 19, 20,* 23, 24, 26, 27, 32	1, 4, 10, *13, 14, 30, 33*
Flanders–Brussels	2, 6, *10*, 28	8, 13, 15, 16, 22, 24, 25, 26, 27, 32, 33	1, 4, 11, 12, 17, 18, 29, 30, *31*	3, 5, 7, 9, 14, 19, 20, 21, 23
Zuid Nederland	18, 20, 32	2, 3, 15, 31	4, 8, 16, *19, 21*, 22, 23, 29	1, *5, 6, 7, 9, 10, 11, 12, 13, 14,* 17, *24, 25, 26, 27, 28, 30, 33*
Stockholm–Östra Mellansverige	8, 11, 15, 17, 18, 33	1, 2, 3, 6, 13, *14, 19,* 22, 23, 30, 31	7, 10, 21, 25, 32	4, 5, 9, *12,* 16, *20,* 24, 26, 27, 28, 29
Basel region	3, 5	1, 2, 4, 8, 9, 10, 11, 12, 13, 14, 15, 17, 18, 19, 20, 21, 22, 23, 24, 25, 26, 27, 28, 29, 30, 31, 32, 33	6, 7	*16*

Legend: (Italics denote sectors that have moved around 1)

Mobility effect: based on the regression residuals (RES_{ij})
Stability: $-0.1 < RES_{ij} < +0.1$
 Stable specialisation ranking: $RTA_{ij} > 1$ in either period
 Stable despecialisation ranking: $RTA_{ij} < 1$ in either period

Change: $RES_{ij} < -0.1$ or $RES_{ij} > +0.1$
 Gain of ranking: $RES_{ij} > 0$
 Loss of ranking: $RES_{ij} < 0$

Regression effect: based on $(RTA_{ij} - RTA_{ijt-2}) - (M_{it} - M_{it-2}) = X$
Concentration:
 consolidating: $X > 0$ and $RTA_{ijt-2} > M_{it-2}$
 falling further behind: $X < 0$ And $RTA_{ijt-2} < M_{it-2}$
Diversification:
 slipping back: $X < 0$ And $RTA_{ijt-2} > M_{it-2}$
 catching up: $X > 0$ And $RTA_{ijt-2} < M_{it-2}$

ANOVA results, which have shown that, having allowed for cross-sectoral variance, cross-regional variation does matter, supporting our third proposition of the distinctiveness of regional technological patterns and development. However, from Table 9.5, although in many cases a negative co-specialisation seems to have occurred within Europe over time (with the regional cores becoming increasingly different to one another), some positive co-specialisation trends can be observed over the three periods analysed. Indeed, a positive correlation holds for Lombardia and the South East UK, in which the strengthening of specialisation profiles has implied a greater closeness between the first and the second period, which has been reinforced between 1978–86 and 1987–95. Lombardia is actually the higher order region that shows the highest co-specialisation pattern; between the three periods, the co-specialisation with Flanders-Brussels has also substantially increased, while in the most recent years an association with Zuid Nederland's profile has emerged. This might imply a relatively higher risk for the Italian region to be beaten in the competitive bidding across EU regions, taking into account the relative weakness in diversifying its technological competence towards the fastest growing areas. Finally, Île de France shows a strong co-specialisation with the Swiss region at the beginning and at the end of the years considered – which, however, seems to weaken between 1978 and 1986 – while the significant difference between its sectoral profile and that of Flanders-Brussels has been attenuated over time (the latter region showing a certain degree of co-specialisation with Basel in the final years).

MNC technological strategies: EU versus non-EU MNCs

The analysis of the pattern of technological specialisation of foreign-owned affiliates based in each higher order region – distinguished by nationality of parent companies, namely EU-owned and non-EU-owned MNCs – is an essential piece of information in order to reach a more precise description of the overall profile of regional innovation systems. As pointed out in Chapter 2, a crucial element in the model of local accumulation of knowledge involves the attraction of outside resources, which may set off cumulative processes. Furthermore, it has been shown that foreign research is associated with a significantly higher probability of entry into new and more distantly related technological areas, creating a long-term drift into new and spillover-generating technological competencies (Zander, 1999b).

It is necessary to bear in mind that our present analysis refers to the regions at the top of the geographical hierarchy and that all of these regions have a relatively broad spectrum of innovative activities, being therefore treated by MNCs as sources of general expertise and skills in the European area. However, as also confirmed by the results shown in the previous section, if a top centre offers entrenched points of technological advantage, showing simultaneously an institutional environment relatively less sensitive to new

Table 9.5 Regional bi-lateral technological specialisation index (correlation coefficients), 1969–77, 1978–86, 1987–95

	Lombardia	Baden Württemberg	Île de France	Flanders-Brussels	Zuid Nederland	Stockholm-Östra Mellan.	Basel region
Period 1969–77							
South East UK	0.081	−0.127	0.150	−0.086	0.137	−0.107	0.026
Lombardia	–	0.053	0.024	0.052	−0.137	−0.211	0.196
Baden Württemberg	–	–	0.288	−0.223	−0.102	−0.058	−0.147
Île de France	–	–	–	−0.349**	−0.002	−0.110	0.461***
Flanders-Brussels	–	–	–	–	−0.053	−0.072	−0.083
Zuid Nederland	–	–	–	–	–	−0.071	−0.186
Stockholm-Östra Mellan.	–	–	–	–	–	–	−0.175
Period 1978–86							
South East UK	0.411**	−0.034	0.247	0.194	−0.042	−0.109	0.138
Lombardia	–	−0.009	−0.106	0.390**	−0.103	−0.068	0.182
Baden Württemberg	–	–	0.038	−0.232	0.190	0.034	0.034
Île de France	–	–	–	−0.318*	0.151	0.062	0.230
Flanders-Brussels	–	–	–	–	−0.049	−0.218	−0.136
Zuid Nederland	–	–	–	–	–	−0.201	−0.219
Stockholm-Östra Mellan.	–	–	–	–	–	–	−0.221
Period 1987–95							
South East UK	0.445***	−0.097	0.009	0.267	−0.143	−0.172	0.236
Lombardia	–	−0.163	−0.084	0.463***	0.347**	−0.189	0.013
Baden Württemberg	–	–	–	−0.245	−0.191	0.065	0.118
Île de France	–	–	–	0.166	−0.218	−0.059	0.597***
Flanders-Brussels	–	–	–	–	−0.060	−0.207	0.350**
Zuid Nederland	–	–	–	–	–	−0.011	−0.204
Stockholm-Östra Mellan.	–	–	–	–	–	–	−0.177

Notes
No. of observations: 33
two-tailed significance: ***significant at 1% level; ** significant at 5% level; *significant at 10% level.

technological opportunities, it is likely to attract MNCs that want to upgrade their expertise by specialising according to the local strengths, the result being that corporate technological activity is broadened, while the technological specialisation of regions tends to become narrower (Cantwell, 1992b). On the other hand, when foreign research has a more pronounced exploratory nature, particularly towards emerging technological fields, it is likely to be attracted by those higher order centres showing a greater flexibility and able to switch to new related technological competencies.

Although these considerations would need to be supported by wider empirical evidence (based on a larger set of indicators), they seem to be in line with the prediction of the general theory of clusters, which – besides the usual congestion effects – identifies a higher degree of flexibility of economic activities, and therefore of competitiveness renewal, in those clusters that are at an intermediate stage of maturity and which are affected by changes in the forces of geographical agglomeration.

On the other hand, as stated above, the formation of an economically integrated space has been conceptualised as an exogenous shock affecting both the geography of economic activities in general and the *modus operandi* of MNCs, therefore bringing about changes in how and where they develop their operations both intra- and inter-bloc (Tavares and Pearce, 1999). Hence, it is plausible to conjecture a different behaviour, in carrying out research strategies, between EU-owned firms and non-EU-owned affiliates, the latter being clearly affected by the integration process to a different extent, not only in terms of market orientation, export propensity, intra-firm trade flows and overall perception of market space, but also in the plurality of motivations for internationalisation of both production and innovation – i.e. resource-seeking, market-seeking, efficiency-seeking and strategic asset-seeking networks (Dunning, 1993).

A first representation of the pattern of technological specialisation of foreign-owned firms in higher-order regional locations in Europe is provided in Figure 9.1, which shows, for each European higher order region, the shares of patents by the home country of large firms (nationally-owned and foreign owned, the latter distinguished between EU and non-EU). The first general observation is that the degree of internationalisation of technology creation is very different among the locations considered. The highest contribution of foreign research to the regional system of innovation for the whole period 1969–95 is recorded by Flanders-Brussels, where 87 per cent of patents granted to large firms for research located there is foreign-owned. Here, we find an outstanding percentage of EU-owned research, 52 per cent of the total, which is likely to be due, at least to a certain extent, to the relatively 'new' institutional environment of the country as a whole, which hosts EU organisations as well as the most relevant representative offices of the business world. Conversely, the least internationalised region is Basel, in which only 4 per cent of overall local research is attributable to foreign subsidiaries: it should be noticed that this is the only regional core in our sample whose home country is not a member of the EU,

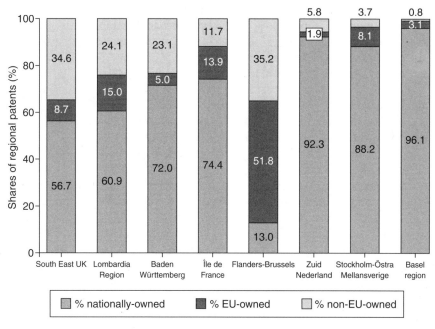

Figure 9.2 Shares of regional patents by the home country of large firms, 1969–95.

although the same can be said for the Stockholm-Östra Mellansverige region – which only joined the EU in 1995, the last year of the period considered in the present analysis. Nonetheless, it is true that the Swiss attitude towards the process of economic integration has always been somehow different from that of the other partners of the European Economic Area (of which Sweden, Finland and Austria joined the Union in 1995), although the largest Swiss firms have had close historical ties with their major German counterparts.

The regions belonging to 'large countries' – namely the South East UK, Lombardia, Île de France and Baden Württemberg – are all rather inter-nationalised, the foreign share of total regional research accounting for between 43 per cent in the UK region and 26 per cent in the French region. Among them, the highest percentage of EU-owned firms is recorded in Lombardia (15 per cent of total regional research), closely followed by Île de France (14 per cent), while the other two locations are relatively more attractive for non-EU MNCs. The foreign contribution to innovation in both the Stockholm-Östra Mellansverige region and Zuid Nederland displays rather low values, the shares being 12 per cent and 8 per cent respectively; in the case of Stockholm-Östra Mellansverige has the bulk of this percentage which originated in other EU-owned foreign firms.

In general terms, it turns out that non-EU foreign companies seem to have been relatively more highly represented in the EU higher-order regional cores, despite these companies' lower propensity to internationalise their innovative capacity with respect to their European counterparts (Cantwell, 1995).[10] As shown by other studies on FDI, the US and Asian MNCs are relatively more 'Europeanised' and their asset-seeking strategy is likely to have followed a pan-European approach, thus leading to a strong geographical concentration in technological centres of excellence (which may have also been a reflex to the fear of the 'EU fortress').

Turning to the sectoral picture, Table 9.6 – showing the regional RTA index for nationally-owned firms, foreign EU-owned firms and foreign non-EU-owned firms, relative to the world as a whole – reveals a different orientation between EU and non-EU foreign research.

Looking at the regional cores that have strengthened their traditional technological advantages over time, overall, the highest shares of EU-owned foreign research are definitely found in the (interrelated) broad group of electrical equipment (sectors from 18 to 22), and particularly in the 'general purpose' high-opportunity IT group (i.e. sectors 18, 19, 22 and 23). Moreover, with the only exception of Basel, EU-owned research records a greater sectoral concentration of innovative activity relative to the other categories of firms, as can be seen from the coefficient of variation reported in Table 9.6. On the other hand, non-EU firms seem to be relatively more sensitive to the distinctiveness of regional environments across Europe, rather than to opportunities offered by specific sectors. This also emerges from the correlation between the profile of technological specialisation of non-EU-owned subsidiaries, which is more closely related to the equivalent pattern of specialisation of indigenous firms than is the profile of technological specialisation of EU-owned subsidiaries in four out of five regions (and particularly in the Basel region) – Stockholm-Östra Mellansverige being the only higher order location in this group where the correlation of indigenous firms with the non-EU-owned technological profile is lower than that with EU-owned firms.

Looking at the pattern of technological specialisation, the South East UK and Lombardia show some similarities, which seems to confirm the increasing degree of co-specialisation of the two regions, as previously pointed out. First of all, in both regions, which have reinforced their sectoral specialisation over time, the increasingly strong advantage in Pharmaceuticals (7) is due to the strength of all firms in that sector, independent of nationality – although in terms of shares of the regional totals, the non-EU-owned contribution is, in both cases, much higher than that of foreign EU MNCs. The latter, instead, are highly specialised in another consolidating point of strength of the South East UK, namely Agricultural chemicals (3), which does not seem to attract non-EU research efforts. The consolidating advantage of Lombardia in Specialised industrial equipment (14) is also sustained by local and non-EU-owned firms, which contribute, to the same extent, to the regional patenting in the sector, in which the share of the EU-owned MNCs is negligible. The South East's comparative advantage – reducing over time – in Telecommunications (18) and Other instruments (32) is a point of strength for all firms located in the region, while the remarkable value of the RTA for EU-owned research in IT sectors such as Image and sound equipment (19) and Semiconductors (22) – in which, moreover, the region has lost its specialisation through time – is not detected in the other cases. Again, EU-owned subsidiaries located in Lombardia have rather high values of RTA in some IT sectors (20 and 22) – where the Italian region has in fact registered a gain over time – in which the EU shares of the regional total research are also among the highest.

Similar to the two previous regions, Île de France records a higher concentration of technological activities carried out by foreign EU-owned firms relative to the others, and a high correspondence between the technological profile of nationally-owned and non-EU MNCs. The latter, in fact, display both a very strong advantage and relatively high shares of total regional research in those fields where the region as a whole has experienced the strongest consolidation of technological competence, i.e. Bleaching and dyeing processes (5), General industrial equipment (15) – the latter being a 'general purpose' technological field that is likely to give rise to significant spillovers between local and foreign research – and Power plants (16). The traditional strength in Telecommunications (18), which has, however, suffered a loss of ranking over time, seems to be supported by the innovative efforts of all large firms.

As said above, the Swedish region is the only one in this group of higher order centres whose technological profile is more closely related to that of EU-owned subsidiaries. Some sectors in particular show the coincidence between local research and foreign innovation capacity (both EU and non-EU); i.e. Telecommunications (18), Other instruments (32) – the only sector receiving a substantial contribution (29 per cent) to the regional total by EU-owned subsidiaries – and Other manufacturing and non-industrial (33). In other sectors where technological specialisation has been concentrating over time, the comparative advantage is instead registered by indigenous and non-EU affiliates: this is the case of Metallurgical processes (8) and, particularly, General industrial equipment (15). The outstanding reinforcement of technological competence in Nuclear reactors (17) is exclusively supported by nationally-owned firms, which contribute 100 per cent to the sectoral patenting activity.

The last higher order regional core that has strengthened its technological competence in the last three decades is the Basel region, where the creation of new technology is almost entirely attributable to nationally-owned firms, whose profile is the one that is matched to the greatest extent by non-EU MNCs. Not surprisingly, the variance of RTAs for all company groups is the highest: technological advantages are strongly and increasingly concentrated in Bleaching and dyeing processes (5) for both nationally-owned and foreign-owned firms, while only non-EU-owned subsidiaries have an advantage, which corresponds to the advantage of Swiss firms in Agricultural chemicals (3) and Other organic chemicals (6). It should be noted that the foreign

Table 9.6 RTA index for eight European regions (nationally-owned firms, EU-owned firms and non-EU-owned firms) relative to the world by technological category, 1969-95

Sectors	Regions											
	South East UK			Lombardia			Baden Württember			Île de France		
	UK-owned firms	EU-owned firms	non-EU-owned firms	Italian-owned firms	EU-owned firms	non-EU-owned firms	German-owned firms	EU-owned firms	non-EU-owned firms	French-owned firms	EU-owned firms	non-E owned firms
1	2.742	0.086	0.749	0.000	0.000	0.412	0.257	1.004	0.709	0.181	0.162	0.640
2	0.648	0.876	0.354	1.371	0.348	0.000	0.592	0.339	0.146	1.723	0.128	0.252
3	3.076	2.322	0.458	1.553	0.000	0.000	1.030	0.205	1.496	0.202	1.237	0.091
4	0.645	0.581	1.260	0.928	0.250	0.971	0.341	0.581	0.543	0.639	0.296	0.712
5	0.377	0.309	0.270	0.981	0.399	0.000	0.606	0.259	3.114	4.766	0.586	1.039
6	1.070	0.553	0.971	2.396	0.922	1.519	0.647	0.459	0.640	0.565	1.482	0.228
7	3.480	1.941	3.868	2.990	3.634	2.698	0.969	0.190	1.118	1.588	4.174	0.568
8	0.751	0.687	0.615	0.218	0.444	0.322	0.536	0.576	0.794	0.883	0.272	0.749
9	0.678	0.404	1.455	0.634	0.487	1.038	1.070	0.858	0.990	1.273	1.654	0.745
10	0.941	0.581	0.561	1.046	0.626	1.140	0.610	1.109	1.197	0.787	0.327	0.579
11	0.617	1.047	0.577	1.193	1.026	1.274	0.863	1.996	1.313	1.042	1.051	0.513
12	0.541	0.463	0.751	0.490	0.398	0.866	0.779	0.775	1.360	0.436	0.098	1.008
13	0.184	0.000	0.564	0.000	0.000	0.121	0.122	0.000	0.027	1.277	0.000	2.082
14	0.795	0.270	0.955	1.442	0.580	3.714	0.942	2.786	1.642	0.831	0.412	0.588
15	1.279	0.707	0.622	0.412	0.266	0.402	3.056	0.938	0.966	1.590	0.503	3.614
16	0.832	0.234	0.195	0.743	0.201	0.375	3.023	0.131	0.870	2.303	0.099	2.039
17	0.098	0.000	0.161	0.273	0.000	0.000	0.149	1.078	5.172	0.177	1.492	0.321
18	1.283	2.715	1.365	0.192	0.861	0.637	0.334	2.128	1.640	1.846	2.441	2.409
19	0.575	1.930	1.041	0.117	0.396	0.197	0.134	2.464	0.981	0.830	1.667	0.275
20	1.070	2.183	0.902	0.524	2.681	1.105	0.800	1.544	1.247	1.275	0.853	0.899
21	0.575	1.282	0.505	0.326	1.909	1.210	1.080	0.960	1.173	0.942	0.658	0.507
22	0.343	4.111	0.606	0.067	4.900	0.564	0.495	0.236	1.404	0.724	1.067	0.709
23	0.468	0.639	0.843	0.199	1.881	1.205	0.523	2.047	1.097	0.810	0.581	2.178
24	1.017	0.490	0.580	1.246	0.084	0.262	8.438	0.110	0.200	1.213	0.786	0.342
25	3.626	0.240	0.000	0.153	0.000	0.000	0.055	0.000	1.124	2.969	0.759	0.179
26	0.514	0.000	0.604	0.512	0.000	0.352	2.815	0.368	2.214	1.354	0.324	0.602
27	0.435	0.634	1.742	1.007	0.000	0.508	2.158	0.000	1.027	1.082	0.200	0.237
28	1.185	0.356	0.326	4.636	0.153	0.381	0.301	0.994	0.235	0.657	0.263	0.177
29	0.689	0.409	0.516	0.506	0.056	0.725	0.278	0.721	0.534	0.641	0.368	1.094
30	1.230	0.094	0.648	1.408	0.244	0.076	0.098	0.079	0.000	1.250	0.060	0.106
31	0.041	0.039	1.272	0.024	0.100	0.062	0.596	0.065	1.221	0.104	0.146	0.086
32	1.123	1.170	1.037	0.601	0.331	0.399	1.366	1.208	1.275	1.108	1.272	1.635
33	0.950	0.844	1.054	1.402	0.168	0.104	0.262	0.870	0.327	1.315	0.903	0.582
CV	0.878	1.083	0.809	1.075	1.578	1.162	1.447	0.923	0.838	0.764	1.056	0.957

contribution to the whole group of chemicals and pharmaceuticals – in which the region has strengthened its specialisation over time – is negligible. EU-owned firms show – as already pointed out as a general tendency – high comparative advantages in some sectors of mechanical engineering and electrical equipment, where the region as a whole is relatively despecialised, which contributes – in particular – to the strong gain registered in Power plants (16).

Regions

	Flanders-Brussels			Zuid Nederland			Stockholm-Östra Mellansverige			Basel Region		
	Belgian-owned firms	EU-owned firms	non-EU-owned firms	Dutch-owned firms	EU-owned firms	non-EU-owned firms	Swedish-owned firms	EU-owned firms	non-EU-owned firms	Swiss-owned firms	EU-owned firms	non-EU-owned firms
.000	0.289	1.278	0.071	1.719	1.128	0.861	0.691	0.763	0.102	0.457	0.000
.802	0.739	1.007	0.585	0.000	0.000	0.100	0.000	0.000	0.196	1.080	0.000
.411	0.000	1.065	0.151	0.000	0.000	0.046	0.000	0.000	8.143	0.000	12.361
.682	5.221	1.426	0.728	0.648	0.505	0.358	0.130	0.648	0.656	0.431	2.121
.519	0.261	0.769	0.032	0.000	0.000	0.058	0.000	0.000	13.772	4.123	3.124
.148	0.768	1.577	0.502	0.779	1.124	0.225	0.021	0.277	3.818	0.138	1.255
.435	0.368	4.588	0.424	0.325	0.053	0.861	0.196	0.577	3.889	0.259	0.654
.348	0.338	0.570	0.781	0.575	1.320	1.898	0.577	1.022	0.313	1.987	0.000
.091	0.546	1.274	0.440	0.541	0.888	1.094	2.392	2.404	0.189	0.000	2.180
.575	1.390	0.944	0.293	1.459	0.638	1.528	0.195	1.440	0.416	0.603	1.959
.457	0.396	0.719	0.492	18.127	5.945	3.322	1.311	0.644	0.284	1.349	0.730
.518	1.106	1.151	0.470	0.774	1.904	1.278	1.244	1.719	0.099	0.823	0.780
.000	0.064	0.000	0.031	0.000	0.000	0.897	0.000	0.000	0.000	0.000	0.000
.831	0.284	2.461	0.603	0.903	4.293	1.230	0.363	1.804	0.257	0.480	1.363
.050	0.211	0.183	0.310	1.924	0.534	1.718	0.416	3.023	0.282	3.068	0.000
.000	0.000	0.097	0.805	0.782	0.000	1.422	0.314	1.390	0.785	9.983	0.000
.000	0.181	1.067	0.133	0.000	2.119	9.107	0.000	0.000	0.220	2.290	0.000
.000	1.018	1.047	1.439	0.319	0.784	1.650	1.793	2.832	0.108	0.848	0.000
.000	0.569	0.114	3.429	0.308	0.000	0.388	0.247	0.000	0.016	0.327	2.478
.000	0.606	0.567	3.342	0.000	3.387	1.138	0.822	0.433	0.338	2.538	1.374
.167	0.496	0.300	1.106	0.303	0.248	1.658	1.460	0.404	0.283	1.772	0.915
.000	0.178	0.394	2.104	0.000	0.231	0.393	0.142	0.000	0.228	3.001	0.711
.000	0.492	0.223	1.940	0.225	0.332	0.472	0.723	1.999	0.040	0.239	0.907
.000	0.000	0.041	0.068	1.969	0.000	0.584	0.264	0.000	0.056	0.000	0.000
.000	0.000	0.000	0.050	0.000	0.000	2.415	4.843	0.000	0.000	0.000	0.000
.000	0.000	0.455	0.106	0.000	0.000	1.200	0.295	0.653	0.025	0.000	0.000
.000	0.267	2.760	0.065	9.545	0.000	0.472	1.278	0.000	0.000	6.765	0.000
.995	1.101	0.664	0.760	1.191	0.195	0.420	0.000	0.000	0.193	0.633	1.200
.941	0.690	1.125	0.791	1.513	0.850	0.473	0.087	0.768	0.228	0.345	0.435
.538	0.040	0.646	0.078	0.000	0.000	0.070	0.000	0.000	0.032	0.000	0.000
.000	1.789	0.048	0.207	0.000	0.508	0.029	0.155	0.000	0.007	0.206	0.000
.162	0.669	0.309	1.183	0.563	0.475	1.227	5.624	1.358	0.224	1.240	0.324
.873	0.383	0.727	0.201	0.652	0.214	5.488	2.618	2.315	0.288	0.000	0.000
.690	1.500	1.036	1.202	2.516	1.609	1.323	1.556	1.153	2.598	1.567	2.088

Turning to the three regions that have most diversified their technological specialisation over the 27 years considered, all of these regions show the lowest (and, in the case of Baden Württemberg, even negative) correlation between the indigenous profile and that of all foreign subsidiaries, independent of the nationality of parent companies.

In the German region, the catching up tendency registered in some chemicals and pharmaceuticals – such as Agricultural chemicals (3) and Bleaching and dyeing processes (5), where the region has gained a comparative advantage in the period 1978–86 – was sustained mostly by non-EU-owned firms, which represent a relevant share of total regional patents (in the case of sector (5) almost 62 per cent). In other mechanicals (10–12 and 14), it turns out that diversification was carried out mainly by foreign MNCs: both EU-owned and non-EU-owned have indeed an RTA above one (while indigenous firms are relatively despecialised), although only the latter category of large firms also records remarkable shares of total regional research. In line with the general tendency observed for the 'concentrating' group of regions, EU-owned innovation has the highest shares in IT sectors – namely Telecommunications (18), Image and sound equipment (19) and Office equipment (23), in which all foreign MNCs show technological advantages and relatively high contributions to regional patenting. Moreover, contrary to what is generally observed in the 'concentrating' regions, the strongest and consolidating advantages in General industrial equipment (15), Other transport equipment (26) and Textiles and wood products (27) are mainly due to nationally owned firms, whose shares are between 80–90 per cent of the regional patents in those sectors.

In the case of Flanders-Brussels, the outstandingly high proportion of EU-owned firms in local innovative activity lies beneath the positive (although rather weak) correlation between the specialisation profile of these MNCs and that of Belgian-owned firms. The region, which, as in the case of Baden Württemberg, records a high sectoral variance for indigenous firms, is catching up in some chemicals and pharmaceuticals sectors (namely, Agricultural chemicals and Pharmaceuticals), thanks to the efforts of non-EU-owned firms, which are actually responsible for almost all research carried out in such sectors (87 per cent of total patents in both cases). In Other metal products (9), non-EU firms own a share above 60 per cent and are the only category showing a RTA greater than one. However, while the noticeable and persistent advantage in Inorganic chemicals (2) and Other organic chemicals (6) is mainly attributable to indigenous and non-EU firms, it is the strength and the large presence of EU-owned subsidiaries located in the region that sustains the remarkable specialisation in Chemical processes (4) and the lessening of technological disadvantages in some ICT sectors.

Finally, for Zuid Nederland the highest variance is found in the sectoral distributions of the RTA index of EU-owned subsidiaries. The strong comparative technological advantage of Zuid Nederland in sectors belonging to the IT group – some of which have experienced a strengthening, while others have slightly slipped back over time – is, as also in the case of Other instruments (32), strictly national, as is confirmed by the very high Dutch-owned shares of regional patents (nearly 100 per cent for all sectors from 18 to 23). Conversely, EU-owned subsidiaries have substantially encouraged the emergence of specialisation in other catching up technological fields, such as Motor vehicles (24) and Textiles and wood products (27), where in fact they contribute substantially to the regional generation of new technology (37.5

per cent and 75 per cent in each sector respectively). However, diversification into other mechanicals is largely attributable to foreign-owned research, with a relatively higher contribution of non-EU subsidiaries (with the exception of Metal working equipment (11), where the foreign patenting activity carried out in the region is shared equally among EU-owned (30 per cent) and non-EU-owned (30 per cent) MNCs).

To summarise, in those regions that have experienced a reinforcement of their technological profiles over time, a greater contribution to this pattern of strengthening is due to non-EU firms, which are more prone than their EU-owned counterparts to tap into local fields of innovative expertise, hence they are relatively more oriented towards asset-seeking, local-competence-acquiring strategies. MNCs from other EU partner countries seem, instead, to have a relatively higher propensity to expand their own lines of technological specialisation, assuming a more sectorally-oriented perspective in the process of rationalisation of their innovative operations within the integrated area.

Conclusions

Increasing technological interrelatedness has been found to be a significant explanation for corporate technological diversification in the recent period. On the other hand, some analyses have shown that countries have tended to follow a reverse trend, becoming more technologically concentrated as part of the locational specialisation associated with the process of globalisation and internationalisation of technological activity (Cantwell, 1989b).

Following the evolutionary tradition and assuming that the creation of innovation follows local specificities, it has been shown that regional profiles of specialisation are rooted in local environments and that the sectoral patterns of MNC technological activity gradually changes as new industries develop and new technological linkages are forged between sectors. However, at a more detailed geographical level of analysis, such as that represented by the regions, specialisation tends to move along a cumulative path in which the creation of new technological competencies depends on the pattern of advantages previously established. In other words, the broadening of specialisation is one of the possible forms of incremental change in the composition of regional innovation, while in other cases regional profiles may be reinforced and concentrated in their established areas of technological expertise.

Multinational firms may fit into the profiles of specialisation of regional innovation systems, thus supporting the process of local technological concentration. In contrast, depending upon the initial pattern of regional specialisation, MNCs may spur the diversification of the regional profile towards areas of interrelated technological competence. As an example, the recent information technology revolution has caused a great increase in research in some closely related electrical/electronic technologies (Santangelo, 2002a, 2002b): such interrelatedness might therefore have pushed the broadening of technological specialisation in those regional cores that show greater expertise in information and communications technology (because of more complementary activities and higher potential spillover effects).

Our empirical findings show that, in the European area, which has been influenced by a process of strong economic restructuring as a consequence of integration processes, two different paths may be observed over the last few decades.

- Higher order regions, especially those characterised by more mature clusters of activity, which have become more narrowly specialised in their technological activities, might experience a slower process of convergence between old and new technologies because of a 'lock-in' trend due to both the initial pattern of specialisation and the institutional environment.
- Higher order regions – especially those in which geographical agglomeration of general economic activity has been strongly affected by EU integration, being now closer to the EU institutional core – which have broadened their specialisation, might experience a faster process of convergence between old and new technologies, reaching a potentially greater competitiveness.

Furthermore, the above tendencies seem to be reinforced by differences between EU-owned and non-EU-owned MNCs in the strategic approaches to developing, upgrading and diversifying technological competencies, non-EU-owned affiliates being affected differently by the integration process and showing a more pan-European perspective than MNCs from the EU partner states. This might be because non-EU-owned firms are more locationally mobile in Europe than are EU-owned firms and because, within any given geographical spread of activity across Europe, non-EU-owned firms have a greater scope for EU-wide integration strategies than do their European counterparts (being probably less constrained by the inherited control of many functions by a home centre that lies within the EU area).

Therefore, our results suggest that the local profiles of technological specialisation in the principal EU regions are distinctive, and the fact that only some regional innovation systems are able to adjust their profiles of specialisation to the highest technological opportunities confirms that the location-specific nature of technological change might eventually imply the rise and the decline of technological poles within Europe.

10 Conclusions: the global–local nexus in technological innovation

What implications are there for the future?

Some issues for public policies

Our EU case-studies have provided support for the hypothesis that the pattern of MNC networks for innovation conforms to an internal (*within* national boundaries) hierarchy of regional centres, as large firms appear extremely sensitive to the characteristics of regional systems. Furthermore, we have also shown that a geographical hierarchy of regional locations can also be established *across* national boundaries in the European area. In such a context, it becomes clear that if, for the MNC, the imperative to create global R&D networks has grown all the more pressing, the ability of regions to reap the best technological opportunities will be increasingly crucial to meet the challenges of the new characteristics of the interdependent geography of innovation.

By investigating the degree to which the technological profile of foreign-owned firms complements the existing knowledge base within the regions of location, we have differentiated between *higher order* and *intermediate* research locations. This differentiation has enabled us to distinguish between the form of potential knowledge spillovers and technological networks in operation between foreign-owned firms and their indigenous counterparts in different regions in Europe.

On the other hand, it has been shown that the regional hierarchy is far from being a clear-cut and rigid classification of local contexts within and across EU national borders. A categorisation without distinctions would have implied an oversimplification of the complex interactions between the global and the local dimensions of the generation of new technology and, in particular, an oversight of the role of the State as the intermediary between these 'extreme points of a dialectical continuum' (Dicken, 1994, p. 103).

This book constitutes a contribution to the analysis of sub-national innovative activity within the EU area and highlights a vital component in the formulation of the future technological and industrial policy of the Union, which aims to sustain the development of the 'Europe of regions'.

The effects of the globalisation of innovation by MNCs cannot be assessed in general terms, as they depend principally upon the technological profiles and strategies of MNCs, as well as upon the characteristics of regional systems. However, despite the wealth of discussion on the changing division of labour within MNCs across national borders, a paucity of both theory and empirical evidence still exists on the beneficial or detrimental interactions between MNCs' innovation activities and regional systems of innovation.

Indeed, the major risk of regarding the innovative process as non-specific in the locational context in which it is developed is to underestimate, or even to overlook completely, the distribution of costs and benefits triggered by the globalisation of innovation. This is all the more true in the presence of an in-depth process of economic integration, as is the case of the EU, which arose from the need to define the problems – and the policies aimed at solving them – in terms of geographical location and centre/periphery economic convergence. The problem of regional imbalances becomes how to keep pace with the structural changes in the generation of innovation due to both integration and globalisation processes. In fact, the importance of the spatial dimension of innovation, in the new European context, becomes something of a paradox (Iammarino *et al.*, 1995). At first glance, it may appear that – by removing the barriers between European markets, encouraging the spread of the new information technologies, improving telecommunication systems, etc. – the direction of the change is one way, i.e. it has helped lessen geographical constraints and localisation. On the other hand, as argued above, since the creation of new networks of transactions is extremely sensitive to geography, the knowledge base matters increasingly at a local/regional level, and economic growth requires the creation and the improvement of endogenous capabilities, which are highly path-dependent and geographically-specific. The centrality of local forward and backward linkages and the emergence of a 'performance' type of MNC, identified by a 'heterarchical' internal structure and innovation-based competitiveness (Dunning, 1993; Cantwell, 1992a, 1994; Amin and Tomaney, 1995), tend to make the geographical polarisation of innovative activities stable and self-organising. Insofar as innovation is essential to any explanation of growth differentials, it is clear that a central role is played by regions as basic units in the cost/benefit evaluation of EU economic integration and in explaining the dynamics of economic convergence within the area.

We believe that the increasing role played by MNCs (both European and extra-European), as global creators of innovation, need not imply a weakening in the economic influence of public policies. On the contrary, in a highly interdependent world, and even more in a unified Europe, public policies form a crucial determinant of the pattern of production and innovation (Cantwell, 1989b), and using the region as a 'unit' of economic analysis can help determine the policies implemented at the community level, in an obvious reversal of the top/down relationship typically followed by public institutions.

In general terms, strengthening public intervention at the level of a regional system should occur in two directions: (1) supporting the endogenous capacity to produce knowledge and to absorb knowledge generated outside the regional environment; (2) increasing the degree of attractiveness of the region in order to capture global flows of innovation. This is central for policies implemented at the national and local level, as well as for the increasingly relevant EU action in this field.

As argued in this book, the technological globalisation of multinational corporations might give rise to a tougher competitive bidding between technologically advanced regional systems and backward regions, as well as between higher order and intermediate regional locations across Western European countries. This makes it increasingly important to consider more carefully the distribution of benefits and costs of integration processes, and the potential gaps between the private and social returns to innovative activity.

One of the first issues in building up or upgrading the 'learning region' seems to be cooperation. As emphasised in this book, cooperation is becoming the necessary condition to develop competitiveness. Firms cannot grow by relying only on their own inputs and innovation ability, but need to participate in the local networks with other market and non-market forces that operate in their own specific geographical context. The intensity of the relationships between firms located in the same region is important at different levels: vertically (linkages, both static and dynamic, transactions, cooperation); horizontally (both competition and collaboration); and spatially (proximity, shared cultural and institutional environment). All three types of relationships imply not only physical flows of inputs and outputs, but also exchanges of information, knowledge and expertise. The degree to which firms are linked not only to local networks but also to interregional ones is extremely important. In this respect, the role of national systems of innovation still occupies a central position in spite of European integration (Asheim and Dunford, 1997). Firms integrated in such dynamic 'constellations' – i.e. linked through local and external networks – are more prone to adapt to changes and to reap information from outside sources (Malecki, 1997).

Therefore, the link between 'global' and 'local' needs to be shaped by government action. As Hirst and Thompson have properly remarked, 'the nation state is central to this process of "suturing": the policies and practices of states in distributing power upwards to the international level and downwards to sub-national agencies are the sutures that will hold the system of governance together. Without such explicit policies to close gaps in governance and arrange a division of labour in regulation, vital capacities will be lost' (Hirst and Thompson, 1996, p. 184). It is thus suggested that the aim of public policy is not to maximise the values of nationally-owned assets, but rather to stimulate high value-added activities in local contexts and communities (Archibugi and Iammarino, 1999).

Supporting regional technology agencies, consortia, entrepreneurs' associations and a systematic public–private cooperation may secure a sufficient collective learning capacity. Moreover, by facilitating economic and knowledge spillovers between the 'cores' of successful agglomerations and the less advanced regions that surround them, it may be possible to set in motion positive cycles. To a certain extent, the promotion of wider cooperation can also be applied at the European level, where the support given to the R&D joint projects and exchange of scientific and technological knowledge via EU networks has recently been extended to cooperation with partners outside the area, given the dramatically growing possibilities for global collaboration and information exchange (Meyer-Krahmer and Reger, 1997).

The process of 'dematerialisation' of technology has brought about a new role to be played by human capabilities, which increasingly constitute the most important strategic resource and the principal means to change the cultural matrix of a regional context. The emphasis on information and knowledge as factors of production and the search for comparative advantages through the enhancement of human capital – deeply embedded in the socio-economic environment – represents the shift from the 'capital-intensive' industrial age to the 'knowledge-intensive' post-industrial era (Vaccà, 1995). This is particularly relevant in order to promote endogenous development in technologically backward regions, where the formation of a sufficient human potential and learning capacity is crucial to bringing about the structural changes necessary to accomplish the main objectives: to transform successfully the regional production system into a learning system; to exploit the benefits of the learning-based competitiveness on global markets (Asheim and Isaksen, 1997).

On the other hand, a crucial factor of regional attractiveness towards foreign research and technologically advanced operations has often proved to be the combined availability of highly qualified human resources as well as relatively low-cost workers. This provides a base for both specialised innovative and production activities (Malecki, 1997). From this perspective, the conventional 'deglomerative tendencies' highlighted by traditional economics – such as, for example, the incentives represented by lower costs in peripheral regions – might actually act as a means of convergence, provided that the preconditions of development towards the 'learning region' are met.

The notion of skilled labour has a very elastic meaning and often refers to the behavioural characteristic of human resources, such as responsibility, discipline, experience and quality. The practice of choosing location on the basis of such characteristics has frequently been associated with Japanese corporations, but that is not the only case. In many Japanese MNCs, excellent use has been made of basic research abroad as an instrument for opening up promising fields of business in the long run. This example shows not only the importance of 'global technology sourcing', but also that linking and embedding into the research system of the host location is becoming a necessary practice (Meyer-Krahmer and Reger, 1997). In contrast to the classic supply of facilities, it is task distribution and networking between actors – i.e. organisational structural characteristics – that determine the comparative advantage (or disadvantage) of both firms and regional contexts. This, in turn, implies that the 'absorptive capacity' of local systems is increasingly important, i.e. the ability and the speed with which they can absorb knowledge produced worldwide and disseminate it amongst local firms. As large differences in terms of absorptive capacity give rise to a considerable degree of geographical agglomeration, knowledge will flow more easily and economic activity in general will be more widely spread if high absorptive capacity exists across space. The trend in the most industrialised economies with respect to foreign investments is one of a progressive convergence between FDI policies and development policies, by acting through both normative instruments and ad hoc institutional structures for the promotion of innovation. Nevertheless, how to attract asset-seeking foreign investments in R&D, or how to promote a research-conducive environments, is something much less clear than with respect to FDI in production.

Turning to the 'competitive bidding' between higher-order and inter-mediate regional systems, different locational factors are likely to influence the choices of MNCs, insofar as relatively advanced techno-economic and political-institutional structures are supposed to characterise these locations. In the previous chapters, it has been argued that quality of life factors and urban agglomeration advantages are by far the most important considerations for the attraction of foreign research activities in advanced regional systems of innovation. The strong concentration of innovation carried out by foreign affiliates in the South Eastern regions of the UK, particularly around London, in the Paris region in France or in the surroundings of Milan in Italy, con-firms the importance of urbanisation economies as centripetal forces drawing multisectoral research activities and Local-for-global MNC strategies. In addi-tion, the strength of the regional industrial base, the presence of fully-evolved technological markets, the quality of the local science and technology infra-structure (i.e. universities, research centres, etc.), as well as that of institu-tional relationships, services and various facilities (i.e., banking, finance, insurance and business services), help attract and expand new technological activities from abroad. In regions defined as intermediate centres, in which the attraction of foreign resources is likely to be motivated by the willingness of MNCs to tap into sectoral-specific local expertise and increase their own technological advantage in some particular technological fields, attention should be paid to the monitoring and evaluation of MNC strategy. As argued in Chapter 2, if the strategies are Centre-for-global or Local-for-local, the appreciable spillover effects might only be moderate and the competitive erosion of indigenous firms might arise.

More in general, the relationship of 'global versus local' for regional centres of excellence in Europe implies a mounting competitive bidding in order to attract external sources of knowledge and technological competence, by which to enhance the regional knowledge base and tap into the full growth potential of globalisation. The sufficient condition to take part in this competitive bidding is clearly the dynamics (upgrading/diversification) of regional technological advantage and the ability to provide opportunities in the most promising technological fields. Such an ability is strictly related to the regional capacity to engage in 'institutional learning', i.e. to adjust the local institutional structure in order to support, sustain and enhance the development of new technologies and to adapt to the prevailing technological paradigm. Thus, the 'institutional comparative advantage' of the regional economy is often the underlying reason for a more dynamic technological performance and for the gradual shift of the regional specialisation towards the fastest growing areas of innovative activity.

Obviously, not all regional cores are able to adjust their profiles of specialisation to the highest technological opportunities: thus, we have suggested that the cumulative and location-specific nature of technological processes brings about an increasing risk of a rise and decline of technological poles within Europe.

Public policies on a far wider range than those currently practised in the majority of countries are necessary, so that nations should exploit the opportunities associated with the globalisation of innovation and offset the risk of winners and losers. The global generation of innovation by MNCs might give rise to more dramatic imbalances, as they occur in national environments which are supposed to be – at least in principle – more economically and socially homogeneous than the international one (Archibugi and Iammarino, 1999). The globalisation process thus offers many opportunities to strengthen public policy effectiveness, both by enabling a government's structure to function in an interdependent world and by examining more carefully the impact on development in different regional contexts. The growing role of regional innovation systems calls for advanced instruments aiming at promoting localised innovation processes in order to secure regional growth and convergence in the unified Europe.

Some open questions for future research

The limited attention paid to the role of MNC innovation networks for regional development in industrialised economies needs to be overcome once and for all by future research efforts. There are a number of issues in this area that should be urgently addressed and it would be impossible here to recall them all. We will, therefore, just mention those more closely related to the research presented in this book, which will represent guidelines for our ongoing work.

The first issue, which is rather conceptual in nature, has to do with the definition of a regional innovation system. Any step in the direction of accomplishing a more suitable notional depiction of RSI, however, has to take into account two major problems. The national innovation system, in fact, has been conceptualised and operationalised looking at actors, institutions and linkages that operate and are governed mainly on a national scale (i.e. R&D system and infrastructure, S&T policy making process, educational structures, etc.). This sort of 'national bias' calls for a substantial rethinking of which are the relevant actors, institutions and relationships at regional level and of how this regional dimension could be meaningfully picked up. The top-down or comprehensive perspective applied to NSI could certainly be used to define a hypothetical RSI, but it is not entirely appropriate to justify different performance and innovative patterns (Evangelista *et al.*, 2002). A complementary problem – which is rather general in regional economics – has to do with the scarcity of data at the sub-national scale. The availability of figures on the role and performance not only of firms, but of the multitude of actors and institutions that shape an innovation system, is even more severe than at the national level. The methodology of data and information collection for R&D and innovative activities is, in practice, still heavily dependent on the custom of the 'territorialisation' of national data and this has so far constrained the possibility of exploring the existence and nature of regional systems of innovation on the basis of statistically robust evidence.

The second issue, related to the previous one, is that too little is still known on the linkages between the global and the local. Much of the literature on local systems as centres for innovation suffers from the defect that it focuses almost entirely on the interchanges that occur within such areas between small and medium-sized enterprises. This literature has rarely paid much attention to the role of larger leader companies within such localities, or to the connections with complementary innovation in other distant sites that are provided when these larger firms are part of a multinational corporation.[1] The need to redress the balance by considering the role of MNCs shares the perspective that both localised and international knowledge exchanges are important and that the co-evolution of interactions between local systems of SMEs (with their tacit and contextual knowledge) and the codified knowledge generated at the global level, are crucial factors for future growth and competitiveness.

These considerations are all the more important as structural upgrading has clearly dynamic consequences, as do the spillovers of MNC operations but, rather surprisingly, there is not yet even a comprehensive theory of MNC and economic growth. More conceptual work is needed, especially to investigate the most recent, innovation-driven stage of MNC-facilitated growth, particularly in regional economics. The literature on economic geography and regional development suggests some possible routes through which the MNC may act as an 'engine of growth' (for instance, Markusen and Venables, 1999). This is consistent with the insights gathered from the *new growth theory*, although we believe that, in this respect, factors underlying growth – such as business organisation, the role of institutions and government intervention – are essential. Theoretical and conceptual work in this direction is today still rather undeveloped.

In addition, there is some empirical evidence pointing out differences in the quality of foreign investment, not only between core and backward regions, but also among the latter group itself. On the one hand, for example, the lack of the prerequisite – i.e. the 'necessary condition' of possessing a minimum threshold stock of technological competence or 'critical mass of absorptive capacity' – to become part of a global network for innovation, is one of the explanations underlying the lagging behind of some backward regions and the substantial absence of much foreign-owned technological activity even at the country level. On the other hand, some peripheral regions – such as those of the UK outside England, namely Wales and Scotland, or Mediterranée in France – have recorded substantial benefits in terms of employment, productivity levels, innovation rates and, ultimately, economic growth, as a reflex of the observed increase in both the magnitude and the quality of foreign investments in research attracted there. What is, and how to build, a 'critical mass' needs to be explored more in depth and at a comparative level, given its relev-ance for the overall social and economic cohesion of the European Union.

As far as the empirical evidence retrieved in this book is concerned, the aim is to proceed in the direction of further improving our understanding of some aspects of the effects of innovation and globalisation on firms and regions – i.e. technological spillovers – by examining more in detail the patterns of technological (by the technological field of the largest firms) and production (by industry of the output of the largest firms) specialisation in each region. As also emerged in the case of the French regions in Chapter 8, differences between the two specialisation profiles may be indicative of technological diversification by industry, and hence potential technological overlaps between industries. Furthermore, the patterns of technological diversification of industries should be further explored by looking at which firms are responsible for a positive technological specialisation in the case of a region that lacks specialisation in the equivalent industrial category, and how this fits into the overall pattern of technological diversification of the firms in question. We believe that this integrated view of MNC production and innovation would add substantial insight to our comprehension of 'local versus global' processes of knowledge creation.

Appendices

Appendix 1(a) The EU7 regions

Regional code	Region	Regional code	Region
Germany (NUTS1)		*France (NUTS1)*	
GER1	Baden-Württemberg	FR1	Île De France
GER2	Bayern	FR2	Bassin Parisien
GER3	Berlin	FR3	Nord-Pas-De-Calais
GER4	Brandenburg	FR4	Est
GER5	Bremen	FR5	Ouest
GER6	Hamburg	FR6	Sud-Ouest
GER7	Hessen	FR7	Centre-Est
GER8	Mecklenburg-Vorpommern	FR8	Mediterranee
GER9	Niedersachsen	FR9	Departements D'outre-Mer
GER10	Nordrhein-Westfalen	*Netherlands (NUTS1)*	
GER11	Rheinland-Pfalz	NL1	Noord-Nederland
GER12	Saarland	NL2	Oost-Nederland
GER13	Sachsen	NL3	West-Nederland
GER14	Sachsen-Anhalt	NL4	Zuid-Nederland
GER15	Schleswig-Holstein	*Belgium (NUTS1)*	
GER16	Thuringen	BL1	Reg. Bruxelles-Cap.
United Kingdom (NUTS1)		BL2	Vlaams Gewest (Flanders)
UK1	North	BL3	Region Wallonne
UK2	Yorkshire and Humberside	*Sweden (NUTS2)*	
UK3	East Midlands	SE1	Stockholm
UK4	East Anglia	SE2	Ostra Mellansverige
UK5	South East	SE3	Smaland Med Oarna
UK6	South West	SE4	Sydsverige
UK7	West Midlands	SE5	Vastsverige
UK8	North West	SE6	Norra Mellansverige
UK9	Wales	SE7	Mellersta Norrland
UK10	Scotland	SE8	Ovre Norrland
UK11	Northern Ireland		
Italy (NUTS2)[a]			
IT1	Piemonte		
IT2	Valle D'aosta		
IT3	Liguria		
IT4	Lombardia		
IT5	Trentino-Alto Adige		
IT6	Veneto		
IT7	Friuli-Venezia Giulia		
IT8	Emilia-Romagna		
IT9	Toscana		
IT10	Umbria		
IT11	Marche		
IT12	Lazio		
IT13	Abruzzo		
IT14	Campania		
IT15	Puglia		
IT16	Calabria		
IT17	Sicilia		
IT18	Sardegna		

Note
a The Italian NUTS2 regions are 20, but Molise and Basilicata were excluded since no USPTO patents were attributed in the period 1969–95.

Appendix 1(b) Selected EU regions

Regional code	Region
BL1+BL2	Flanders-Bruxelles
GER1	Baden Württemberg
GER2	Bayern
GER6	Hamburg
GER7	Hessen
GER9	Niedersachsen
GER10	Nordrhein-Westfalen
GER11	Rheinland Pfalz
GER15	Schleswig-Holstein
FR1	Île de France
FR2	Bassin Parisien
FR4	Est
FR7	Centre Est
FR8	Mediterranee
IT1	Piemonte
IT4	Lombardia
NL2	Oost-Nederland
NL3	West-Nederland
NL4	Zuid Nederland
SE1+SE2	Stockholm-Ostra Mellansverige
UK1	North
UK2	Yorkshire and Humberside
UK3	East Midlands
UK4	East Anglia
UK5	South East
UK6	South West
UK7	West Midlands
UK8	North West
UK9	Wales
UK10	Scotland

Appendix 2(a) The 56 technological sectors

Tech 56		Tech 56	
1	Food and tobacco products	29	Other general industrial equipment
2	Distillation processes		
3	Inorganic chemicals	30	Mechanical calculators and typewriters
4	Agricultural chemicals		
5	Chemical processes	31	Power plants
6	Photographic chemistry	32	Nuclear reactors
7	Cleaning agents and other compositions	33	Telecommunications
		34	Other electrical communication systems
8	Disinfecting and preserving		
9	Synthetic resins and fibres	35	Special radio systems
10	Bleaching and dyeing	36	Image and sound equipment
11	Other organic compounds	37	Illumination devices
12	Pharmaceuticals and biotechnology	38	Electrical devices and systems
		39	Other general electrical equipment
13	Metallurgical processes		
14	Miscellaneous metal products	40	Semiconductors
15	Food, drink and tobacco equipment	41	Office equipment and data processing systems
16	Chemical and allied equipment	42	Internal combustion engines
17	Metal working equipment	43	Motor vehicles
18	Paper making apparatus	44	Aircraft
19	Building material processing equipment	45	Ships and marine propulsion
		46	Railways and railway
20	Assembly and material handling equipment	47	equipment Other transport equipment
21	Agricultural equipment	48	Textiles, clothing and leather
22	Other construction and excavating equipment	49	Rubber and plastic products
		50	Non-metallic mineral products
23	Mining equipment	51	Coal and petroleum products
24	Electrical lamp manufacturing	52	Photographic equipment
25	Textile and clothing machinery	53	Other instruments and controls
26	Printing and publishing machinery	54	Wood products
		55	Explosive compositions and charges
27	Woodworking tools and machinery		
28	Other specialised machinery	56	Other manufacturing and non-industrial

Appendix 2(b) The 33 categories of technological activity, and their relationship to
the 56 sector classification

Technological categories	56 codes included
1 Food and tobacco products	1
2 Inorganic chemicals	3
3 Agricultural chemicals	4
4 Chemical processes	2, 5, 6, 7
5 Bleaching and dyeing processes	8, 10
6 Other organic chemicals	9, 11
7 Pharmaceuticals	12
8 Metallurgical processes	13
9 Other metal products	14
10 Chemical and allied equipment	15, 16, 18, 19
11 Metal working equipment ·	17
12 Assembly equipment	20
13 Mining equipment	23
14 Specialised industrial equipment	21, 22, 24, 25, 26, 27, 28
15 General industrial equipment	29
16 Power plants	31
17 Nuclear reactors	32
18 Telecommunications	33, 34, 35
19 Image and sound equipment	36
20 Electrical systems	37, 38
21 General electrical equipment	39
22 Semiconductors	40
23 Office equipment	30, 41
24 Motor vehicles	42, 43
25 Aircraft	44
26 Other transport equipment	45, 46, 47
27 Textiles and wood products	48, 54
28 Rubber products	49
29 Non-metallic mineral products	50
30 Coal and petroleum products	51
31 Photographic instruments	52
32 Other instruments	53
33 Other manufacturing and non-industrial	55, 56

Appendix 2(c) The 18 classes of technological activity, and their relationship to the 56
            sector classification

Technological classes	56 codes included
1 Food products	1
2 Chemicals nes	2–11
3 Pharmaceuticals	12
4 Metals	13–14
5 Mechanical engineering	15–29
6 Power plants	31
7 Nuclear reactors	32
8 Electrical equipment nes	33–40
9 Office equipment	30, 41
10 Motor vehicles	42–43
11 Aircraft	44
12 Other transport equipment	45–47
13 Textiles	48, 54
14 Rubber products	49
15 Non-metallic mineral products	50
16 Coal and petroleum products	51
17 Professional instruments	52–53
18 Other manufacturing	55–56

Note
nes, not elsewhere specified.

Appendix 3 Regional economic-contextual indicators

Indicator	Description
1 DENPOP = Population density	inh/km² (1994)
2 POPRATE = Population growth	% average growth (1984–94)
3 YOUPOP = Young population	% pop < 25 (1994)
4 OLDPOP = Old population	% pop > = 65 (1994)
5 ACTRATE = Total activity rate	% (1996)
6 ACTRATEF = Female activity rate	% (1996)
7 DEPEND = Dependency rate	% (1996)
8 UNEMPL = Unemployment rate	% (1996)
9 UNEMPLF = Female unemployment rate	% (1996)
10 AGRIEMP = Employment in Agriculture	total = 100 (1996)
11 INDEMP = Employment in Manuf. Industry	total = 100 (1996)
12 SEREMP = Employment in Services	total = 100 (1996)
13 GDPCAP = Per capita GDP	gdp/inhab pps EU15 = 100 (1994)
14 VAEMP = Value added per employee	value added at factor costs/empl (1994)
15 R&D = R&D expenditure	% totr&dexp/gdp (1995)[a]
16 R&DPER = R&D Personnel	% r&dper/thousempl (1994)[b]
17 EPOPAT = EPO patent applications	EPOpat/mioinhab (1995)
18 USPTOPAT = USPTO granted patents	Uspat91–95/mioinhab[c]
19 HIGHWAY = Highways	highwaykm/mioinhab (1994)[d]
20 AIRTRAF =Air traffic	airpassengers/inhab (1994)[e]
21 VEHICLE = Circulating vehicles	vehicles/thousinhab (1994)
22 HIGHEDU = Higher education	students enrolled/thousinhab (1994/95)[f]

Source of data: REGIO Database; University of Reading Database for USPTOPAT.

Notes
a UK = 1994; Sweden = national data used as proxy; Netherlands = national data regionalised on the basis of EPO patents.
b Government sector only; Netherlands = national data regionalised on the basis of EPO patents.
c Population at 31 December 1994.
d Netherlands = channels km.
e Air passengers = embarked + disembarked.
f Netherlands = national data used as proxy.

Notes

2 Regional systems of innovation in Europe and the globalisation of technology

1 However, as also recalled by Caniëls (2000), the *pôles de croissance* à la Perroux are an 'effect' of agglomeration economies, which in turn means 'the economies inducing people and activities to cluster together, not the effects of agglomeration' (Richardson, 1978a, p. 156).

2 Among the studies in regional economics aimed at identifying the endogenous elements of 'territorialised' innovative systems it is necessary to recall the approaches based on the concepts of *milieux innovateur* (Aydalot, 1986) and the industrial or technological district (Becattini, 1987). More recently, attention has focused on specifically defined regional systems of innovation (Saxenian, 1994; Storper, 1995; Howells, 1999). As a consequence of the echoes of the 'new economic geography' (Krugman, 1991a,b,c; Fujita *et al.*, 1999), empirical analyses have proliferated in relation to the geography of innovation, both in the US (see, among others, Jaffe *et al.*, 1993; Audretsch and Feldman, 1995, 1996; Feldman and Audretsch, 1999) and, more recently, in the EU (for instance, Fagerberg *et al.*, 1997; Breschi, 2000; Paci and Usai, 2000a,b; Caniëls, 2000).

3 The distinction between these two types of agglomeration economies – investigated over a long period of time (from Marshall to Krugman, to mention but two) – is obviously not clear-cut. We believe, however, that it turns out to be central in the assessment of the forces at work in analysing the geographical pattern of MNC networks for innovation, as will be shown in the following chapters.

4 The issue of the empirical identification of RSIs is rather broad and actually one of the most discussed in this field of research: the conceptualisation of the regional innovation system has never overcome the serious drawback of measurement and data collection related to sub-national geographical units of reference. Thus, the data and the analysis presented in this book may, hopefully, add further useful insights both to the conceptualisation and to the measurement of RSIs.

5 Among those who claim that globalisation has largely influenced the bulk of the economic and social life see Ohmae (1990), Chesnais (1994), Perraton *et al.* (1997); for a most sceptical view on its actual quantitative relevance see Ruigrok and van Tulder (1995), Michie and Grieve Smith (1995), Hirst and Thompson (1996).

6 For the ongoing academic debate on the extent of the international creation of technology see, for instance, Cantwell (1995) and Patel (1995). For an interpretation of the two sets of results see Archibugi and Michie (1995).

7 See Chapter 4 in this book for a description of the extent of the internationalisation of innovative activities.

8 Indeed, the use of networks external to the firm is not at all confined to MNCs, as the

empirical evidence on small and medium enterprises (SMEs) and SME clusters (such as the industrial districts) has extensively shown.

9 The idea that cumulative causation may give rise to a widening of regional inequalities is not a new one: it goes back to Young (1928), Perroux (1950), Myrdal (1957) and Kaldor (1970, 1981), in its broader formulation within development economics. More recently, however, it has received renewed attention by some scholars interested in giving a fuller account of its interdependence with the process of economic integration and the dynamics of technological globalisation (see, among others, Cantwell, 1987, 1989b; Cantwell and Dunning, 1991).

10 Indeed, as our higher order regions coincide, by and large, with capital regions, it should be reminded that, as highlighted by Richardson (1978b), large urban centres are more likely to be receptive to innovation due to their disproportionate concentration of innovation elites (such as R&D personnel, university researchers, technologists, etc.), a favourable social environment and the location of decision-making centres of MNCs.

11 See Chapter 9 in this book for some empirical evidence and discussion.

3 MNC technological activities and economic wealth: an analysis of spatial distribution in the European Union

1 One of the pioneering works is Nelson *et al.* (1967).

2 Fagerberg and Verspagen (1996), for instance, considered the differences in innovative capabilities across European regions – which are much more pronounced than at country level – showing that they account for a good deal in explaining the diverging trends in economic growth.

3 Notwithstanding these limits, some fresh empirical evidence on knowledge spillovers and their agglomeration across space has provided further support to the observation that the relevance of asset-augmenting research strategies is higher among EU multinationals, confirming the incisiveness of large MNCs as creators of knowledge flows and connections in the integrated area (Criscuolo *et al.*, 2001).

4 The data used in this book are patents granted to 792 of the world's largest industrial firms, derived from the listings of the Fortune 500. Of these 792 companies, 730 had an active patenting presence during the period 1969–95. To these 730 firms, 54 companies were added, making a total of 784 large corporate groups. These companies include (mainly for recent years, but occasionally historically) enterprises that occupied a prominent position in the US patent records, some of which are firms that were omitted from Fortune's listing for classification reasons (e.g. RCA and AT&T were classified in the service sector).

5 Since Switzerland is the only non-EU country in our database, the regionalisation was undertaken on the basis of a geographical subdivision devised to make it generally compatible with the EU territorial classification. However, Switzerland has not been included in the present chapter because of the lack of comparable data on economic and contextual indicators at the sub-national level.

6 The original 399 original classes identified by the US Patent and Trademark Office were grouped into 56 technological sectors in the University of Reading database, collecting together technologically related patent classes. No problems arise in keeping the classification consistent over time because the USPTO reclassifies all earlier patents if a change in the system of patent classes occurs.

7 The NUTS levels (1 and 2) used in the present work are those which Eurostat statistics refer to and which are generally used in the application of regional policies, being thus the most appropriate to analyse regional–national problems (Eurostat, 1995). The NUTS was recently revised to take into account administrative alterations, but our database has not yet been updated to the new version (NUTS99). It should be noted

that despite the aim of comparing equivalent regions among EU countries, the NUTS classification still implies considerable differences between sub-national units in terms of their area, population, economic weight and administrative powers (on the disadvantages of using a classification based on administrative units see, for example, Molle, 1980). However, by choosing the NUTS level corresponding to the 'standard regions' for each country, difficulties in comparisons can be partially compensated, while the 'administrative' character of the classification can be considered an advantage from the perspective of policy implications.

8 As also shown by Paci and Usai (2000a), such a result does not significantly change when using other measures of concentration (Gini, Herfindal).

9 The CV of MNC patent counts across the 69 regions is equal to 1.6 for the first sub-period (1969–77) covered by the database, rising to 1.8 in the last sub-period (1987–95).

10 The EU regions represented in Figure 3.1 total 65, as IT2, IT5, IT18 and FR9 have no patents in the sub-period 1991–5.

11 More than 77 per cent of the overall patents' stock in Italy (1969–95) is concentrated in Lombardia and Piemonte (see Chapter 5 in this book).

12 The structural factor also explains some differences in our regional ranking as compared with other analyses based on EPO data (cf. Paci and Usai, 2000a, 2000b, 2001): the latter, in fact, reflects the weight of small and medium enterprises, not taken into account in our study.

13 The regions included in Figures 3.2(a) and (b) are only those with a minimum number of US patents in all three sub-periods.

14 Cf. Chapter 6 in this book.

15 It is worth mentioning that some Swedish areas have indeed recorded highly dynamic technological performances: to give an example, the high-technology hub in Kista, a large research centre located north west of Stockholm, in 2001 was ranked second after Silicon Valley among the centres of excellence in digital technologies at the worldwide level.

16 Cf. Chapter 7 in this book.

17 Also relevant, in the case of Lazio, is the 'institutional effect' on innovative activities of being the capital region (see Iammarino *et al.*, 1998).

18 The regions of Brussels and Flanders in Belgium, and Stockholm and Östra Mellan-sverige in Sweden were merged for consistency with the analysis carried out in Chapter 9 of this book.

19 Actually, as previously mentioned, since one of the two criteria for the selection of the regions to be analysed more in depth in this chapter was that of 'attractiveness' (in terms of patents granted to foreign-owned firms for research carried out in the region), five regions that were in the first 30 positions of the ranking 87–95 for technological size (FR6, GER3, SE4, SE5 and BL3) were excluded on the basis of a low share of foreign patenting. They were substituted with those immediately following in the rank and which were more significant for foreign-owned technological activity. However, it should be noted that the excluded regions were anyway not in the top 20, which has not exhibited exceptional changes in its composition over the time span considered here (except for the already mentioned outstanding climb of Mediterranée, that of the French Est (more moderate), and a few dramatic drops in the ranking of some UK regions such as Wales and West Midlands).

20 As shown in Table 3.3(b), the value of the Bartlett's test of sphericity, used to test the hypothesis that the correlation matrix is an identity matrix, is highly significant (1 per cent), therefore H_0 was rejected. The Kayser–Meyer–Olkin (KMO) measure of sampling adequacy is 0.62, which supports the use of the PCA.

21 The method used for the CA is that of Ward, an agglomerate hierarchical clustering in which clusters are formed by grouping cases into larger and larger clusters until all cases are members of a single cluster.

22 It is worth pointing out that the rather tiny share of MNC patenting of the remaining 39 'technologically backward' regions of the EU7 stayed fairly steady over time, having increased only by 0.5 percentage points between the first (1969–77) and the last (1987–95) sub-periods considered here (from 6.3 per cent to 6.7 per cent of the total EU7).

23 For the decisive role played by the government in the French NSI, see Chapter 8 in this book.

4 Geographical hierarchies of research locations in the European Union

1 For a description of the data used to identify national and regional technological profiles see the third section in Chapter 3.

2 Nevertheless, more recently, US and Japanese large firms have made increasing use of foreign research facilities (Dunning, 1993, 1994). For the explanations underlying the strong centralisation of technological activities in Japan see Papanastassiou and Pearce (1995) and Pearce and Papanastassiou (1996).

3 Although figures and relative shares may vary according to the research perspective and the unit of analysis adopted (e.g. patents, R&D expenditure, R&D personnel, etc.), they are substantially in line in showing the same uniform trend towards greater and more complex internationalisation and globalisation of technology.

4 This is also confirmed by very recent studies at the firm level. For example, von Zedtwitz and Gassmann's study (2002), based on a direct survey to 81 MNCs, found a substantial amount of intra-European internationalisation: of a total of 352 R&D locations in Europe, no less than 133 sites were owned by companies from other European countries.

5 Germany hosts the largest absolute number of patent grants but records a significant imbalance between those attributed to foreign-owned versus indigenous research. As highlighted, while foreign-owned firms' share of patents has been increasing over time in both the UK and Italy – it averages approximately half of the total in the 1991–5 period – and has been rising in the most recent years in France, it is substantially lower in Germany throughout the three decades under observation.

6 Note that this is a proxy for *relative* (as opposed to *absolute*) advantage. A small region could demonstrate a high RTA in a particular sector but this could actually be associated with a relatively low patent count. Conversely, a region with an RTA below one – thus showing a relative technological disadvantage – may still patent but it does not as much as all other regions or as much as in other sectors.

7 These restrictions have led to imposing different cut-off points at the regional or sectoral level, therefore only some regions and not all sectors for each national case are considered in detail in the subsequent analysis.

8 This differing pattern for Germany can be explained by considering the type of technological activity associated with Nordrhein-Westfalen (cf. Chapter 7 in this book).

9 This is consistent with the general results shown in Chapter 3 for the 69 EU regions. See also Appendix 1(b).

10 As highlighted in the country-studies reported below, the fact that a number of regions were dropped from the analysis due to having inadequate numbers for statistical purposes, in itself supports the hypothesis that internal geographical hierarchies exist in these economies.

5 Multinational corporations and the Italian regional systems of innovation

* This chapter was adapted from Cantwell and Iammarino (1998) MNCs, technological innovation and regional systems in the EU: some evidence in the Italian case, *International Journal of the Economics of Business*, Special Issue, 5(3): pp. 383–408.

1 As already stated in Chapter 3, the NUTS applied in the Italian case is level 2 (see Appendix 1(a)).
2 See the conceptual framework in Chapter 2.
3 For the description of data cf. Chapter 3, section 3.
4 As highlighted in most empirical analyses of Italian national and regional innovation systems, the strongly uneven geographical distribution has rendered cross-regional comparisons based on the use of the NUTS2 level biased or even meaningless, particularly in the case of regions with a weak technological industrial base (see, inter alia, Evangelista *et al.*, 2001).
5 Some of the technological sectors were dropped from the tables on the grounds of the relatively small number of patents for corporate research in the country as a whole, the outcome being that only 28 sectors are reported in Tables 5.1–5.3 and commented upon in the text. Total 56, however, refers to the total number of patents for all 56 technological sectors.
6 Note, however, the sharp decline registered by Piemonte in the technological field of office equipment, which is largely ascribable to that of Olivetti, which, between the 1980s and the 1990s, progressively lost the capacity to expand its innovative activities significantly (Breschi *et al.*, 1999; Balcet and Cornaglia, 2002).
7 In particular, the local system of Milan is characterised by a strong specialisation in pharmaceuticals and chemicals. Among the main actors in this field we find Ciba-Geigy, Farmitalia Carlo Erba (acquired by the Swedish Pharmacia in 1993), the Lepetit Group (acquired in 1995 by the German Hoechst from the US Dow Chemical) and the groups of Montedison and Eni.
8 This is in line with what was observed by other empirical studies based on EPO patents: the regional system of Lombardia not only holds the absolute technological leadership in terms of both patent counts and shares on the Italian total, but represents almost the sole location of some of the most advanced technologies in which the country as a whole appears to be completely despecialised (Breschi and Mancusi, 1997). The relevant role of Milan in some office equipment and electronic components technologies is mainly due to the dynamic presence of Sgs-Thomson.
9 The technological activity of large firms in the Textile and clothing machinery is indeed related to the presence of industrial districts that are specialised in textiles and clothing, which is rather remarkable in the region. As highlighted elsewhere, the technological level of textiles and clothing products strikingly increased during the 1980s because of the diversification processes that mainly occurred through the specialisation, within industrial districts, in complementary sectors, such as machinery and equipment for textiles and garments (cf. Guerrieri and Iammarino, 2001).
10 For the subscripts see the legend in Table 5.4.

6 Multinational corporations and the UK regional systems of innovation

* This chapter was adapted from Cantwell and Iammarino (2000), Multinational corporations and the location of technological innovation in the UK regions, *Regional Studies,* 34(3): pp. 317–22.
1 Indeed, much more work has been done on the foreign ownership in UK manufacturing production at the territorial level (see, among others, Dicken and Lloyd, 1980; Hill and Munday, 1992; Stone and Peck, 1996).
2 As stated in Chapter 3, the UK study refers to the NUTS1 level in order to ensure as much as possible the comparability among European regions. According to Eurostat Basic Principles, NUTS1 in the UK is the level corresponding to 'standard regions' (11) (see Eurostat, 1995); see Appendix 1(a).
3 As seen in Chapter 4, in the UK the total number of patents registered in the Reading database over the period 1969–95 is more than five times that registered for Italy.

4 Just for the sake of clarity, the two output indicators are different not only insofar as the EPO reflects 'patent requests' and the USPTO 'patents granted', but also because, in the first case, the overall number of requests is reported, while in the second the Reading database includes only corporate patents – i.e. patents granted to the largest industrial firms. See Chapter 3, third section, for clarifications about the database.

5 More specifically, taking the period 1977–91 as a whole, GDP per capita in most regions shows a tendency to fall relative to that of Greater London, moving towards an asymptotic level of 56 per cent of Greater London GDP. Looking at the subperiods, however, the analysis suggests that the UK regions exhibit a stronger tendency to converge in periods of slow national growth than they do in boom conditions (Chatterji and Dewhurst, 1996).

6 Some of the technological sectors were dropped from the table on the grounds of the relatively small number of patents for corporate research in the country as a whole, the outcome being that only 32 sectors are reported in Tables 6.2 and 6.3 and thus discussed in the text. However, the total 56 refers to the total number of patents for all 56 technological sectors. The key to the sectoral codes is given in Appendix 2(a).

7 Cf. Chapter 5 in this book.

8 However, this would need a closer analysis of the sectoral composition of the fall in UK-owned company patenting, in comparison with the recent rise in technological development abroad by British-owned firms: this lies beyond the scope of this chapter.

9 Historically, pharmaceuticals was a traditional British strength – deriving partly from food industries, just as some other chemical areas were linked to textiles or to oil – but it fell away for much of the middle part of the last century. It recovered its tradition in the 1970s and 1980s and, as argued by Cantwell (1987), this was due in part to the favourable interaction between research in US-owned and indigenous British firms in this industry, which seems from our current data to have had a regional focus in the North West.

10 For the assumptions of this methodology see the third section of Chapter 5.

11 Furthermore, by analogy with the exercise carried out for Italy, the period was subdivided into 1969–82 and 1983–95 in order to test the validity of our hypothesis at different geographical levels over time. We thus adopted a Granger notion of sequential causality, and we run the regression for 47 technological sectors (cf. Chapter 5, third section, for methodological clarifications). As expected, the results were not significant in all cases except the North West, for which the overlap in technological specialisation of UK-owned and foreign-owned firms also holds in the regression over time (at the 1 per cent level of significance).

7 Multinational corporations and the German regional systems of innovation

* This chapter was adapted from Cantwell and Noonan (2001) The regional distribution of technological development. Evidence from foreign-owned firms in Germany. In M.P. Feldman and N. Massard (Eds) *Knowledge Spillovers and the Geography of Innovation* (Dordrecht: Kluwer Academic).

1 Although Germany continues to be the largest recipient of patents within the EU (accounting for approximately 40 per cent of the EU total), the number of patents secured has declined each year since 1983 (see also Table 4.6 in Chapter 4).

2 The regions of Rheinland-Pfalz and Niedersachsen were also included in the analysis of the German case because of the relatively high absolute number of patents granted to firms located there.

3 See Table 4.6 in Chapter 4 in this book.

4 As in previous country-studies, technological sectors that recorded an insufficient number of patents over the 1969–95 period were excluded. The analysis therefore

includes the 35 most prominent technology sectors in Germany. See Appendix 2(a) for the sectoral codes.

5   The main focus of regional industrial policy in this state has been to help small- and medium-sized (*Mittelstand*) firms absorb new technology. This has been achieved inter alia through the unique service offered to small firms via the Steinbeis Stiftung für Wirtschaftsförderung (StW). Indeed Baden Württemberg is unique on many fronts – it hosts the greatest number of Max Plank Institutes, Fraunhofer gesellschaften and second largest number of Universities in Germany (Bundesbericht Forschung, 1996). Such an infrastructure is believed to heighten the incidence of knowledge transfer and explain spatial distribution of firm activity (Jaffe *et al.*, 1993).

6   This is the case for all indigenous and foreign firms with the exception of those located in Rheinland-Pfalz and, interestingly, Baden Württemberg, which hosts the greatest patenting activity by foreign firms. This exercise was indeed also repeated for indigenous firms' RTA as a dependent variable (for clarity this result was omitted from the figure), supporting the findings obtained for foreign-owned firms.

8 Multinational corporations and the French regional systems of innovation

1   It is interesting to note that, according to some empirical studies on EU regions, a negative correlation seems to be found between the sectoral concentration of technological activities and aggregate productivity – i.e. the regions that show a wider sectoral spread in the distribution of technological capabilities are also characterised by higher productivity levels (Paci and Usai, 2000a). These results give further support to our hypothesis of positive inter-industry spillover effects in higher order regions and therefore to the significance of the categories of the regional hierarchy.

2   See, respectively, Chapters 5, 6 and 7 in this book.

3   For the regional codes see Appendix 1(a).

4   It is worth mentioning that, in 1995, the capital region accounted for nearly 50 per cent of total national R&D expenditure (Eurostat, 1999).

5   The Departements d'Outre-mer are not considered here, as they do not register any US patents by large firms in the period observed. Thus, there are eight regions included in the tables and charts, instead of the nine NUTS1 French regions. See Appendix 1(a) for the regional NUTS codes.

6   France is ranked between the UK and Germany in terms of both the foreign affiliates' share of R&D expenditure and share of production (turnover) in manufacturing (OECD, 1999).

7   The Survey referred to the innovative activities undertaken in the period 1986–91. The source of information is Dupont (1994).

8   As in the previous country-studies, some of the technological sectors were dropped from the table on the grounds of the relatively small number of patents for corporate research in the country as a whole, the outcome being that only 31 sectors are reported in Tables 8.2 and 8.3 and are thus discussed in the text. However, the total 56 refers to the total number of patents for all 56 technological sectors. The key to the sectoral codes is given in Appendix 2(a).

9   It is interesting to recall the position of Île de France in the cluster analysis performed in Chapter 3, attributing the capital region to the group of 'highly dynamic metropolitan contexts'. The other two French regional technological cores were classified as 'medium industrial potential, scarcely urbanised regional contexts' in terms of our socio-economic indicators; however, in contrast with a GDP growth lower than the EU average, both Bassin Parisien and Centre-Est displayed a remarkable growth of MNC technological activities over the time span considered here (see also Figures 3.2(a) and (b)).

10 Cf. Chapter 3 in this book.

11 It is worth mentioning the high comparative advantage of French-owned firms in Aircraft (44), shown by Île de France, Bassin Parisien and France as a whole: in this sector, a traditional point of strength in the country, no foreign patents are recorded at all.

12 The adjusted RTA is given by: $\mathrm{adjRTA}_{ij} = (\mathrm{RTA}_{ij} - 1)/(\mathrm{RTA}_{ij} + 1)$
ranging from -1 to $+1$: values between 0 and 1 (between 0 and -1) indicate a comparative advantage (disadvantage) of region (i) in sector (j) relative to the world.

13 For the acronyms see the Legend in Table 8.4.

14 As stated previously, the reason for having a smaller number of sectors in the lagged cross-section model is that, when we subdivided the period 1969–95, we dropped all the technological sectors with an overall number of patents less than 600 in the world total in both 1969–82 and 1983–95. The purpose was to avoid the inclusion of sectors with a relatively low propensity to patent at the world level.

15 The regression results for France as a whole (equations (8.2) and (8.4)) are not reported, as they are significant neither in the aggregate nor in the lagged equation.

16 This is consistent with what is shown in Chapter 9 in this book, which reports a more in-depth inspection of change, stability and strengthening of technological comparative advantages across higher-order European regions over time.

17 As highlighted in Chapter 3, these considerations also apply in the case of a rather 'peripheral' region, such as Mediterranée, which has shown an impressive State-pushed technological convergence over recent decades.

9 The geographical hierarchy across European national borders

* This chapter draws upon Cantwell and Iammarino (2001) EU regions and multi-national corporations: change, stability and strengthening of technological comparative advantages, *Industrial and Corporate Change,* Special Issue on Geography of Innovation and Economic Clustering, 10(4), pp. 1007–37.

1 As emphasised also by Swann (1997), the benefits of the sectoral specialisation depend on the life-cycle of the territorial cluster: if it is in a phase of expansion, then specialisation in one sector is advantageous; if it is in a phase of maturity, then specialisation becomes less desirable. Clusters entering in the maturity phase might start to decline, and their possible resurgence, more than to the traditional price mechanism (in the declining cluster costs fall, but so also do benefits), is due to the convergence between old and new technologies: if they converge, spillovers generated even in an old specialised cluster may attract entry in a newer sector, causing a shift in the cluster specialisation and eventually its recovery (see also Brezis and Krugman, 1993).

2 It should be noted that the proposition of cumulativeness of technological development here refers to the sectoral composition of innovation rather than to its overall rate or rapidity for each region.

3 For Baden Württemberg, the regional share of patents attributable to the largest indigenous German firms is below that of two other German regions, namely Nordrhein-Westfalen and Bayern. The share of the selected core regions in the patenting of foreign-owned firms from local sources exceeds the share of the same regions in patenting by indigenous firms in Baden Württemberg, South East UK, Lombardia, Flanders-Brussels and Stockholm-Östra Mellansverige. However, the regional share of domestically-owned corporate patenting is greater than the equivalent regional share of foreign-owned firms in Île de France, Zuid Nederland and Basel.

4 Cf. Chapter 7 in this book.

5 For the purpose of the present chapter, the 56 technological sectors have been rearranged in 33 broader categories of technological activity. The key to sectoral codes and the concordance between Tech 33 and Tech 56 are given in Appendix 2(b).

6 The standard assumption of this analysis is that the regression is linear and that the error term ε_{ijt} is independent of RTA_{ijt-k}. It has been shown that, with a distribution across 30 or so sectors, a minimum count of about 1,000 patents is, in general, needed to have an RTA index that roughly conforms to a normal distribution (Cantwell, 1993). For this reason, the regression analysis described below has been carried out by grouping the 56 technological sectors into 33 categories, in order to reach a sufficiently large number of patents ($>1,000$ in all three periods considered here) for all eight selected European regions.

7 The regressions were run on both $t-1$ (1978–86) and $t-2$ (1969–77), but only in the latter case are the results reported here. However, it has to be noted that the results obtained are consistent throughout the three periods.

8 In Table 9.4 the term 'specialisation' denotes the usual meaning of an RTA value greater than one in the context of the analysis of the mobility effect, but also refers to an RTA value greater than the mean in the context of the subdivision of the regression effect.

9 Indeed, from the picture reported in Chapter 3, the Belgian regions of Brussels and Flanders emerged as particularly dynamic in terms of MNC overall patenting activity growth, especially since the 1980s.

10 Cf. Table 4.1 in this book.

10 Conclusions: the global–local nexus in technological innovation

1 Extensive work has been done on this issue in the Asian New Industrialised Economies. See, for all, Ernst (1998, 2001) and Ernst *et al.* (2001).

Bibliography

Abramovitz, M. (1986) Catching up, forging ahead, and falling behind, *Journal of Economic History*, 46, 385–406.

Almeida, P. (1997) Knowledge sourcing by foreign multinationals: patent citation analysis in the US semiconductor industry, *Strategic Management Journal*, 17, 155–65.

Almeida, P. and Kogut, B. (1997) Exploration of technological diversity and the geographic localization of innovation, *Small Business Economics*, 9, 21–31.

Amin, A. and Thrift, N. (1994) *Globalization, Institutions, and Regional Development in Europe* (Oxford: Oxford University Press).

Amin, A. and Tomaney, J. (1995) The regional development potential of inward investment in the less favoured regions of the European Community. In A. Amin and J. Tomaney (eds) *Behind the Myth of the European Union* (London: Routledge).

Antonelli, C. (1986) *L'attività innovativa in un distretto tecnologico* (Torino: Fondazione Agnelli).

Antonelli, C. (2000) Collective knowledge communication and innovation: the evidence of technological districts, *Regional Studies*, 34, 535–47.

Archibugi, D. (1992) Patenting as an indicator of technological innovation: a review, *Science and Public Policy*, 19, 357–68.

Archibugi, D. and Iammarino, S. (1999) The policy implications of the globalisation of technology, *Research Policy*, 28(2–3), 317–36.

Archibugi, D. and Iammarino, S. (2002) The globalisation of technological innovation: definition and evidence, *Review of International Political Economy*, 9(1), 98–122.

Archibugi, D. and Imperatori, G. (eds) (1997) *Economia globale e innovazione. La sfida dell'industria italiana* (Rome: Donzelli).

Archibugi, D., Howells, J. and Michie, J. (eds) (1999) *Innovation Policy in a Global Economy* (Cambridge: Cambridge University Press).

Archibugi, D. and Lundvall, B.Å. (eds) (2001) *The Globalising Learning Economy* (Oxford: Oxford University Press).

Archibugi, D. and Michie, J. (1995) The globalisation of technology: a new taxonomy, *Cambridge Journal of Economics*, 19(1): 121–40.

Archibugi, D. and Pianta, M. (1992) *The Technological Specialisation of Advanced Countries. A Report to the EC on International Science and Technology Activities* (Dordrecht: Kluwer).

Asheim, B.T. (1995) Industrial districts as learning regions: a condition for prosperity?, STEP Report no. 3 (Oslo: STEP Group).

Asheim, B.T. and Dunford, M. (1997) Regional futures, *Regional Studies*, 31(5), 445–55.

Asheim, B.T. and Isaksen, A. (1997) Location, agglomeration and innovation: towards regional innovation systems in Norway?, *European Planning Studies*, 5(3), 299–330.

Audretsch, D.B. and Feldman, M.P. (1995) Innovative clusters and the industry life cycle, *CEPR Discussion Paper*, 1161.

Audretsch, D.B. and Feldman, M.P. (1996) Knowledge spillovers and the geography of innovation and production, *American Economic Review*, 86(3), 630–40.

Aydalot, P. (ed.) (1986) *Milieux Innovateurs in Europe* (Paris: Gremi).

Balassa, B. (1965) Trade liberalisation and 'revealed' comparative advantage, *The Manchester School of Economics and Social Studies*, 33(2), 99–124.

Balcet, G. (1999) Multinazionali in Piemonte. Fattori localizzativi, strategie di investimento e impatto regionale, Quaderni di Ricerca IRES 89 (Turin: IRES Piemonte).

Balcet, G. and Cornaglia, F. (2002) The innovative activities of multinational firms in Italy. In R. Lipsey and J.L. Mucchielli (eds) *Multinational Firms, and Impacts on Employment, Trade and Technology. New Perspectives for a New Century* (London: Harwood Press).

Balcet, G. and Enrietti, A. (1998) Global and regional strategies in the European car industry: the case of Italian direct investments in Poland, *Journal of Transnational Management Development*, 1, 197–230.

Balcet, G. and Enrietti, A. (2002) The impact of focused globalisation in the Italian automotive industry, *Journal of Interdisciplinary Economics*, 13(1/3), 97–133.

Baptista, R. and Swann, G.M.P. (1998) Do firms in clusters innovate more?, *Research Policy*, 27, 525–40.

Beaudry, C. and Breschi, S. (2000) Does 'clustering' really help firms' innovative activities?, *Manchester Business School*, Working Paper 412.

Becattini, G. (1987) *Mercato e forze locali: il distretto industriale* (Bologna: Il Mulino).

Beckouche, P. (1991) French high-tech space: a double cleavage. In G. Benko and M. Dunford (eds) *Industrial Change and Regional Development: the Transformation of New Industrial Spaces* (London and New York: Belhaven Press).

Beise, M. and Spielkamp, A. (1996) Technologietransfer von Hochschulen: ein insider-outsider effect, ZEW-Discussion Paper No. 96–100 Mannheim.

Beise, M. and Stahl, H. (1999) Public research and industrial innovations in Germany, *Research Policy*, 28, 397–422.

Benko, G. and Dunford, M. (eds) (1991) *Industrial Change and Regional Development: the Transformation of New Industrial Spaces* (London and New York: Belhaven Press).

Blind, K. and Grupp, H. (1999) Interdependencies between science and technology infrastructure and innovation activities in German regions: empirical findings and policy consequences, *Research Policy*, 28, 451–68.

Braunerhjelm, P. and Ekholm, K. (eds) *The Geography of Multinational Firms* (Boston, Dordrecht and London: Kluwer).

Breschi, S. (2000) The geography of innovations: a cross-sector analysis, *Regional Studies*, 34(3), 213–29.

Breschi, S. and Mancusi, M.L. (1997) Il modello di specializzazione tecnologica in Italia: un'analisi basata sui brevetti europei. In D. Archibugi and G. Imperatori (eds) *Economia globale e innovazione. La sfida dell'industria italiana* (Rome: Donzelli).

Breschi, S., Mutinelli, M. and Palma, D. (1999) Sistemi locali nei settori ad alta tecnologia in Italia. In S. Ferrari, P. Guerrieri, F. Malerba, S. Mariotti and D. Palma (eds) *L'Italia nella competizione tecnologica internazionale*, 2nd Report (Milan: FrancoAngeli).

Breschi, S. and Palma, D. (1999) Localised knowledge spillovers and trade competitiveness: the case of Italy. In M.M. Fischer, L. Suarez-Villa and M. Steiner (eds) *Innovation, Networks and Localities* (Berlin: Springer-Verlag).

Brezis, E.S. and Krugman, P. (1993) Technology and the life cycle of cities, *NBER Working Paper*, 4561.

Bundesbericht Forschung (1993/1996) *Bundesministerium fuer Bildung*, Wissenschaft, Forschung und Technologie, Bonn.

Caniëls, M.C.J. (2000) *Knowledge Spillovers and Economic Growth: Regional Growth Differentials Across Europe* (Cheltenham: Edward Elgar).

Caniëls, M.C.J. and Verspagen, B. (2001) Barriers to knowledge spillovers and regional convergence in an evolutionary model, *Journal of Evolutionary Economics*, 11, 307–29.

Cantwell, J.A. (1987) The reorganization of European industries after integration: selected evidence on the role of multinational enterprise activities, *Journal of Common Market Studies*, XXVI(2).

Cantwell, J.A. (1989a) *Technological Innovation and Multinational Corporations* (Oxford: Basil Blackwell).

Cantwell, J.A. (1989b) The changing form of multinational enterprise expansion in the twentieth century. In A. Teichova, M. Lévy-Leboyer and H. Nussbaum (eds) *Historical Studies in International Corporate Business* (Cambridge: Cambridge University Press).

Cantwell, J.A. (1991) Historical trends in international patterns of technological innovation. In J. Foreman-Peck (ed.) *New Perspectives on the Late Victorian Economy* (Cambridge: Cambridge University Press).

Cantwell, J.A. (1992a) The effects of integration on the structure of multinational corporation activity in the EC. In M.W. Klein and P.J.J. Welfens (eds) *Multinationals in the New Europe and Global Trade* (Berlin: Springer-Verlag).

Cantwell, J.A. (1992b) The internationalisation of technological activity and its implications for competitiveness. In O. Granstrand, L. Håkanson and S. Sjölander (eds) *Technology Management and International Business. Internationalization of R&D and Technology* (Chichester: Wiley).

Cantwell, J.A. (1993) Corporate technological specialisation in international industries. In M.C. Casson and J. Creedy (eds) *Industrial Concentration and Economic Inequality* (Aldershot: Edward Elgar).

Cantwell, J.A. (ed.) (1994) *Transnational Corporations and Innovatory Activities* (London: Routledge).

Cantwell, J.A. (1995) The globalisation of technology: what remains of the product cycle model?, *Cambridge Journal of Economics*, 19(1), 155–74.

Cantwell, J.A. (2000) Technological lock-in of large firms since the interwar period, *European Review of Economic History*, 4, 147–74.

Cantwell, J.A. and Bachmann, A. (1998) Changing patterns of technological leadership: evidence from the pharmaceutical industry, *International Journal of Innovation Management*, 2(1), 45–77.

Cantwell, J.A. and Barrera, P. (1998) The localisation of corporate technological trajectories in the interwar cartels: co-operative learning versus an exchange of knowledge, *Economics of Innovation and New Technology*, 6, 257–90.

Cantwell, J.A. and Dunning, J.H. (1991) MNEs, technology and the competitiveness of European industries, *Aussenwirtschaft*, 46, 45–65.

Cantwell, J.A. and Fai, F.M. (1999) The changing nature of corporate technological diversification and the importance of organisational capability. In S.C. Dow and P.E. Earl (eds) *Contingency, Complexity and the Theory of the Firm: Essays in Honor of Brian J. Loasby* (Cheltenham: Edward Elgar).

Cantwell, J.A. and Harding, R. (1998) The internationalisation of German companies' R&D, *National Institute Economic Review*, 163, 99–115.

Cantwell, J.A. and Hodson, C. (1991) Global R&D and UK competitiveness. In M.C. Casson (ed.) *Global Research Strategy and International Competitiveness* (Oxford: Basil Blackwell).

Cantwell, J.A. and Iammarino, S. (1998) MNCs, technological innovation and regional systems in the EU: some evidence in the Italian case, *International Journal of the Economics of Business*, Special Issue, 5(3), 383–408.

Cantwell, J.A. and Iammarino, S. (2000) Multinational corporations and the location of technological innovation in the UK regions, *Regional Studies*, 34(3), 317–22.

Cantwell, J.A. and Iammarino, S. (2001) EU regions and multinational corporations: change, stability and strengthening of technological comparative advantages, *Industrial and Corporate Change*, Special Issue on Geography of Innovation and Economic Clustering, 10(4), 1007–37.

Cantwell, J.A. and Iammarino, S. (2002) The technological relationships between indigenous firms and foreign-owned multinational corporations in the European regions. In P. McCann (ed.) *Industrial Location Economics* (Cheltenham: Edward Elgar).

Cantwell, J.A., Iammarino, S. and Noonan, C. (2000) Inward investment, technological change and growth: the impact of multinational corporations on the UK economy. In N. Pain (ed.) *Inward Investment, Technological Change and Growth* (London: Macmillan).

Cantwell, J.A. and Janne, O.E.M. (1999) Technological globalisation and the innovative centres: the role of corporate technological leadership and locational hierarchy, *Research Policy*, 28(2–3), 119–44.

Cantwell, J.A. and Janne, O.E.M. (2000) The role of multinational corporations and national states in the globalisation of innovatory capacity: the European perspective, *Technology Analysis & Strategic Management*, 12(2), 243–62.

Cantwell, J.A. and Narula, R. (2001) The eclectic paradigm in the global economy, *International Journal of the Economics of Business*, 8(2), 155–72.

Cantwell, J.A. and Noonan, C.A. (2001) The regional distribution of technological development. Evidence from foreign-owned firms in Germany. In M.P. Feldman and N. Massard (eds) *Knowledge Spillovers and the Geography of Innovation* (Dordrecht: Kluwer).

Cantwell, J.A. and Piscitello, L. (1999) The emergence of corporate international networks for the accumulation of dispersed technological capabilities, *Management International Review*, 39(1), 123–47.

Cantwell, J.A. and Piscitello, L. (2000) Accumulating technological competence: its changing impact on corporate diversification and internationalisation, *Industrial and Corporate Change*, 9, 21–51.

Cantwell, J.A. and Piscitello, L. (2002) The location of technological activities of MNCs in European regions: the role of spillovers and local competencies, *Journal of International Management*, 8, 69–96.

Cantwell, J.A. and Santangelo, G.D. (2000) Capitalism, profits and innovation in the new techno-economic paradigm, *Journal of Evolutionary Economics*, 10(1), 131–57.

Cantwell, J.A. and Santangelo, G.D. (2002) The new geography of corporate research in Information and Communication Technology (ICT), *Journal of Evolutionary Economics*, 109, 1–38.

Carlsson, B. and Stankiewicz, R. (1991) On the nature, function and composition of technological systems, *Journal of Evolutionary Economics*, 1, 93–118.

Casson, M.C. (ed.) (1991) *Global Research Strategy and International Competitiveness* (Oxford: Basil Blackwell).

Casson, M.C. and Creedy, J. (eds) (1991) *Industrial Concentration and Economic Inequality* (Aldershot: Edward Elgar).

Castellani, D. and Zanfei, A. (2002) Multinational experience and the creation of linkages with local firms: evidence from the electronic industry, *Cambridge Journal of Economics*, 26(1), 1–25.

Cesaratto, S., Mangano, S. and Silvani, A. (1993) L'innovazione nell'industria italiana secondo l'indagine Istat-CNR: tipologie settoriali e dinamiche territoriali, *Economia e politica industriale*, 79, 167–200.

Chandler, A.D., Hagström, P. and Sölvell, O. (eds) (1998) *The Dynamic Firm. The role of Technology, Strategy, Organisation and Regions* (Oxford: Oxford University Press).

Chatterji, M. and Dewhurst, J.H.L. (1996) Convergence clubs and relative economic performance in Great Britain: 1977–1991, *Regional Studies*, 27(8), 727–43.

Chesnais, F. (1988) Technical co-operation agreements between firms, *Science Technology Industry Review*, 4, 57–119.

Chesnais, F. (1992) National Systems of Innovation, foreign direct investment and the operations of multinational enterprises. In B.Å. Lundvall (ed.) *National Systems of Innovation* (London: Pinter).

Chesnais, F. (1993) The French national system of innovation, in R.R. Nelson (ed.) *National Systems of Innovation* (New York: Oxford University Press).

Chesnais, F. (1994) *La mondialisation du capital* (Paris: Syros).

Chiesa, V. (1995) Globalizing R&D around centres of excellence, *Long Range Planning*, 28(6), 19–28.

Cohen, W.M., Nelson, R. and Walsh, J. (2000) Protecting their intellectual assets, appropriability conditions and why US manufacturing firms patent (or not). NBER working paper, W7552.

Cooke, P., Gomez Uraga, M. and Etxebarria, G. (1997) Regional innovation systems: institutional and organisational dimensions, *Research Policy*, 26, 475–91.

Cooke, P. and Morgan, K. (1994) The regional innovation system in Baden Wuerttemberg, *International Journal of Technology Management*, Special Issue on Technology, Human Resources and Growth, 394–430.

Coronado, G.D. and Acosta, S.M. (1997) Spatial distribution of patents in Spain: determining factors and consequences on regional development, *Regional Studies*, 31(4), 381–90.

Cosh, A. and Hughes, A. (1996) The changing state of British enterprise: growth, innovation and competitive advantage in small and medium sized firms 1986–95, ESRC Centre for Business Research, University of Cambridge.

Criscuolo, P., Narula, R. and Verspagen, B. (2001) Measuring knowledge flows among European and American multinationals: a patent citation analysis, *Eindhoven Centre for Innovation Studies*, September.

Dearlove, D. (2001) The cluster effect. Can Europe clone Silicon Valley?, *Strategy+Business*, 24, 67–75.

De Bresson, C. (1987) I poli tecnologici dello sviluppo, *L'industria*, 3, 301–35.

Dicken, P. (1994) The Roepke Lecture in economic geography: global–local tensions: firms and states in the global space economy', *Economic Geography*, 70(2), 101–28.

Dicken, P. and Lloyd, P.E. (1980) Patterns and processes of change in the spatial distribution of foreign-controlled manufacturing employment in the United Kingdom, 1963 to 1975, *Environment and Planning, A*, 12(1), 404–26.

Dicken, P. and Lloyd, P.E. (1990) *Location in Space. Theoretical Perspectives in Economic Geography,* 3rd edn (New York: HarperCollins).

Dosi, G. (1988) Sources, procedures and microeconomic effects of innovation, *Journal of Economic Literature*, 26, 1120–71.

Dosi, G. (2000) *Innovation, Organization and Economic Dynamics* (Cheltenham and Northampton, MA: Edward Elgar).

Dosi, G., Freeman, C., Nelson, R., Silverberg G. and Soete, L. (eds) (1988) *Technical Change and Economic Theory* (London: Pinter).

Dunford, M. (1996) Regional disparities in the European Community: evidence from the REGIO databank, *Regional Studies*, 30(1), 31–40.

Dunning, J.H. (1992) *The Globalization of Business* (London: Routledge).

Dunning, J.H. (1993) *Multinational Enterprises and the Global Economy* (Wokingham: Addison–Wesley).

Dunning, J.H. (1994) Multinational enterprises and the globalisation of innovatory capacity, *Research Policy*, 23, 67–88.

Dunning, J.H. (1958 [1998]) *American Investment in British Manufacturing Industry,* (London: Allen & Unwin). 1998 edition published by Routledge, London and New York.

Dunning, J.H. and Lundan, S.M. (1998) The geographical sources of competitiveness of multinational enterprises: an econometric analysis, *International Business Review*, 7, 115–33.

Dunning, J.H. and Narula, R. (1995) The R&D activities of foreign firms in the US, *International Studies in Management and Organisation*, 25, 39–73.

Dunning, J.H. and Robson, P. (eds) (1987) *Multinational and the European Community* (Oxford: Basil Blackwell).

Dunning, J.H. and Wymbs, C. (1999) The geographical sourcing of technology based assets by multinational enterprises. In D. Archibugi, J. Howells and J. Michie (eds) *Innovation Policy in a Global Economy* (Cambridge: Cambridge University Press).

Dupont, M.J. (1994) Les filiales étrangères en France: des atouts maîtres pour innover. In Ministère de l'Industrie, des Postes et Télécommunications et du Commerce Extérieur, les chiffres clés. *L'innovation technologique dans l'industrie* (Paris: Ministère de l'Industrie).

Enright, M. (1998) Regional clusters and firm strategy. In A.D. Chandler, P. Hagström and O. Sölvell (eds) *The Dynamic Firm. The role of Technology, Strategy, Organisation and Regions* (Oxford: Oxford University Press).

Ernst, D. (1998) High-tech competition puzzles. How globalization affects firm behaviour and market structure in the electronics industry, *Revue d'Economie Industrielle*, 3, 9–30.

Ernst, D. (2001) Small firms competing in globalized high-tech industries: the co-evolution of domestic and international knowledge linkages in Taiwan's computer industry. In P. Guerrieri, S. Iammarino and C. Pietrobelli (eds) *The Global Challenge to Industrial Districts. The case of Italy and Taiwan* (Cheltenham, UK and Northampton, MA, USA: Edward Elgar).

Ernst, D., Guerrieri P., Iammarino, S. and Pietrobelli, C. (2001) SME clusters facing global restructuring: What can be learnt comparing Italy and Taiwan?. In P. Guerrieri, S. Iammarino and C. Pietrobelli (eds) *The Global Challenge to Industrial Dis-*

tricts. The case of Italy and Taiwan (Cheltenham, UK and Northampton, MA, USA: Edward Elgar).

Eurostat (1995) *NUTS. Nomenclature of Territorial Units for Statistics* (Luxembourg: Eurostat).

Eurostat (1999, 2000) *Regions: Statistical Yearbook* (Luxembourg: European Communities).

Evangelista, R. (1999) *Knowledge and Investment. The Sources of Innovation in Industry* (Cheltenham, UK and Northampton, MA, USA: Edward Elgar).

Evangelista, R., Iammarino, S., Mastrostefano, V. and Silvani, A. (2001) Measuring the regional dimension of innovation: lessons from the Italian innovation survey, *Technovation*, 21(11), 733–45.

Evangelista, R., Iammarino, S., Mastrostefano, V. and Silvani, A. (2002) Looking for regional systems of innovation. Evidence from the Italian innovation survey, *Regional Studies*, 36(2), 173–86.

Fagerberg, J. and Verspagen, B. (1996) Heading for divergence? Regional growth in Europe reconsidered, *Journal of Common Market Studies*, 34(3), 431–48.

Fagerberg, J., Verspagen, B. and Caniëls, M.C.J. (1997) Technology gaps, growth and unemployment across European regions, *Regional Studies*, 31(5), 457–66.

Fagerberg, J., Verspagen, B. and von Tunzelman, N. (eds) (1994) *The Dynamics of Technology, Trade and Growth* (Aldershot: Edward Elgar).

Feldman, M.P. (1994) *The Geography of Innovation* (Boston: Kluwer Academic Publishers).

Feldman, M.P. and Audretsch, D.B. (1999) Innovation in cities: science-based diversity, specialization and localized competition, *European Economic Review*, 43, 409–29.

Feldman, M.P. and Massard, N. (2001) (eds) *Knowledge Spillovers and the Geography of Innovation* (Dordrecht: Kluwer).

Ferrari, S., Guerrieri, P., Malerba, F., Mariotti, S. and Palma, D. (eds) (1999) *L'Italia nella competizione tecnologica internazionale*, 2nd Report (Milan: FrancoAngeli).

Ferrari, S., Guerrieri, P., Malerba, F., Mariotti, S. and Palma, D. (eds) (2002) *L'Italia nella competizione tecnologica internazionale*, 3rd Report (Milan: FrancoAngeli).

Fischer, M.M., Suarez-Villa, L. and Steiner, M. (eds) (1999) *Innovation, Networks and Localities* (Berlin: Springer-Verlag).

Foray, D. and Freeman, C. (eds) (1993) *Technology and the Wealth of Nations* (London: Pinter).

Fors, G. (1998) Locating R&D abroad: the role of adaptation and knowledge-seeking. In P. Braunerhjelm and K. Ekholm (eds) *The Geography of Multinational Firms* (Boston, Dordrecht and London: Kluwer).

Freeman, C. (1987) *Technology Policy and Economic Performance* (London, Pinter).

Freeman, C. (1994) The economics of technical change, *Cambridge Journal of Economics*, 18, 463–514.

Freeman, C. (1995) The national system of innovation in historical perspective, *Cambridge Journal of Economics*, 19(1), 5–24.

Freeman, C. and Soete, L. (eds) (1990) *New Explorations in the Economics of Technical Change* (London: Pinter).

Freeman, C. and Soete, L. (1994) *Lavoro per tutti o disoccupazione di massa?* (Milan: EtasLibri).

Fromhold-Eisebith, M. (1992) Messbarkeit und Messung des regionalen Wissens- und Technologientransfers aus Hochschulen. In NIW (ed.) *Erfolgskontrollen in der Technologiepolitik* (Hannover: NIW workshop).

Frost, T.S. (1996) From exploitation to exploration: the geographic sources of sub-sidiary innovations and the evolutionary theory of the multinational enterprise. University of Western Ontario, mimeo.

Frost, T.S. (2001) The geographic sources of foreign subsidiaries' innovations, *Strategic Management Journal*, 22, 101–23.

Fujita, M., Krugman, P. and Venables, A.J. (1999) *The Spatial Economy* (Cambridge, MA: MIT Press).

Garofoli, G. (ed.) (1992) *Endogenous Development and Southern Europe* (Aldershot: Avebury).

Geroski, P. (1995) Markets for technology: knowledge, innovation and appropria-tion. In P. Stoneman (ed.) *Handbook of the Economics of Innovation and Technological Change* (Oxford: Basil Blackwell).

Ghoshal, S. and Barlett, C.A. (1990) Innovation processes in multinational corpora-tions, *Strategic Management Journal*, 11, 499–518.

Granstrand, O., Håkanson, L. and Sjölander, S. (eds) (1992) *Technology Management and International Business. Internationalization of R&D and Technology* (Chichester: Wiley).

Griliches, Z. (1990) Patent statistics as economic indicators: a survey, *Journal of Economic Literature*, XXVIII, 1661–707.

Grossman, G.M. and Helpman, E. (1991) *Innovation and Growth in The Global Economy* (Cambridge, MA: MIT Press).

Grotz, R. and Braun, B. (1997) Territorial or trans-territorial networking: spatial aspects of technology oriented co-operation within the German mechanical engin-eering industry, *Regional Studies*, 31, 545–57.

Guerrieri, P. and Iammarino, S. (2001) The dynamics of Italian industrial districts. In P. Guerrieri, S. Iammarino and C. Pietrobelli (eds) *The Global Challenge to Industrial Districts. The case of Italy and Taiwan* (Cheltenham, UK and Northampton, MA, USA: Edward Elgar).

Guerrieri, P., Iammarino, S. and Pietrobelli, C. (eds) (2001) *The Global Challenge to Industrial Districts. The case of Italy and Taiwan* (Cheltenham, UK and Northampton, MA, USA: Edward Elgar).

Hagedoorn, J. (1993) Understanding the rationale of strategic technology partnering: interorganizational modes of cooperation and sectoral differences, *Strategic Management Journal*, 14, 371–85.

Hägerstrand, T. (1967) *Innovation Diffusion as a Spatial Process* (Chicago: University of Chicago Press).

Hall, B. and Ham, R.M. (1999) The patent paradox revisited: determinants of patenting in the US semiconductor industry, 1980–1994. IBER Working Paper No. E99–268.

Harris, R.I.D. (1988) Technological change and regional development in the UK: evidence from the SPRU database on innovations, *Regional Studies*, 22, 361–74.

Harrison, B. and Bluestone, B. (1991) *The Great U-Turn* (New York: Basic Books).

Harrison, B., Kelley, M.R. and Gant, J. (1996) Innovative firm behaviour and local milieu: exploring the intersection of agglomeration, firm effects, and technological change, *Economic Geography*, 72(3), 233–58.

Hart, P.E. (1976) The dynamics of earnings, 1963–1973, *The Economic Journal*, 86(3), 551–65.

Hart, P.E. and Prais, S.J. (1956) The analysis of business concentration: a statistical approach, *Journal of the Royal Statistical Society*, Series A, 119, 150–91.

Henderson, R. and Clark, K. (1990) Architectural innovation, *Administrative Science Quarterly*, 35, 9–30.

Hill, S. and Munday, M. (1992) The UK regional distribution of foreign direct investment: analysis and determinants, *Regional Studies*, 26, 535–44.

Hirschman, A. (1958) *The Strategy of Economic Development* (New Haven: Yale University Press).

Hirst, P. and Thompson, G. (1996) *Globalization in Question* (Cambridge, UK: Polity Press).

Howells, J. (1999) Regional systems of innovation?. In D. Archibugi, J. Howells and J. Michie (eds) *Innovation Policy in a Global Economy* (Cambridge: Cambridge University Press).

Howells, J. and Wood, M. (1993) *The Globalisation of Production and Technology* (London: Belhaven Press).

Iammarino, S., Prisco, M.R. and Silvani, A. (1995) On the importance of regional innovation flows in the European Union: some methodological issues in the Italian case, *Research Evaluation*, 5(3), 189–206.

Iammarino, S., Prisco, M.R. and Silvani, A. (1998) The geography of production and innovation: how regional styles play in the global scenario, *Regional Science Review*, 18, 31–45.

Iammarino, S., Prisco, M.R. and Silvani, A. (1999) Alla ricerca di un modello vincente di innovazione regionale: alcune considerazioni sull'esperienza italiana, *L'industria*, 3, 537–65.

Jaffe, A.B., Trajtenberg, M. and Henderson, R. (1993) Geographic localization of knowledge spillovers as evidenced by patent citations, *Quarterly Journal of Economics*, 63(3), 577–98.

Johnson, B. (1992) Institutional learning. In B.Å. Lundvall, *National Systems of Innovation* (London: Pinter).

Kaldor, N. (1970) The case for regional policies, *Scottish Journal of Political Economy*, 17, 337–47.

Kaldor, N. (1981) The role of increasing returns, technical progress and cumulative causation in the theory of international trade and economic growth, *Economie appliquée*, 34(4), 593–617.

Keeble, D. (1997) Small firms, innovation and regional development in Britain in the 1990s, *Regional Studies,* 31(2), 281–93.

Keeble, D. and Bryson, J. (1996) Small firms creation and growth, regional development and the north-south divide in Britain, *Environment and Planning, A*, 28, 909–34.

Klein, M.W. and Welfens, P.J.J. (eds) (1992) *Multinationals in the New Europe and Global Trade* (Berlin: Springer-Verlag).

Kline, G.J. and Rosenberg, N. (1986) An overview of innovation. In R. Landau and N. Rosenberg (eds) *The positive Sum Strategy: Harnessing Technology for Economic Growth* (Washington DC: National Academy Press).

Krugman, P. (1991a) *Geography and Trade* (Cambridge, MA: MIT Press).

Krugman, P. (1991b) History and industry location: the case of manufacturing belt, *American Economic Review*, 81(2), 80–3.

Krugman, P. (1991c) Increasing returns and economic geography, *Journal of Political Economy*, 99(33), 483–99.

Krugman, P. and Venables, A.J. (1995) Globalization and the inequality of nations, *Quarterly Journal of Economics*, 110(4), 857–80.

Kuemmerle, W. (1999) The drivers of foreign direct investment into research and development: an empirical investigation, *Journal of International Business Studies*, 30(1), 1–24.

Landau, R. and Rosenberg, N. (eds) (1986) *The positive Sum Strategy: Harnessing Technology for Economic Growth* (Washington DC: National Academy Press).

Le Bas, C. and Sierra, C. (2002) Location versus home country advantages in R&D activities: some further results on multinationals' locational strategies, *Research Policy*, 31, 589–609.

Le Galès, P., Anniello, V. and Tirmarche, O. (1999) The governance of local economies in France: after the State and national champions, emerging structure of local governance?. Mimeo.

Lösch, A. (1954) *The Economics of Location* (New Haven: Yale University Press).

Lundvall, B.Å. (1988) Innovation as an interactive process: from user-producer interaction to the national system of innovation. In G. Dosi, C. Freeman, R. Nelson, G. Silverberg and L. Soete (eds) *Technical Change and Economic Theory* (London: Pinter).

Lundvall, B.Å. (ed.) (1992) *National Systems of Innovation* (London: Pinter).

McCann, P. (1995) Rethinking the economics of location and agglomeration, *Urban Studies*, 32(3), 563–77.

McCann, P. (2001) *Urban and Regional Economics* (Oxford: Oxford University Press).

McCann, P. (ed.) (2002) *Industrial Location Economics* (Cheltenham: Edward Elgar, forthcoming).

Maillat, D. and Grosjean, N. (1999) Globalisation and territorial production systems. In M. Fischer, L. Suarez-Villa and M. Steiner (eds) *Innovation, Networks and Localities* (Berlin: Springer-Verlag).

Malecki, E.J. (1980) Dimensions of R&D location in the United States, *Research Policy*, 9, 2–22.

Malecki, E.J. (1983) Technology and regional development: a survey, *International Regional Science Review*, 8, 89–125.

Malecki, E.J. (1997) *Technology and Economic Development: The Dynamics of Local, Regional and National Competitiveness*, 2nd edn (Harlow: Longman).

Malerba, F. (1992) Learning by firms and incremental technical change, *Economic Journal*, 102, 845–59.

Malerba, F. (1993) Italy. The national system of innovation. In R.R. Nelson (ed.) *National Systems of Innovation* (New York: Oxford University Press).

Malerba, F. (2002) Sectoral systems of innovation and production, *Research Policy*, 31(2), 247–64.

Malmberg, A., Sölvell, O. and Zander, I. (1996) Spatial clustering, local accumulation of knowledge and firm competitiveness, *Geografiska Annaler*, 78B(2), 85–97.

Mansfield, E. (1995) Academic research and industrial innovation, *Research Policy*, 20, 1–20.

Mansfield, E. and Lee, J.-Y. (1996) The modern university: contributor to industrial innovation and recipient of industrial R&D support, *Research Policy*, 25, 1047–58.

Markusen, A. (1996) Sticky places in slippery space: a typology of industrial districts, *Economic Geography*, 72, 293–313.

Markusen, J. and Venables, A.J. (1999) Foreign direct investment as a catalyst for industrial development, *European Economic Review*, 43, 335–56.

Marshall, A. (1891) *Principles of Economics*, 2nd edn (London: Macmillan).

Martin, R. (1999) The new 'geographical turn' in economics: some critical reflections, *Cambridge Journal of Economics*, 23, 65–91.

Martin, P. and Ottaviano, G. (1998) Growth and agglomeration, Center for Economic Policy Research, Discussion paper no. 1529.

Meyer-Krahmer, F. and Reger, G. (1997) European Technology Policy and Internationalisation: an analysis against the background of the International Innovation Strategies of Multinational Enterprises. Mimeo.

Michie, J. and Grieve Smith, J. (eds) (1995) *Managing the Global Economy* (Oxford: Oxford University Press).

Miller, R. (1994) Global R&D networks and large-scale innovations: the case of the automobile industry, *Research Policy*, 23, 27–46.

Ministère de l'Industrie, des Postes et Télécommunications et du Commerce Extérieur (1994) *Les chiffres clés. L'innovation technologique dans l'industrie* (Paris).

Molle, W. (1980) *Regional Disparity and Economic Development in the European Community* (Farnborough: Saxon House).

Myrdal, G. (1957) *Economic Theory and the Under-developed Regions* (London: Ducksworth).

Narula, R. (1995) *Multinational Investment and Economic Structure* (London: Routledge).

Narula, R. (1999) Explaining strategic R&D alliances by European firms, *Journal of Common Market Studies*, 37(4), 711–23.

Narula, R. and Dunning, J.H. (1998) Explaining international R&D alliances and the role of the governments, *International Business Review*, 7, 377–97.

Narula, R. and Hagedoorn, J. (1999) Innovating through strategic alliances: moving towards international partnerships and contractual agreements, *Technovation*, 19, 283–94.

Nelson, R. and Wright, G. (1992) The rise and fall of American technological leadership: the postwar era in historical perspective, *Journal of Economic Literature*, 30(4), 1931–64.

Nelson, R.R. (ed.) (1993) *National Systems of Innovation* (New York: Oxford University Press).

Nelson, R.R., Peck, M.J. and Kalachek, E.D. (1967) *Technology, Economic Growth and Public Policy* (London: Allen and Unwin).

Nelson, R.R. and Rosenberg, N. (1993) Technical innovation and national systems, in R.R. Nelson (ed.) *National Systems of Innovation* (New York: Oxford University Press).

Nelson, R.R. and Winter, S.G. (1977) In search of useful theory of innovation, *Research Policy*, 6(1), 36–76.

Nelson, R.R. and Winter, S.G. (1982) *An Evolutionary Theory of Economic Change* (Cambridge, MA: Harvard University Press).

Neven, D.J. and Gouyette, C. (1994) Regional convergence in the European community, *CEPR Discussion Paper*, 914.

OECD (1999) *Measuring Globalisation. The Role of Multinationals in OECD Economies*, (Paris: OECD).

Ohmae, K. (1990) *The Borderless World: Management Lessons in the New Logic of the Global Market Place* (London: Collins).

Paci, R. and Usai, S. (2000a) Technological enclaves and industrial districts. An analysis of the regional distribution of innovative activity in Europe, *Regional Studies*, 34(2), 97–104.

Paci, R. and Usai, S. (2000b) The role of specialisation and diversity externalities in the agglomeration of innovative activities, *Rivista Italiana degli Economisti*, 2, 237–68.

Paci, R. and Usai, S. (2001) Externalities, knowledge spillovers and the spatial distribution of innovation, *GEOjournal*, 52, 12.

Papanastassiou, M. and Pearce, R.D. (1995) The research and development of Japanese multinational enterprises in Europe. In F. Sachwald (ed.) *Japanese Firms in Europe* (Chur: Harwood).

Patel, P. (1995) Localised production of technology for global markets, *Cambridge Journal of Economics*, 19(1), 141–53.

Patel, P. and Pavitt, K.L.R. (1991) Large firms in the production of the world's technology: an important case of non-globalisation, *Journal of International Business Studies*, 22(1) 1–21.

Patel, P. and Pavitt, K.L.R. (1994) National innovation systems: why they are important and how they might be measured and compared, *Economic Innovation and New Technology*, 3, 77–95.

Patel, P. and Pavitt, K.L.R. (1997) The technological competencies of the world's largest firms: complex path dependent, but not much variety, *Research Policy*, 26, 141–56.

Patel, P. and Pavitt, K.L.R. (1998) The wide (and increasing) spread of technological competencies in the world's largest firms: a challenge to conventional wisdom. In A.D. Chandler, P. Hagström and O. Sölvell (eds) *The Dynamic Firm. The role of Technology, Strategy, Organisation and Regions* (Oxford: Oxford University Press).

Patel, P. and Vega, M. (1999) Patterns of internationalisation of corporate technology: location versus home country advantages, *Research Policy*, 28(2/3), 145–55.

Patrucco, P.P. (2001a) The production of technological knowledge: some European evidence from metropolitan areas. University of Turin, mimeo.

Patrucco, P.P. (2001b) Institutional variety, networking and knowledge exchange: communication and innovation in the case of the Brianza technological district. University of Turin, mimeo.

Pavitt, K.L.R. (1982) R&D, patenting and innovative activities: a statistical exploration, *Research Policy*, 2, 33–51.

Pavitt, K.L.R. (1988a) International patterns of technological accumulation. In N. Hood and J. Vahlne (eds) *Strategies in Global Competition* (London: Croom Helm).

Pavitt, K.L.R. (1988b) Uses and abuses of patent statistics. In A. van Raan (ed.) *Handbook of Quantitative Studies of Science Policy* (Amsterdam: North Holland).

Pearce, R.D. (1999) Decentralised R&D and strategic competitiveness: globalised approaches to generation and use of technology in multinational enterprises (MNEs), *Research Policy*, 28(2), 157–78.

Pearce, R.D. and Papanastassiou, M. (1996) The technological competitiveness of Japanese multinationals. The European dimension, *Thames Essays on Contemporary International Economic Issues* (Michigan: The University of Michigan Press).

Pearce, R.D. and Papanastassiou, M. (2000) 'Funding sources and the strategic roles of decentralised R&D in multinationals'. University of Reading Discussion Papers in International Investment & Management, 278.

Pearce, R.D. and Singh, S. (1992) *Globalizing Research and Development* (London: Macmillan).

Perraton, J., Goldblatt, D., Held, D. and McGrew, A. (1997) The globalisation of economic activity, *New Political Economy*, 2(2).

Perroux, F. (1950) Economic space: theory and applications, *Quarterly Journal of Economics*, LXIV, 1, 89–104.

Perroux, F. (1955) Note sur la notion de pôle de croissance, *Économie appliquée*, 7, 307–20.

Phene, A. and Tallman, S. (2002) The effects of regional clusters on knowledge stocks and flows: Evidence from the biotechnology industry. University of Utah, mimeo.

Pitelis, C. (2000) A theory of the (growth of the) transnational firm: a Penrosean perspective, *Contributions to Political Economy*, 19, 71–89.

Pitelis, C. and Sugden, R. (eds) (1999) *The Nature of the Transnational Firm*, 2nd edn (London: Routledge).

Porter, M.E. (1990) *The Competitive Advantage of Nations* (Basingstoke & London: Macmillan).

Porter, M.E. (1994) The role of location in competition, *Journal of the Economics of Business*, 1, 35–9.

Porter, M.E. (1998) Clusters and the new economics of competition, *Harvard Business Review*, November–December, www.hbsp.harvard.edu/hbr.

Pred, A. (1967) *Behaviour and Location. Part I. Foundations for a Geographic and Dynamic Location Theory* (Lund: Gleerup).

Pred, A. (1977) *City Systems in Advanced Economies*, (Cambridge, MA: Harvard University Press).

Quah, D.T. (1996) Regional convergence clusters across Europe, *CEP-LSE Discussion Papers*, 274, February.

Richardson, H.W. (1969) *Elements of Regional Economics* (Harmondsworth: Penguin Books).

Richardson, H.W. (1978a) *Regional and Urban Economics* (Hindsdale: Dryden Press).

Richardson, H.W. (1978b) The state of regional economics: a survey article, *International Regional Science Review*, 3, 1–48.

Rodríguez-Pose, A. (1994) Socioeconomic restructuring and regional change: rethinking growth in the European community', *Economic Geography*, 79(4), 325–43.

Rodríguez-Pose, A. (1996) Growth and institutional change: the influence of the Spanish regionalisation process on long term growth trends, *Environment and Planning C*, 14(1), 71–87.

Rodríguez-Pose, A. (1998) *Dynamics of Regional Growth in Europe. Social and Political Factors* (Oxford: Clarendon Press).

Rosenberg, N. (1976) *Perspectives on Technology* (Cambridge: Cambridge University Press).

Rosenberg, N. (1982) *Inside the Black Box: Technology and Economics,* (Cambridge: Cambridge University Press).

Ruigrok, W. and van Tulder, R. (1995) *The Logic of International Restructuring* (London: Routledge).

Sachwald, F. (ed.) (1995) *Japanese Firms in Europe* (Chur: Harwood).

Santangelo, G.D. (2002a) The regional geography of corporate patenting in information and communications technology (ICT): domestic and foreign dimensions, *Regional Studies*, 36(5), 495–514.

Santangelo, G.D. (2002b) *Innovation in Multinational Corporations in the Information Age: the Experience of the European ICT Industry* (Cheltenham, UK and Northampton, MA, USA: Edward Elgar).

Saxenian, A. (1994) *Regional Advantage. Culture and Competition in Silicon Valley and Route 128* (Cambridge, MA and London: Harvard University Press).

Schmookler, J. (1966) *Invention and Economic Growth* (Cambridge, MA: Harvard University Press).

Sharp, M. and Pavitt, K.L.R. (1993) Technology policy in the 1990s: old trends and new realities, *Journal of Common Market Studies*, 31(2): 129–51.

Silvani, A., De Bresson, C., Berni, A. and Hu, X. (1993) La localisation regionale des grappes d'innovation en Italie: troisieme Italie ou Lombardie?, *Revue d'Economie Regionale et Urbaine*, 2, 289–307.

Soete, L. (1987) The impact of technological innovation on international trade patterns: the evidence reconsidered, *Research Policy*, 16, 101–30.

Sölvell, Ö. and Bengtsson, M. (1997) The role of industry structure, climate of competition and cluster strength. Stockholm School of Economics, mimeo.

Stone, I. and Peck, F. (1996) The foreign-owned manufacturing sector in UK peripheral regions, 1979–1993: restructuring and comparative performance, *Regional Studies,* 30(1), 55–68.

Stoneman, P. (ed.) (1995) *Handbook of the Economics of Innovation and Technological Change* (Oxford: Basil Blackwell).

Storper, M. (1995) The resurgence of regional economies, ten years later: the region as a nexus of untraded interdependencies, *European Urban and Regional Studies*, 2, 191–221.

Storper, M. (1997) *The Regional World. Territorial Development in a Global Economy* (New York and London: Guildford Press).

Suarez-Villa, L. (1993) The dynamics of regional invention and innovation: innovative capacity and regional change in the twentieth century, *Geographical Analysis*, 25, 147–64.

Swann, G.M.P. (1997) Towards a model of clustering in high-technology industries. In G.M.P. Swann, M. Prevezer and D. Stout (eds) *The Dynamics of International Clusters: International Comparisons in Computing and Biotechnology* (Oxford and New York: Oxford University Press).

Swann, G.M.P., Prevezer, M. and Stout, D. (eds) (1997) *The Dynamics of International Clusters: International Comparisons in Computing and Biotechnology* (Oxford and New York: Oxford University Press).

Tavares, A.T. and Pearce, R. (1999) Economic integration and the strategic evolution of MNEs' subsidiaries in a peripheral European economy. University of Reading Discussion Papers in International Investment & Management, 266.

Thwaites, A. and Wynarczyk, P. (1996) The economic performance of innovative small firms in the South East region and elsewhere in the UK, *Regional Studies*, 30(2), 135–49.

Ullman, E.L. (1958) Regional development and the geography of concentration, *Papers and Proceedings of the Regional Science Association,* 4, 179–98.

Vaccà, S. (1995) Impresa locale distrettuale e transnazionale, *Economia e politica industriale*, 86, 53–68.

Venables, A.J. (1996) Equilibrium locations of vertically linked industries, *International Economic Review*, 37, 341–59.

Vernon, R. (1966) International investment and international trade in the product cycle, *Quarterly Journal of Economics*, 80(2), 190–207.

Verspagen, B. (1997) European regional clubs: do they exist, and where are they heading? On economic and technological differences between European regions. Paper presented at the 3rd Conference *on Economic Growth and Change, A Comparative Analysis*, Cagliari, Italy, 19–21 June.

Vertova, G. (1998) Technological similarity in national styles of innovation in a historical perspective, *Technology Analysis & Strategic Management*, 10(4), 437–49.

Vertova, G. (2001) National technological specialisation and the highest technological opportunities historically, *Technovation*, 21, 605–12.

Vertova, G. (2002) A historical investigation of the geography of innovative activities, *Structural Change and Economic Dynamics*, 13(3), 259–83.

von Hippel, E. (1989) *The Sources of Innovation* (Oxford: Oxford University Press).

von Hippel, E. (1994) Sticky information and the locus of problem solving: implications for innovation', *Management Science*, 40, 429–39.

von Zedtwitz, M. and Gassmann, O. (2002) Market versus technology drive in R&D internationalization: four different patterns of managing research and development, *Research Policy*, 31, 569–88.

Weber, A. (1929) *Theory of the Location of Industries* (Chicago: University of Chicago Press).

Young, A. (1928) Increasing returns and economic progress, *Economic Journal*, 38(152), 527–42.

Young, S. and Hood, N. (1995) Attracting, managing and developing inward investment in the single market. In A. Amin and J. Tomaney (eds) *Behind the Myth of European Union* (London: Routledge).

Zander, I. (1997) Technological diversification in the multinational corporation – historical evolution and future prospects, *Research Policy*, 26, 209–27.

Zander, I. (1999a) Whereto the multinational? Evolution of technological capabilities in the multinational network, *International Business Review*, 8, 261–91.

Zander, I. (1999b) How do you mean global? A taxonomy of innovation networks in the multinational corporation, *Research Policy,* 28(2–3), 195–213.

Zander, I. and Sölvell, O. (1997) Internationally integrated innovation – an unexplored aspect of the multinational corporation. Mimeo.

Zanfei, A. (2000) Transnational firms and changing organisation of innovative activities, *Cambridge Journal of Economics*, 24(5), 515–42.

Index

Abramovitz, M. 11
Acosta, S.M. 44
affiliate networks 15
agglomeration 8, 9, 10, 11, 13, 15, 19,
    56–60, 113–14
Almeida, P. 4
Amin, A. 17, 158
ANOVA 38–40
Antonelli, C. 26
Archibugi, D. 14, 17, 50, 60, 159, 162
architectural knowledge 25–6
Asheim, B.T. 11, 159, 160
attractiveness of regions 33–40
Audretsch, D.B. 1, 3

Bachmann, A. 100
backward regions 12, 13, 19
Baden Württemberg 114, 134, 138, 142,
    143, 149, 153; see also Germany
Balassa, B. 56
Baptista, R. 13
Barrera, P. 27
Bartlett, C.A. 16
Basel region 151; see also Switzerland
Bassin Parisien 111, 113, 114, 116, 118,
    119, 122, 125; see also France
Beaudry, C. 25
Beckouche, P. 127
Beise, M. 104
Belgium 31, 33, 48; Flanders-Brussels 142,
    143, 146, 148, 154
Bengtsson, M. 9
Blind, K. 94
bottom/up approach 11–12
Braun, B. 104
Breschi, S. 1, 24, 25, 62
Bryson, J. 77
buyer-supplier networks 1

Caniëls, M.C.J. 1, 24, 28, 50
Cantwell, J.A. 2, 3, 5, 14, 17, 18, 19, 20,
    21, 27, 30, 47, 48, 49, 50, 52, 56, 57,
    60, 70, 85, 100, 105, 110, 129, 130, 131,
    135, 136, 148, 155, 158
Carlsson, J.A. 11
Castellani, D. 25
Centre-Est 112, 113–14, 116, 117, 118,
    122, 125, 129; see also France
Centre-for-global patterns 16
Cesaratto, S. 62
change: concepts 128–31; methodology
    131–7; results 137–46; technological
    change 5
Chatterji, M. 78
Chesnais, F. 2, 14, 126
Chiesa, V. 25
Clark, K. 25
cluster analysis 23, 37–8, 42–3, 57
Cohen, W.M. 3
competencies 46, 47, 50, 130
competitive bidding 18, 161
component knowledge 25
concentration of production 1
Cooke, P. 1, 12, 98
cooperation 159
Coronado, G.D. 44
Cosh, A. 77
costs, transaction costs 15
creation of knowledge 4
critical mass 164
cumulativeness 17–21; concepts 128–31;
    methodology 131–7; results 137–46

De Bresson, C. 9
Dearlove, D. 43
decentralisation 14–15, 116–17
deglomerative tendencies 13, 160

Delors Plan 72
dematerialisation of technology 160
Dewhurst, J.H.L. 78
diamond approach 13
Dicken, P. 5, 10, 46, 157
differentiation 13, 19; concepts 128–31;
    methodology 131–7; results 137–46
diffusion of knowledge 9, 9–10
diversification 17, 131, 140, 143
Dunford, M. 79, 159
Dunning, J.H. 2, 15, 17, 50, 130, 148, 158
Dupont, M.J. 113

economies of agglomeration 8
economies of scale 9, 10, 14
economies of scope 2, 46
England *see* United Kingdom
European Union: geographical
    agglomeration 56–60; features 50–5;
    technological specialisation 56
Evangelista, R. 12, 31, 63, 66, 163
external (inter-firm) networks 2, 16, 17,
    108, 131

Fagerberg, J. 11, 24, 78
Fai, F.M. 100
Feldman, M.P. 1, 3
Fiat group 68
Flanders-Brussels 142, 143, 146, 148, 154
Foray, D. 24
Fors, G. 2, 50
France 28, 31, 33, 38, 43, 48, 50, 52, 54,
    57, 59, 108–27; Bassin Parisien 111, 113,
    114, 116, 118, 119, 122, 125; Centre-
    Est 112, 113–14, 116, 117, 118, 122,
    125, 129; characteristics of innovation
    system 126–7; Île de France 111, 116,
    118, 122, 125, 141–2, 149, 151; location
    of technological activities 109–17;
    product innovation 113; regional
    hierarchies 117–25; Sophia Antipolis 31,
    43; sources of innovation 113;
    technological specialisation 117–25
Freeman, C. 11, 23, 24, 26
Fromhold-Eisebith, M. 104
Frost, T.S. 24
Fujita, M. 130

Galtonian regression model 134–5
Gassmann, O. 47, 50
GDP (Gross Domestic Product) 28–33
geographical agglomeration *see*
    agglomeration
Germany 29, 31, 33, 37, 38, 42, 48, 50,
    52, 54, 57, 59, 93–107, 131–2; Baden
    Württemberg 114, 134, 138, 142, 143,
    149, 153; geographical concentration
    110; location of technological activities
    93–9, 109; regional hierarchies 100–6,
    110; small and medium-sized enterprises
    98; technological specialisation 100–6
Geroski, P. 3
Ghoshal, S. 16
globalisation 7, 14–21, 22, 49, 157–8, 159,
    162
Grosjean, N. 12
Grotz, R. 104
Grupp, H. 94

Hagedoorn, J. 17
Hägerstrand, T. 10
Hall, B. 3
Ham, R.M. 3
Harding, R. 85
Harris, R.I.D. 77
Harrison, B. 10
Hart, P.E. 135
Henderson, R. 25
hierarchies *see* regional hierarchies
Hirschman, A. 25
Hirst, P. 159
Hodson, C. 49
Honestly Significant Difference (HSD) test
    38, 39
Howells, J. 11, 14
Hughes, A. 77

Iammarino, S. 14, 17, 28, 62, 63, 158, 159,
    162
Île de France 111, 116, 118, 122, 125,
    141–2, 149, 151; *see also* France
industrial composition 129
industrial structures 30
information 3
inter-firm networks 2, 16, 17, 108, 131
internal (intra-firm) networks 16, 19, 108,
    128, 131
internal market 49
internationalisation of technological
    activities 47–50
intra-firm networks 16, 19, 108, 128, 131
Isaksen, A. 160
Italy 29, 30, 31, 33, 43, 48, 50, 54, 57–8,
    59, 61–75, 109; geographical
    concentration 109–10; location of
    activities 62–8; Lombardia 62, 63, 65,
    66, 67, 68, 74, 110, 142, 146, 149;
    Piemonte 62, 63, 66, 68, 74, 129;

Italy *continued*
    regional hierarchies 68–73, 110;
    technological specialisation 68–73

Jaffe, A.B. 1, 4
Janne, O.E.M. 19, 48, 49, 50
Japan 48, 50, 54, 160

Kaldor, N. 9, 10
Keeble, D. 77, 91
Kline, G.J. 9
knowledge: architectural knowledge 25–6;
    component knowledge 25; creation 4;
    diffusion 9, 9–10; and information 3;
    local accumulation 18; networks 2;
    property rights 3; and the public good 3;
    spillover effect 1, 4, 7, 20, 25, 46; sticky
    knowledge 3; tacit knowledge 9–10, 11;
    transfer 2–3
Kogut, B. 4
Korea 48
Krugman, P. 1, 10
Kuemmerle, W. 50

labour force 160
Le Bas, C. 50
Le Galès, P. 117, 127
learning 11
Lee, J.-Y. 104
Lloyd, P.E. 10
local dimension of innovation 7, 8–13,
    17–21, 46
Local-for-global strategy 16, 19
Local-for-local strategy 19
location of activities 8; France 109–17;
    Germany 93–9, 109; Italy 62–8; United
    Kingdom 77–85
Lombardia 62, 63, 65, 66, 67, 68, 74, 110,
    142, 146, 149; *see also* Italy
Lösch, A. 8
Lundan, S.M. 50
Lundvall, B.A. 9, 10, 11

McCann, P. 8
Maillat, D. 12
Malecki, E.J. 8, 159, 160
Malerba, F. 4, 25
Malmberg, A. 8, 10
Mancusi, M.L. 62
Mansfield, E. 104
market failure 3
Markusen, A. 18, 25, 163
Marshall, A. 8
metropolitanisation process 117

Meyer-Krahmer, F. 160
Michie, J. 50
midway regions 12
Morgan, K. 1, 98

Narula, R. 17, 20
National Innovation Survey 111, 113
Nelson, R.R. 3, 11, 23, 129
Netherlands 29, 31, 33, 37, 43, 48; Zuid
    Nederland 134, 138, 143, 149, 154
networks 4, 5, 11, 20, 50, 128, 158; of
    affiliates 15; buyer-supplier 1; external
    (inter-firm) 2, 16, 17, 108, 131; internal
    (intra-firm) 16, 19, 108, 128, 131;
    knowledge 2
Noonan, C.A. 3
North West UK 129; *see also* United
    Kingdom

Paci, R. 1, 28, 50
Papanastassiou, M. 44
Patel, P. 44, 50, 56, 105
patent statistics 1, 14, 26–8, 33, 42, 48–50,
    52, 57–8
Patrucco, P.P. 26
Pavitt, K.L.R. 44, 56, 105, 129
Pearce, R. 4, 14, 44, 109, 148
peripheral regions 164
Perraton, J. 14
Perroux, François 8
Phene, A. 25
Pianta, M. 60
Piemonte 62, 63, 65, 66, 68, 74, 129; *see
    also* Italy
Piscitello, L. 18, 47, 50
Pitelis, C. 15
Porter, M.E. 13, 24
price mechanism 13, 18
principal component analysis (PCA) 4–6
process innovation 113
product innovation 113
property rights 3
public good 3
public policies 162

Reger, G. 160
regional convergence 23–6
regional cores and attractiveness 33–40
regional dimension 9
regional hierarchies: France 117–25;
    Germany 100–6, 110; Italy 68–73, 110;
    United Kingdom 85–91, 110
Research Council Grants 80, 87
Richardson, H.W. 10

Robson, P. 15
Rodriguez-Pose, A. 24
Rosenberg, N. 3, 9, 11
RSA (Revealed Scientific Advantage)
  index 86–7, 88, 89
RTA (Revealed Technological Advantage)
  index 56, 59, 68, 70, 85–6, 88, 89, 90,
  100, 101, 120, 130, 132, 134, 135, 136,
  154

Santangelo, G.D. 60, 155
Saxenian, A. 61
Scotland 31, 38, 43; *see also* United
  Kingdom
sectoral system of innovation 4–5
Sierra, C. 50
Silvani, A. 62
Singh, S. 14
single currency 49
skilled labour 160
small and medium-sized enterprises 98, 163
social capabilities 11
social embeddedness 108
social returns 3
Soete, L. 56
Sölvell, Ö. 9
Sophia Antipolis 31, 43
South East UK 141, 149, 150; *see also*
  United Kingdom
spatial distribution of technological activity
  28–33
specialisation *see* technological specialisation
Spielkamp, A. 104
spillover effect 1, 4, 7, 20, 25, 46
Stahl, H. 104
Stankiewicz, R. 4, 11
state of the art 47–8
sticky knowledge 3
Stockholm-Östra Mellansverige 141–2,
  149, 150
subsidiary companies 2, 3, 19
Sugden, R. 15
Swann, G.M.P. 13
Sweden 31, 33, 48, 151; Stockholm-Östra
  Mellansverige 141–2, 149, 150
Switzerland 48, 141, 146, 151
systems of innovation 5

tacit knowledge 9–10, 11
Tallman, S. 25
Tavares, A.T. 148
technological change 5

technological congruence 11
technological convergence 42–3
technological growth 23–6, 41–3
technological specialisation 56, 148; France
  117–25; Germany 100–6; Italy 68–73;
  United Kingdom 85–91
technological strategies 146–55
territorial embeddedness 108
Thompson, G. 159
Thwaites, A. 77
Tomaney, J. 17, 158
top/down approach 11–12
transaction costs 15
transfer of knowledge 2–3
Turkey 38, 39

United Kingdom 33, 38, 42, 48, 50, 54,
  57, 76–92; geographical concentration
  109–10; hosting foreign-owned
  patenting activity 109; location of
  technological activities 77–85; North
  West 129; personnel employed in R&D
  77–8; regional hierarchies 85–91, 110;
  Research Council Grants 80, 87;
  Scotland 31, 38, 43; South East 141,
  149, 150; technological specialisation
  85–91; West Midlands UK 129
urbanisation economies 10
Usai, S. 1, 28, 50

Vaccà, S. 160
Venables, A.J. 25, 163
Vernon, R. 2, 47
Verspagen, B. 24, 50, 78
Vertova, G. 27, 56
von Hippel, E. 3, 9
von Zedtwitz, M. 47, 50
vulnerable regions *see* weak regions

weak regions 12, 13, 19
Weber, A. 8, 13
West Midlands UK 129; *see also* United
  Kingdom
Winter, S.G. 3, 23, 129
Wood, M. 14
Wymbs, C. 2, 15, 130
Wynarczyk, P. 77

Zander, I. 20, 108, 130, 146
Zanfei, A. 25
Zuid Nederland 134, 138, 143, 149, 154;
  see also Netherlands